Israeli and Palestinian Identities in Dialogue

Israeli and Palestinian Identities in Dialogue

The School for Peace Approach

Edited by **RABAH HALABI**
Translated from Hebrew by **DEB REICH**

Rutgers University Press
New Brunswick, New Jersey, and London

First published in Hebrew by Hakibbutz Hameuchad Press,
Tel Aviv, Israel, © 2000 by Rabah Halabi

First published in English 2004 by Rutgers University Press,
New Brunswick, New Jersey

Library of Congress Cataloging-in-Publication Data

Dialog ben zekhuyot. English.
    Israeli and Palestinian identities in dialogue : the school for peace approach / edited by
Rabah Halabi ; translated from Hebrew by Deb Reich.
        p.   cm.
Includes bibliographical references and index.
    ISBN 0-8135-3348-1 (hardcover : alk. paper) —
    ISBN 0-8135-3349-X (pbk. : alk. paper)
        1. Multicultural education—Israel.   2. Neveh shalom (School)   3. Israel—
Ethnic relations.   4. Intergroup relations—Israel.   5. Conflict management—Israel.
6. Youth—Israel—Attitudes.   7. Arab-Israeli conflict—1993—Peace.   I. Halabi,
Rabah.   II. Title.
    LC1099.5.I75D5313 2004
    370.117'095694—dc21
                                                                        2003014222

A British Cataloging-in-Publication record is available from the British Library

Manufactured in the United States of America

Contents

Acknowledgments

I have been engaged for over a decade in Jewish-Arab encounter work, a particularly fascinating and instructive endeavor. During these years, we in Israel lived through an uprising—the first intifada—and then the Oslo agreements. As this book goes to press, we are living through the second intifada. This unfolding history has been reflected in the groups I have facilitated, and it resonates within me. I have been a part of the events I have tried to witness. I have been swept along in the turbulent currents, felt the pain of the victims, and tried to hold on to happier moments, moments of optimism. My identity has been reshaped over the course of these years; I've achieved a broader and more profound understanding of the Jewish-Arab conflict and of conflicts in general. I hope I've contributed something to those for whom I've served as facilitator; I hope they've learned something from me. In any case, I have certainly learned a great deal from them.

After a good many years of conducting encounters, we at the School for Peace felt the need to document our experiences and our thoughts on the subject. The initiative took a few more years to mature, perhaps to permit us to formulate our ideas in such a way that they could be committed to writing. I am pleased and proud that it has been my task to edit this book, which offers a unique combination of material that draws both on experience in the field and on scientific theory.

The fruitful outcome presented here could not have come about without the dedicated and skilled School for Peace staff who served as active partners in the writing and editing. I thank everyone who had a hand in the process—beginning with Michal Zak, who, aside from authoring chapters herself, closely supervised the editing of the Hebrew edition and its translation into English. I thank Nava Sonnenschein, Ahmad Hijazi, and Wafa'a Zriek-Srour, who were partners in the design and writing of the book and who read drafts and gave good advice. My thanks to Professor Ariella Friedman and Professor Arie Nadler of Tel-Aviv University and to Dr. Ramzi Suleiman of Haifa University, who agreed to take part in the writing and who endowed the book with its academic flavor. Thanks also to Jermaine Abu Maneh, secretary at the School for Peace, for her unflagging contribution and joyful spirit in typing the material. Thanks to all the other School for Peace facilitators, partners in the project through the ongoing dialogue we maintained; and thanks to all the participants in the workshops we conducted over the years. The thoughts we offer here were shaped through the work we did together.

Thanks to the United States Institute of Peace, whose support for this project enabled the School for Peace staff to devote time to the writing of the text.

Special thanks to Deb Reich, who invested heart and soul in the English translation. Thanks to Joan Scott and the American Friends of Neve Shalom/Wahat al Salam for their help in making possible the book's publication in English. And thanks to Kristi Long and the entire team at Rutgers University Press for their warmth and their devotion to our shared project.

Rabah Halabi

Israeli and Palestinian Identities in Dialogue

INTRODUCTION

THOUGHTS ABOUT THE
PALESTINIAN-ISRAELI CONFLICT

RABAH HALABI

This book presents an educational approach developed at the School for Peace at Neve Shalom/Wahat al Salam to address the Jewish-Arab conflict in Israel. In this introduction I begin by clarifying a few of the relevant concepts that my colleagues and I use in our work and by describing both the ongoing reality in which we live and our frame of reference. I refer briefly to nationality, the Palestinian-Israeli conflict, and relations between Jews and Arabs within Israel. I then address cross-cultural encounter as an educational approach employed to cope with conflicts around the globe. Finally, I describe the book, explain the rationale behind its writing, and survey its contents.

Contrary to the classic notion once common among political scientists and sociologists, collective identities do not fade with increasing progress and development. In fact, we have been witnessing just the opposite: a resurgence of national, ethnic, and religious identities that appears to be gaining momentum (Hobsbawm 1995; Smith 1998). At the beginning of the twenty-first century, the matter of nationality is a major and focal influence on our world. Most countries today are national entities, and liberation movements are overwhelmingly national movements. In addition, national tensions and schisms threaten the integrity of old-line European countries like Spain, France, and the United Kingdom, not to speak of the nations of Eastern Europe and the Third World (Hobsbawm 1995). Indeed, many conflicts and wars have an ethnic, national context: in the Sudan, the Kurdish struggle, the conflict in Northern Ireland now moving (perhaps) toward resolution, and likewise the Palestinian-Israeli conflict, with which our book is concerned (Smith 1992; Isaacs 1989).

The Israeli-Palestinian conflict is among the most longstanding and intractable of the modern era. It is an outcome largely of the national re-awakening around the globe, a direct outgrowth of the Second World War and the Holocaust, to which the Jews were subject. This conflict is between two peoples. It began at the end of the nineteenth century as a struggle between two national movements, the Zionist and the Palestin-ian, over the same bit of land. The decisive juncture in this conflict was the year 1948, when the Zionist movement won the war and established the State of Israel; this fulfillment of Zionist aspirations came about at the expense of the Palestinian people, for whom the same date is remembered as Al Naqba—the Catastrophe.

The Zionist fulfillment tore the Palestinian people in two and cre-ated the particular reality with which we are still contending today. Dur-ing the 1948 war, some 750,000 Palestinians lost their homes and became refugees; the Palestinians then found themselves divided between those who had remained in Israel and those who were now outside Israel (Mor-ris 1987). That moment was a turning point for the Israeli-Palestinian conflict, sundering it into two channels. The first, the external conflict, was led on the Palestinian side by the Palestine Liberation Organiza-tion, which, beginning in the 1960s, fought in the name of the Palestinian people for the right to self-determination and the right of return to their homeland. Today these issues are at the heart of the Israeli-Palestinian agenda. In the late 1990s, they appeared to be on their way to eventual resolution, with the establishment of a Palestinian state alongside the State of Israel.

The second channel is the internal conflict, which involves those Pal-estinians who remained within the State of Israel and were transformed almost literally overnight from a majority controlling most of the land and resources of an extensive territory to a small minority dispossessed of most of its land, bereft completely of national rights, and broadly discriminated against in terms of civil rights. Before 1948 approximately 1.4 million Pal-estinians and approximately 620,000 Jews lived in the territory of Pales-tine, while immediately after the war approximately 120,000 Palestinians remained in the territory of the State of Israel. This remnant was like a body without a head because the elite—virtually the entire social, com-mercial, and political leadership—had emigrated or had been exiled

(Morris 1987; Kimmerling and Migdal 1999). It was a frightened minority, lacking everything, at the mercy of the Israeli establishment.

Israel, finding itself "stuck with" all these Palestinians inside its boundaries, didn't know what to do with them initially. Once recovered, the state ruled with an oppressive hand over the Palestinian minority in every possible way. Beginning in 1948 and continuing through 1966, a military administration governed the areas where the Palestinians lived; it limited the Palestinians' freedom of movement and of expression and thwarted any exercise of their freedom to organize (Kimmerling and Migdal 1999). Most of the Arab lands were expropriated, and allotments of water were so minuscule that the Palestinians were forced to give up agriculture, the primary source of such livelihood as remained to them. En masse, they rapidly switched to working for wages for Jewish employers and thus became economically dependent on the establishment (Kimmerling and Migdal 1999; Lustick 1985).

Israel's policy was not limited to subjugating the Arabs by force; it aspired to rule them by constructing their collective identity in a manner different from, cut off from, that of the rest of the Palestinians. The state thus attempted to subdivide the Palestinian minority ethnically and religiously—in other words, divide and rule, a system favored by imperialist nations in the early 1900s (Lustick 1985). Another, perhaps primary instrument for achieving this objective was the state's control of the Arab educational system, which the establishment tried to manipulate so as to inculcate Arab schoolchildren with an indistinct, rootless identity that elided their Palestinian selfhood (Al-haj 1996; Mar'i 1985). This was an identity of obedience, estranged from its own history and culture, which were sacrificed in favor of strengthening the children's identification with their Israeliness and with the state in general (Peres, Ehrlich, and Yuval-Davis 1968).

This massive policy has had an impact on the Palestinian minority in Israel but only within certain limits and not for the long term. The first study of Palestinian identity in Israel, on the eve of the 1967 war, revealed that the Israeli component was strong and deeply engrained. The subjects saw themselves as Israelis first and as Arabs and Palestinians only to a lesser degree (Peres and Yuval-Davis 1969). Many similar studies have been conducted since then. Over the years, the Palestinian component has grown persistently stronger until it has become the dominant element in the identity of Arabs in Israel, and, at the same time, the Israeli component has consistently weakened (Suleiman and Beit-Hallahmi 1997; Rouhana 1984, 1993; Smooha 1983; Tessler 1977).

Smooha (1988) found that 40 percent of the Arabs in Israel describe their identity as combining Palestinian and Israeli components. He ascribes this phenomenon to the "new Arabs," who have succeeded in integrating these two strands of identity within themselves: they feel solidarity with their people, the Palestinian people, on the one hand, and, on the other, loyalty to the State of Israel. Rouhana (1993), by contrast, argues that the Palestinian identity is the core identity, while the Israeli civic identity is secondary and exists on a formal, instrumental level only. Suleiman (1999) attributes Palestinians' ability to encompass within themselves both these seemingly opposing identities, the Palestinian and the Israeli, to their marginal status in both these worlds. This marginality glosses over the contradictions and enables the Palestinian to be, as Suleiman puts it, in two places at once.

The duality inherent in the identity of Palestinians in Israel and its implications for their position within the state have been extensively studied and written about. One of the explanations given for discrimination against Palestinians in Israel is their "double identity" and alleged lack of loyalty to the state. Rouhana (1993) argues that the problem lies not with the Palestinians but rather in the structure of the state and its ideology. He says further that the very definition of the state as Jewish places the Palestinians who live there on the outside and precludes their identification with its symbols, ideology, and narratives. In recent years, the situation of the Arabs in Israel has improved in every way with respect to standard of living, level of education, and civil rights, but the discrimination they confront and the considerable gap between them and Jewish Israelis remains. Discrimination continues in the allocation of public resources and social wealth; the State of Israel continues to be Jewish in its foundations and its agenda; and the Arabs do not enjoy collective rights as a national minority. Within the context of the improvement in their condition in economic and civic terms, the question about their political voice and degree of "Israelization" is merely thrown into sharper relief. Bishara (1999) observes that the Israelization of the Arabs in Israel has become a fact. He contends that the transformation was initially coercive but that social-political circumstances have transformed it into an inseparable part of the existing culture, particularly in light of the concurrent improvement in living conditions.

The questions are whether the State of Israel wants the Palestinians who live in it to be full partners, and, concomitantly, how it is that a group suffers discrimination based on ethnicity in a state that defines itself as democratic. Smooha (1990) solved this conundrum by defining the State of Israel as an ethnic democracy. In this model, the state is an instrument in the hands of a national majority, with members of the minority enjoying civil rights as individuals and theoretically able to aspire to the attainment of collective rights as a national minority.

Bishara (1999) called this model "flawed democracy" and termed it a distortion of reality and an emasculation of the concept of democracy, a temporary phenomenon that would exist in Israel as long as the Arabs living there were resigned to less than full equality as individuals and less than full national rights as a group. The moment the Arabs ceased being resigned to this situation and embraced more radical demands, he reasoned, the model would crash.

Bishara could not have foreseen how quickly he would be proven right. In October 2000, at the start of the second intifada, Palestinians in Israel took to the streets to demonstrate. Their frustration with continuing discrimination and their despair in the face of the domestic and external situation fanned the flames of protest. Israel's police reacted with disproportionate severity and killed a demonstrator at Umm al Fahm; this incident prompted masses of people to come out and join the protests in the streets. The police response escalated further; in the process, thirteen Palestinians (from Israel) were shot to death.

Relations between Jews and Palestinians in Israel have not been the same since. The fracture is not mended and is unlikely to be mended in the near future. Jews have all but disappeared from Arab towns and villages, Arabs have begun avoiding contact with Jews, and an atmosphere of anxiety has taken hold on both sides, tinged with a fear of the unknown.

The explosion of October 2000 was the outcome of a conflict that had been building between Palestinians and Jews in Israel over a period of years and was clearly, sooner or later, going to reach its peak. As already noted, the Palestinians who remained in Israel after 1948 were initially submissive and fearful. As time went on and the next generation grew to maturity, it recovered to some degree from the trauma, developed an understanding of its identity, reclaimed its pride, and stood tall again (Rabinowitz and Abu Baker 2002). This invigoration presented a challenge to the longstanding policy of institutionalized discrimination and to the very structure of the Jewish state, which was unable to make space for the figure of a proud Palestinian with civic and national aspirations. Several struggles ensued over the years, notably on Land Day in 1976, when six Palestinian demonstrators were killed. The explosion in October 2000, a quarter of a century later, was of broader dimensions. At this writing, there is as yet no clear answer to the question of where the relationship may be headed.

The status of national and ethnic minorities in a modern democratic state is of considerable interest to sociologists and social psychologists. Numerous models have been proposed that offer optimal integration of minorities while affording them their own social-political space. Models dealing with the cultural and practical integration of immigrants into a host state range along a continuum from assimilation into the majority culture at one pole to segregation behind the ramparts of the culture of origin at the other. These models deal mainly with immigrants' mechanisms of survival (see, e.g., Hutnik 1991; Birman 1994; Berry 1997). The Palestinians in Israel are original residents, although they sometimes suffer from something like immigrant syndrome—as if they had migrated into Jewish-Western culture rather than vice versa. That being the case, it seems appropriate to examine models dealing with oppressed minorities discriminated against within their own state on account of their ethnic-national identity. These models argue that the optimal way for the minority to deal with the conflict is to construct and reinforce a positive collective identity encompassing ethnic, cultural, and racial components while, at the same time, preserving the ability to communicate and function within the broader society (Phinney 1989; Helms 1989).

One of the leaders in this field has been Helms (1990a), who addresses the racial identity of whites and blacks in the United States. She proposes two models for developing a positive ethnic identity, for both whites and blacks, as the basis for building a healthy, just society. The central tenet of Helms's model is that identity is constructed in the encounter with oneself through the encounter with the other. This is not the ordinary day-to-day encounter but rather a meeting of significance that awakens the individual through a confrontation with reality that cannot be denied and cannot be ignored. (The Helms model is treated in detail in Chapter Five.)

Like whites and blacks in the United States, Arabs and Jews in Israel live together without really meeting in the sense that Helms intends. Arabs more commonly have contact with Jews than vice versa, but this is an instrumental kind of meeting and typically involves an Arab worker with a Jewish boss. In general, Arabs in Israel are "present absentees," in the words of Grossman (1992). Today about a million Palestinians live in Israel, and they constitute about 20 percent of the state's citizens. The vast majority live in their own villages and cities in the Galilee, the Triangle (an area in the north-central coastal plain), and the Negev. A much smaller proportion live in cities that have become "mixed" by force of circumstances: cities like Acre, Jaffa, Ramla, and Lod, which were Arab cities until the establishment of the State of Israel, when Jews came to live there in place of the Arabs who had been expelled. In any case, the Jewish and Arab residents live separate lives for the most part, even in the mixed cities, and this separation obtains in education as well. Arab youngsters study in their own schools, and Jewish youngsters in theirs. For the most part the two peoples have virtually no contact with one another outside official frameworks like government offices or places of employment. This lack of contact is particularly evident on the Jewish side because Jews rarely need to come, and rarely do come, into contact with Arabs in ordinary daily life.

As in all situations involving a majority and a minority, the Arabs have always been the ones with more interest in a relationship and have sought ways of breaking through the barriers to reach out to Jews. Initially meetings were held between Arab intellectuals and Jewish intellectuals, but these were sporadic and not systematic. The most significant contact was via the Israeli Communist Party, a Jewish-Arab party that tried to reach beyond national affiliation and to unite around the themes of social justice and fraternity between peoples. In the early 1970s, the boundaries were breached to some extent, and a number of organizations began holding planned meetings between Jews and Arabs. The approach to these encounters, imported from the United States, was naïve and romantic, and the value of the meetings was essentially that they took place. They met the need of Arabs to pursue contact with Jews and stroked the liberal leftist ego of a marginal Jewish group.

One group of Arabs and Jews went further and decided to conduct an ongoing encounter: by living together. They set up a joint Jewish-Arab village in 1972 and called it Neve Shalom/Wahat al Salam ("Oasis of Peace"). From a small group consisting of a few couples, the village grew and developed over the years and today has forty resident families, half of them Arab, half Jewish. With development came a certain sobering effect: the original handful of revolutionaries intent on breaking down the contemptible barriers of nationality became a complex, multihued community with a diversity of opinion and outlook. The initial attempt to gloss over national origin made way for an engagement through ongoing dialogue between national identities.

Ongoing contact between the two peoples sharpened identities, brought people a high level of awareness, and sometimes caused tension but, overall, stabilized their identities and their social and political outlooks and immunized them against reality—an ever-present reality that intrudes into the community and precludes the option of building a self-contained utopia. Thus, for example, the reigning language in the community is Hebrew, just as in the rest of the state; and in the binational, bilingual school located in the village, the dominance of Hebrew is beyond doubt. The Arab students have complete mastery of Hebrew; the Jewish students are far from mastering the Arabic language.

From this richness and complexity of experience grew the School for Peace, founded by the community in 1976 to reach out beyond the village to a wider public. Since then, the School for Peace has conducted hundreds of encounter activities for young people and adults in which some twenty-five thousand secondary school students, teachers, university students, and others have participated.

Like the community and like other organizations involved in encounter work at the time, the School for Peace began with a naïve outlook. The encounter itself was the object; the magic words were "reduction of stereotypes" and "bringing people together." Over the years, learning from the experience of the village as a whole and from their own work, the staff of the School for Peace developed a more critical way of looking at the encounter. We understood that stereotypes are only the visible, superficial symptom and that, as such, they can reveal the much deeper underlying conceptions held by both Jews and Arabs. These ideas are hard to eradicate: they are formed by the conflict and also reinforce it. We came to see that cordial contact, as contact ("eating hummus together"), may provide a good feeling for the moment but solves nothing; rather it helps preserve the status quo and even fortifies it.

After considerable trial and error, we created an approach to this work that sees the encounter as one between two national identities; the goal is to examine and construct one's own identity through the encounter with the other. The utopian alternative would have been to build bridges beyond nationality and aspire to a universal human society; this approach, alas, does not work in reality. Despite progress, despite technology, fragmentation along ethnic and national lines not only does not disappear but sometimes even intensifies, as we have seen. Hence in the existing reality, our aspiration is to unravel and then reconstruct participants' identities because only an encounter between confident identities can lead to a genuine meeting of equals and permit the option of building a more humane and just society. Our considerable accumulated experience on the subject indicates that only when the Arab group becomes strong, shaking off the sediment of inferiority feelings and uprooting the internalized oppression, can it also help the Jewish group to free itself from being the oppressor; the ensuing dialogue between the two groups is more authentic and egalitarian. Such a process is painful because it involves letting go of a familiar situation and a stable, clear reality, however dreadful; but it is also full of hope for a better future. If the encounter can teach us anything useful about the wider reality, as we believe it can, then a collectively stronger Palestinian minority in Israel and the rehabilitation of its national identity are not only not a threat to the Jewish majority but indeed represent the most reliable road to healthier relations between the two peoples.

While refining our approach to this work and perhaps as an outcome of that effort, we at the School for Peace have revised our view of Jewish-Arab encounter in general. We consider encounter work a profession and believe those who facilitate it should enjoy professional status on a par with that afforded social workers, psychologists, and group facilitators in other fields. To this end, we conduct special training for people wishing to work in the field, and we maintain links with academia in two principal ways: by grounding our work in the existing body of relevant theory and via courses on the Jewish-Arab conflict that we teach at the major universities in Tel Aviv, Jerusalem, Haifa, and Beersheva. These courses give an academic imprimatur to the School for Peace, historically a grass-roots institution, thereby greatly enriching our work. The partnership is also nurturing a new generation of scholars.

In this book, we attempt to portray our approach to encounter work as vividly and richly as possible. We hope in this way to contribute to moving the field another step closer to full professional recognition. The writing style, partly academic and partly experiential, and the content symbolize the duality in which we find ourselves today. The book was written by members of the staff of the School for Peace in cooperation with faculty members from the universities with which we work. Some of the chapters are more descriptive and experiential, and others are more academic in character. We hope that this combination will give the book a special flavor and emphasize that which is different and special in the encounter work that we do.

The book has ten chapters. The first two, by Arie Nadler of Tel-Aviv University and Ramzi Suleiman of the University of Haifa, respectively, provide a theoretical foundation for the overall subject of groups in conflict and for the Jewish-Arab conflict specifically. The third chapter, by Rabah Halabi and Nava Sonnenschein, describes the approach used at the School for Peace with reference to the two preceding chapters and to other theories in this field. The fourth chapter, written jointly by Halabi, Sonnenschein, and Ariella Friedman of Tel-Aviv University, tells the story of the university courses we are teaching via a detailed description of the course at Tel-Aviv University. In the fifth chapter, Halabi describes the training offered by the School for Peace to facilitators who want to do this kind of work professionally.

The sixth chapter, by Michal Zak, Halabi, and Wafa'a Zriek-Srour, describes our project for young people, the school's flagship program and its largest. The seventh chapter, by Halabi and Zak, addresses the subject of language in Jewish-Arab encounter—a central issue. In a special way, via a dialogue between two facilitators, Zak and Halabi, the eighth chapter considers the subject of facilitating with a partner, a fascinating issue in group facilitation generally and in facilitation with groups in conflict in particular. The ninth chapter, by Sonnenschein and Ahmad Hijazi, deals with the uninational forum, its special nature and characteristics. And finally, the concluding chapter, by Gabriel Horenczyk, reexamines the encounter as described in the book in light of more recent contributions to the theoretical literature.

The writing of this book extended over three years, and the outcome is a product of the insight and experience accumulated by both Arabs and Jews at the School for Peace over more than two decades. We found the actual task of writing to be instructive, enriching, and enlightening.

We were unable, in this one volume, to cover every aspect of the encounters we facilitate. We do not, for example, refer to the issue of gender nor to meetings between Israeli Jews and Palestinians from the Palestinian Authority. These and other subjects will, we hope, be addressed in the next book we write.

Finally, we hope that this book will be of help to all those working to bring together Arabs and Jews in Israel and to all who facilitate encounters between groups in conflict anywhere in the world. And it is our hope that the book will contribute to the transformation of our work into a bona fide profession, entitled to the recognition any profession deserves, rather than being considered a well-intentioned hobby, as if the Jewish-Arab conflict could be adequately dealt with during one's spare time. For us, this work is a great deal more than that: not only our life's work, but a matter of life and death.

This book was published in both Arabic and Hebrew in 2000. On October 31 of that year, I was on my way to pick up the first copies of the Arabic edition from the printer in Tel Aviv. En route, I heard that the police had killed a Palestinian demonstrator from Umm al Fahm. Later that same week, another twelve Palestinian demonstrators were killed by the police, and I found myself going from one funeral to another.

The severity of these events was such that, even now, I have yet to fully digest what is going on around me. When the first vivid impressions had paled somewhat and the dust of battle had more or less settled, I sat down with my colleagues at the School for Peace to discuss how to proceed. The outcome was quick and forthright: we decided to strike for a month in mourning and in protest, and we published a declaration to that effect in the newspapers.

This was an extraordinary and, in retrospect, a rather brave step. A few stood with us; others criticized us, arguing that dialogue was more appropriate than ever at such a time. All the other organizations working in this field chose the second option and went on with business as usual. A few even went further and set up ad hoc gathering places—"peace tents"—at major roadside intersections, where Jews and Palestinians could meet and talk. The reality was simply too overwhelming for such gestures, however, and most people realized soon enough that no peace tent could mend what had been shattered in the relations between the two peoples.

Even when we returned to work, the situation was not as it had been. The facilitators, especially the Arabs, had trouble functioning, the more so because the killing did not stop but was escalating to new levels in the Palestinian Authority. Hence most of the work during that period focused on sustaining and strengthening the staff. We held several meetings, most of them uninational, and discussed the options available to us for dealing with the terrible period we were living through. We opted to take action and began organizing contributions and collecting food and medicines for our brothers and sisters over the border.

That year, organized encounter activity was low, particularly in programs involving school-age youngsters. Most such meetings already scheduled were cancelled by the Arab and Jewish schools involved. We facilitated five student encounter workshops during that year, compared with twenty-two during the prior year. Adult encounters, especially institutional ones like the university courses we teach and the facilitators course, met as scheduled. The sessions held immediately following October 2000 were difficult: Voices were raised, and sometimes it was impossible to deal with the level of aggression being expressed, to the point where we began to wonder how useful the encounters were under such conditions. In the few youth encounters that were held, however, the atmosphere was more comfortable. The facilitators were surprised and even resentful—especially the Arab facilitators, who anticipated that the Arab students, after the painful events of October, would evince pride and confidence and possibly a desire to "avenge" our brothers who had been shot by the police.

Even now, we know that we are still far from understanding precisely how the events of October 2000 have affected the encounters we facilitate; we need more time. One immediately obvious outcome, however, was that after October 2000 requests by Jews seeking to participate in such encounters rose, compared with a clear drop in the motivation of Arabs to meet with Jews. From the standpoint of the dialogue and the overall dynamic in the encounter itself, we still have not been able to pinpoint clearly what is different. Apparently more time and greater perspective will be required before we can hope to comprehend how our relations have changed in the wake of the shattering events of October 2000.

1

INTERGROUP CONFLICT AND ITS REDUCTION

A SOCIAL-PSYCHOLOGICAL PERSPECTIVE

ARIE NADLER

I am a social psychologist by profession; hence the study of conflict be-tween groups is central to my professional identity. Researchers in so-cial psychology have always been actively engaged in studying the roots of intergroup conflict, prejudice between groups, and stereotyping of the other. Kurt Lewin, considered by many to be a founding father of the field, published his collected essays under the title *Resolving Social Conflicts* (Lewin 1948). The book still stands as a brilliantly written analysis of conflicts between individuals and groups.

The field has moved a long way since then; yet, although themes have changed and emphases have shifted, one thing has remained con-stant: the centrality of the psychological aspects of intergroup conflicts and their resolution. Beyond that, however, theoretical concepts and re-search methodologies vary. Thus approaches focusing respectively on cognitive processes, social identity, and objective conflict have all been used to explain conflict between groups and the resolution of such con-flict. This diversity has not resulted in a lack of clarity or in ambiguity but is rather a testament to the complex and multicausal nature of these phe-nomena; it has led to a more sophisticated social-psychological analysis of intergroup conflict and has pointed the way toward its resolution.

Another aspect of my identity is that I am an Israeli and a Jew. I am the offspring of parents who survived the Holocaust and came to Israel more than half a century ago to build a new life. I have lived all my life in Israel and have witnessed firsthand all the changes that this society has undergone. Through all these years one reality has remained unchanged—the reality of war, tension, and animosity between Arabs and Jews. I have always felt personally threatened by this reality and have seen and experienced its unbearable costs in human suffering. I remain convinced, however, that this conflict is not a God-given burden that we all must bear. Things can be different.

My personal identity as an Israeli Jew and my professional identity as a social psychologist converge in my efforts to understand Arab-Jewish relations and in my thinking about ways to better them. One of these professional activities has been my involvement, together with friends from Tel-Aviv University and the School for Peace, in the running and observation of the graduate course titled "Intergroup Conflict." In this course, seven or eight Israeli Arabs and an equal number of Israeli Jews meet weekly for the whole academic year. In the first semester, the group is led by experienced and trained group moderators from the School for Peace. During this time, several social psychologists (of whom I am one) observe the group processes taking place and subsequently analyze them jointly with School for Peace colleagues. The second semester is dedicated to a conceptualization of the issues that were discussed and processes that were observed in the first—"experiential"—semester. This involves introducing social-psychological theory and research on intergroup conflicts, cognitive mechanisms of stereotypes and prejudice, social-identity theory, and general knowledge about group processes. Our goal is the integration of academic knowledge with personal experience. The basic assumption that has guided our efforts is that learning of the kind we are seeking to promote occurs only when personal experiences can be understood and conceptualized within the framework of sound theory.

This chapter represents such an integrative effort. I shall consider relevant key concepts and research findings from social psychology against the background of the work that my colleagues from the School for Peace and Tel-Aviv University are doing. In my opinion, their work demonstrates persuasively that an integration of experience and knowledge along the lines described here has great potential for helping lead us—students and faculty, facilitators and participants, and readers of this book—toward a better understanding of intergroup conflicts. Before proceeding, I should emphasize that I do not propose to provide the reader with exhaustive coverage of what social psychology knows about intergroup conflict and its resolution. This task is beyond the scope and purpose of this chapter, and the interested reader is referred elsewhere for this (Brown 2000). My aim is to introduce key concepts and findings that are relevant to the work of the School for Peace.

THE ORIGINS OF CONFLICT BETWEEN GROUPS: "REAL CONFLICT" OR "SOCIAL IDENTITY"

It is said that people are social animals. Generally we begin our life in a small group called a family, grow and develop in small groups of friends at school and work, and find satisfaction of our deepest human needs in the families that we ourselves establish. Beyond this, we are all part of larger groups. These groups are the countries, nations, ethnic groups, and religions to which we belong. Yet, regardless of the breadth or size of the group, social living is often characterized by intergroup conflict, prejudice, and animosity. In extreme cases, of which we in the Middle East are only too aware, such intergroup conflict takes the shape of armed conflict and loss of human life.

What are the origins of this enduring characteristic of social life? Is conflict between groups so common because it is part of our human nature? Or is it perhaps a result of particular circumstances or situations? Numerous philosophers—Thomas Hobbes, Jean Jacques Rousseau, and Sigmund Freud come to mind—have offered provocative and illuminating thoughts on this question, but those writings are beyond the scope of the present chapter. My focus here is on the thinking of modern social psychology on the origins of intergroup conflict and its resolution.

In the early days, a powerful tradition developed within social psychology that viewed hatred of, and aggression toward, the other as an aberration of the soul. Human beings were viewed as basically empathic and benevolent. When they behaved differently, the behavior was considered to be contrary to human nature. Hating the other was viewed as a reflection of the "sick mind." The proponents of this approach included J. W. Adorno and his colleagues (Adorno et al. 1950), who, at the end of World War II, were baffled and alarmed by the atrocities reported from the killing fields in Auschwitz. They continued in their quest for understanding by defining the "authoritarian personality." Individuals with such a personality are said to be predisposed to hate and ultimately to hurt the other. This view was common and influential in the 1950s and 1960s but continued to stimulate research interest through the 1980s (e.g., Altemeyer 1988). Yet, by placing the blame for hatred and aggression toward the other on the "sick mind," we distance ourselves from such phenomena. None of us would admit to being in that loathsome category of people whose warped personality predisposes them to hate. It is always the "them." We all want to maintain a positive self-image, and it is therefore the other who is viewed as having a "hateful," "obnoxious," or "aggressive" personality. Such negative attribution is facilitated if the others belong to a different national or ethnic group. Then it becomes a matter of their "national" or "ethnic" character. "We" remain blameless and in the clear. This externalization of blame for prejudice and conflict is a problematic proposition.

The pervasiveness of social conflict does not support the view that prejudice and hatred are relatively rare and arise because they are part of the maladjusted personality. Rather, such phenomena seem to be part and parcel of group life, as are the phenomena of cooperation, helpfulness, and empathy. The question therefore remains: Why are we so often intolerant of and prejudiced and openly aggressive toward the other? To this there are two main "socio-psychological" answers. One is subsumed under the heading of the "real- (or realistic-) conflict" explanation, and the other under the heading of "social-identity theory." Both these approaches accept the inevitability of conflict and hatred between groups. But while the real-conflict approach centers on the causal role of the situations we live in, the social-identity approach tends to put the onus on our human nature.

Realistic-Conflict Theory: An Optimistic View

The most influential proponents of the realistic-conflict approach were a group of researchers led by Muzafer Sherif (Sherif et al. 1961). Their position was that real conflict between groups over objective and scarce resources precedes the phenomena of prejudice and hatred of the other. Hatred is caused by competition. Introduce competition, and you create intergroup conflict. Take it away, and you eradicate prejudice and hatred. To demonstrate the validity of their ideas, Sherif and his group conducted what they termed the robber's cave experiment. The experiment was conducted at a youth summer camp set up and supervised by the researchers. In most ways this was an ordinary summer camp, but the activities were organized and overseen by the researchers, and the children's behavior was carefully monitored and recorded.

On their arrival, the campers were arbitrarily divided into two groups. Each group chose a typical summer-camp-style name for itself: one became the Rattlers and the other, the Eagles. For a while, the groups were cordial and pleasant toward one another. Then the researchers introduced deliberate competition between the two groups. In these contests (tug of war etc.), the prizes were "scarce resources" that the children coveted (pocket knives etc.). As the competitions progressed, prejudice toward and hatred of the other emerged. The children engaged in name calling, and fistfights ensued. Children who only recently had been "nice kids" who happened to belong to the Rattlers or the Eagles were suddenly viewed as "lazy," "bums," and "cowards." Hostility, intolerance, and prejudice reigned. Indeed it would seem, based on these outcomes, that competition over scarce resources (even pocket knives) precedes hatred of the other.

In the next phase of the study, the researchers attempted to reduce the prejudice that they had created. They tried preaching to the children about the importance of brotherly love and the dangers of intolerance. These, and other common techniques, did not work. Hatred toward the other continued unabated. Yet, one technique did work to reduce prejudice and hatred. The researchers called this technique the creation of superordinate goals.

The idea was simple. Instead of competing to obtain a coveted resource, the groups would now need to cooperate to achieve it. The researchers created situations that would force children from the two warring groups to join forces in order to secure a goal of importance to everyone. If they wanted to see a movie, for example, children from both groups had to cooperate and "chip in" to cover the necessary cost. The telling point is that after only six successive days the atmosphere had changed completely. Animosity decreased, expressions of prejudice disappeared, intolerant behavior vanished, and cross-group friendships developed.

The point to be drawn from this tale is that prejudice and intolerance, on the one hand, and tolerance, on the other, are associated with the existence of, or lack of, competition over resources. Real competition precedes conflict and hatred, and cooperation is the king's road to its elimination. This is an optimistic view of social life because it tells us that prejudice and hatred of the other are not part of human nature but rather are part of the existing circumstances: change the situation, and hatred and prejudice evaporate.

This position—that intergroup attitudes and behavior tend to reflect group interests—was labeled the "realistic group conflict theory" (Campbell 1965). Its validity was demonstrated by other investigators. Thus, for example, Seago (1947) found that Americans' stereotypes of the Japanese became less positive after the attack on Pearl Harbor. In a similar line, Brewer and Campbell (1976) reasoned that geographical proximity should be associated with competition over scarce resources and therefore it should precede hatred of the other. In support of this they found in a study that investigated intertribal perceptions in East Africa that the closer tribes were geographically the higher the tendency to negatively stereotype the other.

These and other findings portray an objective-rational model of intergroup conflict and hatred. Why is there hatred between social groups? Because people need resources, which are scarce, and groups compete with each other over these resources. How does one remedy the situation and restore intergroup harmony? Two routes seem possible. The first is to increase needed resources and do away with scarcity. In an imperfect world this route is unrealistic because we cannot live in everlasting abundance. A second answer was demonstrated by Sherif et al. (1961). Conflict between groups and hatred of the other can be reduced if members of the two groups join forces to obtain the resource coveted by all. By creating a superordinate goal, Sherif and his colleagues forced the competing groups to cooperate; on an ongoing basis, such cooperation did decrease hatred. Overall, this is an optimistic view of intergroup hatred and our ability to control it.

Social-Identity Theory: The View of the Pessimist

A second position, which turns out to be a more pessimistic one, is known as social-identity theory. It rests on the observation that a central part of our personal identity is made up of our group affiliations. When asked to respond to the simple question—"Who am I?"—people reply with group identities. The individual may respond with "Jewish," "Muslim," or "Christian." Alternatively the response may be "Israeli," "Palestinian," "a student," or "a professor." Regardless of their specific contents, all these are social categories. They denote affiliation with social groups. Thus, a central part of our sense of personal identity is our social identity.

This axiom has guided Henry Tajfel and his colleagues in their formulation of the social-identity theory (Tajfel 1978a). Although Tajfel's thinking has undergone revisions and reformulations (as described by, e.g., Turner and Reynolds 2001), I shall limit myself to the original theory because of its conceptual clarity, pioneering status, and relevance to the present analysis of the School for Peace model of dialogue between adversarial groups.

Intergroup Favoritism: "Stepping on the Other to Raise Oneself"

We human beings are motivated to uphold a positive view of ourselves. We need to feel esteemed and appreciated by ourselves and others. Because a major part of our sense of self is anchored in the groups to which we belong, an easy way to enhance our self-esteem is to view the social groups to which we belong as better than other social groups. If my group is better, I am better. Our tendency to downgrade the other, rather than being predicated on competition for scarce resources or other objective external circumstances, is rooted in a basic human motivation to have feelings of personal worth and positive self-esteem.

Numerous studies in social psychology have lent empirical support to this position. Tajfel has demonstrated that random assignment to a group is enough to generate this phenomenon. Such studies typically divide people arbitrarily into two groups (e.g., the A's and the B's or the Greens and the Blues). When individuals are then asked to distribute resources between members of the ingroup (their own group) and members of the outgroup (the other group), a consistent ingroup favoritism is observed. "Their own" people get more than do "others." Furthermore, members of the ingroup are viewed as "better" than members of the outgroup. Bear in mind: these are not Arabs rating a Jew, or Israelis sharing resources with Palestinians. Despite the trivial and arbitrary nature of the group affiliation, it is enough to create a relatively more positive perception of one's own group and favoritism toward its members. It is no coincidence, therefore, that this body of research has come to be known as the "minimal group paradigm" (Bourhis and Gagnon 2001). The inference is that hatred and devaluing of the other are not uncommon or abnormal, nor are they the product of objective circumstances; rather they are a natural and normal part of social life. These studies and their theoretical underpinnings are thus relatively pessimistic about the feasibility of reducing conflict between groups.

What conclusions are to be drawn from this analysis? One choice is to surrender to despair: if prejudice, hatred, and conflict are natural to the human condition, it would seem that little can be done to combat them. An alternative conclusion is that, given the pervasiveness of such phenomena, we should constantly guard against them. Adopting this position implies a responsibility to invest effort and resources in an ongoing fight against prejudice and hatred. Indeed, perhaps one hallmark of a civilized society is to acknowledge the endemic and pervasive nature of our tendency to be prejudiced against the other, while maintaining a never-ending struggle to overcome it.

Outgroup Favoritism: The "Paradox" of Low-Status Groups

The research just mentioned discusses an exception to the rule of ingroup favoritism. When one of the groups is a high-status group and the other is of relatively lower social status, an outgroup rather than an ingroup favoritism was observed. More specifically, members of the low-status group adopted the prevailing view of their ingroup as less worthy and evaluated the high-status outgroup more favorably than they evaluated their own group. A classic study has demonstrated this phenomenon (Clark and Clark [1947] 1955). In this study, black and white children played with black and white puppets. The black children correctly identified the black puppet as being more like themselves but showed a clear preference for playing with the white puppets. Later studies replicated this finding and found that black children view white puppets as nicer and better than black puppets (Asher and Allen 1969).

In the context of social-identity theory, the phenomenon of outgroup favoritism leads to the somewhat untenable conclusion that individuals from low-status groups willingly adopt a negative view of the self. How can this be reconciled with the universal motivation for positive self-evaluation? Social-identity theory suggests a number of ways to resolve this apparent motivational conflict. I will briefly describe two solutions that may be of particular relevance to Arab-Jewish dialogue groups.

One way to maintain a positive self-evaluation under such circumstances is by lowering the intensity of one's identification with one's ingroup. Thus, individuals may choose personal upward mobility to satisfy their need for positive self-evaluation, while at the same time weakening emotional ties to their lowly evaluated ingroup. An Arab citizen in Israel, who belongs to a relatively low-status group in Israeli society, may adopt this solution by dissociating himself or herself from the Arab ingroup and climbing the more universal professional social ladder. By taking this route, the person leaves his or her national group behind and moves as an individual outside the boundaries of the low-status group. This solution is possible only if the boundaries between the low- and high-status groups are relatively permeable and allow such personal movement.

The second solution occurs when individuals in the minority group reject outgroup favoritism in favor of working to change the low status of their group. When this occurs, members of low-status minority groups openly challenge the existing social structure. In contrast to the first solution, which revolves around the individual, this solution revolves around the group.

When is group mobility likely to be sought? The theory suggests that confrontation with the high-status group—an open attempt to change the status of one's own group—is more likely when the existing social order is destabilized or viewed as illegitimate or unjust. Among the many and various factors that can promote such a change: external delegitimization of the social order (e.g., the international community's denunciation of apartheid in South Africa) or a significant internal sociopolitical change (e.g., the effects of the intifadas on Arab-Jewish relations within Israeli society).

Realistic Conflict or Social Identity?

Which of these two approaches (realistic conflict or social identity) is more valid? There is probably no final answer to this question. Both real-conflict elements and identity considerations are important in explaining conflict and its resolution, although their relative relevance may vary from conflict to conflict and also is likely to change over time with respect to a particular conflict. What begins as a competition between two groups over scarce resources may later be transformed into a conflict over whose social identity is more legitimate or worthy. In the complex social world in which we live, then, both identity and objective-reality considerations should be taken into account on the road to conflict resolution.

Before considering the social-psychological principles of reducing intergroup conflict, let me briefly allude to the manifestations of real conflict and social identity in the Arab-Jewish dialogue groups that are the focus of this book. These comments are based on my personal observation of these groups. Conflict over scarce resources seems to be the essential face of the Arab-Israeli conflict. The resources are not pocket knives at a summer camp but land, water, and budgets. Discussions of the justifiability of land confiscation and of the relative availability of government budgets to Israeli Jews and Arabs, among other issues, were quite common in the dialogue groups I observed. Yet beneath all of that ran the deeper current of social identity. Participants were continuously engaged in presenting their own identity as more worthwhile and legitimate than that of the other. For example, in many of these groups the issue of the "legitimate victim" was always present. The Jewish members often referred to the Holocaust to bolster their case for legitimacy. The Arab members kept referring back to the uprooting of the Arab population in 1948 and 1967 as evidence in their quest for legitimacy. By trying to achieve legitimacy, the groups were actually engaged in moral ingroup favoritism. Each was attempting to attain a relatively higher moral justification. Further, in such meetings, one group (Israeli Jews) was of relatively higher social status in Israeli society than the other (Israeli Arabs). These encounters have resulted in demonstrations of the phenomena described in the preceding sections. We have observed instances of outgroup favoritism, as well as confrontations with the existing power relations within Israeli society. These phenomena and processes are the focus of subsequent chapters.

REDUCING CONFLICT: THE EFFECTS OF CONTACT

The wealth of data and theory on conflict reduction and resolution is vast and beyond the scope of this chapter. Given the focus of the whole volume, I will concentrate here on the effects on conflict reduction of contact between members of two conflicting groups and will focus my discussion on what is known as the contact hypothesis.

The Contact Hypothesis

The term *contact hypothesis* was coined by Gordon Allport. In his pioneering book, *The Nature of Prejudice* (1954), Allport suggests that one of the best ways to reduce tension between members of conflicting groups is to simply bring them into contact with one another. In its simplest form, the contact hypothesis suggests that interpersonal contact between members of groups in conflict is all that is needed to reduce tension and hatred. No one has said it better than Allport himself. In trying to capture the spirit of this hypothesis, he describes a conversation between two people (quoted by Brown 1995):

> "See that man over there?"
> "Yes."
> "Well, I hate him."
> "But you don't know him."
> "That's why I hate him."

The contact hypothesis is based on the view that lack of knowledge is the father of all evil. It is predicated on the idea that people in a conflict just need a chance to get to know each other and that once this happens, individuals will soon discover that beneath the mantle of group identity (e.g., Israeli or Palestinian) rests a much deeper and common identity— that of a human being. In somewhat extreme terms, this hypothesis suggests that once people get to know each other as individuals rather than as members of groups, all barriers will fall, intergroup conflict will disappear, and interpersonal harmony will reign. This idea is the basic rationale behind many social programs. It is one of the major rationales for creating ethnically integrated schools or racially mixed neighbor-hoods. It is also the logic that has driven many dialogue groups in count-less spheres of life (e.g., religious and secular, men and women, Arabs and Jews).

Although intuitively appealing, the simplistic version of the contact hypothesis, that all you need is to meet and get to know, does not fare well empirically (Pettigrew 1998). One major issue here is the problem of gen-eralizability. Even when the effects of interpersonal meetings are positive, are these effects generalizable? Will the reduced hatred between Mo-hamed and Yossi, who participate in an Arab-Jewish dialogue group, gen-eralize to less prejudiced perceptions of Arabs and Jews in general? The social-psychological research on prejudice suggests a negative answer be-cause of the process of subtyping (e.g., Weber and Crocker 1983); in this process prejudiced individuals create a distinct social subcategory for the people they meet in the dialogue group: "Mohamed is a nice person, but he is not a typical Arab. Arabs in general are cruel and inhumane." More-over, there is the issue of generalizability of effects over time. Even if the effects of contact were proven to be positive and generalizable beyond the specific context in which contact occurred, are these effects durable? One study, for example, suggests that positive effects of intergroup contact wear off after a period of about one year (Hamilton and Bishop 1976). These questions regarding generalizability over context and time point to the complexity of the issue. It seems that contact may "work" only under certain specified conditions.

When Does Contact "Work"?

What do social-psychological research and theory tell us about the conditions that are conducive to positive interpersonal contact? I shall briefly enumerate some of these conditions and expand on one of them (equal status) that is particularly relevant here (Brown 1995). Four basic conditions are said to promote positive contact: institutional support, acquaintance potential, cooperative atmosphere, and equal status.

Institutional Support

Contact between members of conflicting groups does not take place in a void. It occurs within a larger social context that may support or oppose such encounters. It seems that a supportive social atmosphere is crucial in order for contact to have positive effects on the reduction of prejudice and hatred. If the society at large creates laws and takes steps to reduce discrimination and intergroup hatred, it creates a normative atmosphere that encourages tolerance. Antidiscrimination laws or forced busing cannot by themselves change attitudes and rule out hatred of the other, but they create an overall normative atmosphere that supports this direction. Intergroup contact in such a normative atmosphere is more likely to yield positive results than if the normative atmosphere does not lend support to such efforts.

These effects of broader social context on the outcomes of intergroup contact were quite clear in the Arab-Jewish dialogue groups that I observed. Political shifts, terrorist attacks, or the signing of peace treaties and agreements—all strongly affected the quality of the contact within the small groups. When external conditions were supportive of Arab-Jewish contact (e.g., around the time of the signing of the Oslo Accords), the contact between group members was less conflicted than during other, more strained periods (e.g., after a time of violence between Israelis and Palestinians).

Acquaintance Potential

A second condition that positively affects intergroup contact is what Brown (1995) labels "acquaintance potential." Brief meetings are of no consequence from this perspective. Only contacts that are close and durable can be expected to have a positive impact because such contacts are likely to result in reduced fear of and increased knowledge of the other and, crucially, in the discovery of elements of interpersonal similarity. In light of numerous studies in social psychology that show that interpersonal similarity breeds liking (Byrne 1971), the opportunity to learn about interpersonal similarities (in interests, hobbies, professional aspirations) is extremely important in this regard.

This principle was also at work in the Arab-Jewish groups I observed. The encounter was durable, with meetings taking place over a period of several months and marked by a high level of interpersonal exchanges. The number of group members was relatively small (fifteen to twenty), and the facilitators encouraged an atmosphere of interpersonal closeness.

Cooperative Atmosphere

A third condition that seems to facilitate the positive effects of contact between groups is the cooperative or competitive nature of these meetings. In line with Sherif's idea of superordinate goals, cooperation breeds tolerance. The term *superordinate* may be somewhat misleading in this context. I am not referring here to a monumental task that the groups aim to achieve. Cooperative contact is made up of a succession of small tasks in which cooperation between the two groups is instrumental. There were many such cooperative encounters in our dialogue groups.

Equal Status

A further condition is that of equal status. Contact between members of groups in conflict often occurs between members of groups of unequal status. Whether the contact is between blacks and whites, men and women, or Arab and Jewish Israelis, one group is usually higher in social status than the other. In many societies, men and whites still hold a higher social status than do women and blacks, respectively. In Israeli society, Israeli Jews have a higher social status than Israeli Arabs. If the encounter preserves these traditional status relationships, interpersonal contact will not have positive effects on intergroup relations. Yet, in numerous daily encounters this is exactly what happens. In these the high-status person teaches, gives, or supervises, while the low-status person listens, receives, or is being supervised. Such encounters reinforce existing inequalities and prejudicial perceptions, rather than diminishing them.

If intergroup dialogue is to prove successful, the encounter needs to take place between individuals who are certain of the equality of their social identity. In too many dialogue groups this is not the case. Well-intentioned third parties encourage people of conflicting groups to come into the dialogue group as individuals. They implicitly ask them to leave their robes of social belongingness and social identity outside the room. The operating assumption is that a "pure" interpersonal meeting between members of conflicting groups is possible and advisable. Yet, as emphasized throughout this chapter, our sense of who we are is embedded in the groups to which we belong. Moreover, the elements of our social identity become more salient in situations of conflict with another group. Thus, the simplistic adoption of the contact hypothesis, in which people can easily transcend their sense of social belongingness and meet as human beings, is neither feasible nor instrumental for decreasing conflict. This may account for the somewhat dismal appraisal of the effects of dialogue groups on the reduction of hatred, prejudice, and conflict.

Achieving Equal Status and Generalizability: Emphasizing Social Identity

The importance of equality of status and of social identity, taken together, suggests a different route toward the reduction of hatred and prejudice. It suggests that instead of trying to erase feelings of group belongingness, one should try to nurture and encourage members to identify with their respective groups. Only contact between individuals who feel that they belong to a worthwhile and esteemed group is likely to generate less prejudice and hatred toward the other group. A meeting of this kind is a meeting of individuals who belong to different and unique groups that have equal status.

Building a sense of worthwhile social identity is crucial in creating a sense of personal self-respect and individual self-esteem. Attempting to short-circuit the process is unwise. People who belong to two conflicting groups need to interact as members of two equally esteemed, yet unique and different groups. Recognizing the importance of social identity in people's lives leads to what may sound like a counterintuitive suggestion: to decrease hatred between individuals from two conflicting groups, one needs to strengthen members' identification with their respective groups.

There is a second rationale for this approach. As noted previously, one of the open questions regarding the contact hypothesis is that of generalizability—going beyond the statement "Fatma, whom I met, is a decent person" to "Arabs are decent people." It seems only logical to assume that the more Fatma is viewed as a representative of Arabs in general, the more my changed perceptions of her are likely to be generalized to changed perceptions of the group (Arabs) to which she belongs.

The idea that making group affiliations more salient is an effective vehicle for lessening conflict has not been extensively tested in social psychology. One study is particularly illuminating in this context. Wilder (1984) examined the effects of the typicality of the outgroup member in an intergroup encounter on the perceptions of the outgroup. For the sake of brevity and clarity of presentation, I shall describe here only the procedures and findings relevant to the present discussion.

In this experiment, individuals who were students at a university in the United States met another student from a rival college. As the two colleges were competing institutions, perceptions of members of the outgroup were not flattering. To vary the typicality of the outgroup member, Wilder introduced two experimental conditions. In one, the student supposedly from the other college acted pleasantly but deemphasized his affiliation with the outgroup. His clothes did not bear any insignia associating him with the outgroup, and he presented himself in words and action as "just another student like yourself." In the other situation, the outgroup member behaved pleasantly but made efforts to emphasize his group affiliation. His shirt bore the insignia of the other college, and his speech and behavior emphasized his belongingness to the rival group. In fact, he presented himself as a typical member of the outgroup. His self-presentation proclaimed, "I am a nice person, but I am not just another student like yourself. I am a member of the rival group." Following these interactions, the experimenter measured perceptions of the rival group.

If my earlier comments about the importance of emphasizing group identity in an intergroup encounter are valid, we might predict that only when the other person was pleasant and also presented himself as typical of his group would meeting him alter perceptions of the rival group. Wilder's findings fully support this position. When the student was pleasant and nice but did not present himself as a member of the other group ("I am a student like yourself"), perceptions of the rival group remained negative. However, when the student was pleasant and emphasized his affiliation with the rival group, perceptions of the rival group became significantly more positive. These results imply confirmation of the need to nurture and emphasize respective group identities if we want intergroup encounters to be effective in reducing hatred and prejudice.

THE IMPLICATIONS OF SOCIAL PSYCHOLOGY FOR THE WORK OF THE SCHOOL FOR PEACE: A GENUINE DIALOGUE BETWEEN SECURE IDENTITIES

In the preceding sections, I attempted to highlight some basic concerns that dominate the discussion of intergroup conflict and its resolution in the context of the work of the School for Peace. In this concluding section, I want to summarize by extracting three basic dilemmas from the foregoing discussion and suggesting how they are reflected in the answers provided by the work of the School for Peace.

The first dilemma emanates from the discussion on the origins of intergroup conflict. The real-conflict perspective suggests that conflict is due to the difficulties that two groups face when they need to divide scarce and coveted resources and that it will end when they agree on a formula for the division of these resources. This is a rational-economic model of conflict and its resolution, and it has been fundamental to much of the theoretical and empirical work on conflict resolution in social psychology (Carnevale and Pruitt 1992). The social-identity perspective highlights the emotional needs that fuel and maintain conflict. It focuses on the relative inequality and powerlessness of group members as constituting the psychological component that underlies intergroup conflict. The work at the School for Peace reflects a perspective that is closer to the social-identity approach. It is predicated on the view that unequal power relations between Jews and Arabs are the key factor in understanding the conflict between these groups within the Israeli context and beyond. The work within the parameters of this model aims to lead Arabs and Jews to genuinely and openly address the inequality and the power differences that exist between them. Thus, both the social-identity perspective and the School for Peace model view relative power as the nexus through which greater understanding of the conflict between groups can be achieved.

A second dilemma that is relevant here emanates from the two courses of action that members of low-status groups can take to better their underprivileged situation. As noted in the previous discussion of outgroup favoritism, one such course of action is individual mobility—people downplay their ties to an underprivileged ingroup while attempting to better their personal position in the general society. The second course is group-based and consists of working for social change. Here members of low-status groups confront the privileged group and attempt to change the social structure. The tension between effecting change through personal or group action is echoed in the work of the School for Peace. Although much work within the tradition of the contact hypothesis stresses the positive impact of constructive contact between members of adversarial groups on participants' perceptions of and behavior toward the "enemy," the School for Peace model views a significant dialogue between Jews and Arabs as one that occurs between two adversarial groups and not simply between individuals who come from two adversarial groups. This work focuses on the inequities that exist between the two groups in the Israeli social context and the possibility of creating greater equality and relative harmony between the two groups. From that perspective, this book focuses on work that asserts that a significant dialogue that will lead to change in people's perceptions and behavior is a dialogue that occurs between conflicting groups.

A third dilemma refers to the content of the dialogue. As noted previously, some approaches in social psychology have asserted that intergroup conflict is reduced when there is an emphasis on the commonalities between the groups and a deemphasis on their differences. This is reflected in the classic work of Sherif et al. (1961), which highlights the importance of superordinate goals, and in the more recent work of Gaertner et al. (1999), which indicates that a process of recategorization can produce a new social identity that includes the separate identities of the two rival groups. This, for example, occurs when Israelis and Palestinians are asked to redefine themselves as Middle Easterners. A different line of research and theory has proposed that only a meeting between groups that are fully aware of their own and their adversary's identity can lead to a lowering of intergroup tensions (Wilder 1984). This approach holds that a constructive intergroup dialogue is one that takes place between separate and clearly demarcated identities. The work of the School for Peace has a similar emphasis. It tells us that when people have a clear and demarcated ingroup identity, they are better equipped to conduct a genuine intergroup dialogue, which in turn is a necessary condition for coexistence between equal social groups. Dialogue in the spirit of this model in fact creates a process that helps participants to solidify their ingroup identity.

In summary, the School for Peace model makes clear choices with respect to three major dilemmas that have been identified by extant social-psychological research and theory on intergroup relations. First, it is not aimed at promoting a calculus of interests between rational decision makers — the conflict-resolution — perspective, but rather aims to promote a genuine and direct dialogue between Arabs and Jews in Israel concerning the inequities and inequality that characterize the situation of Arabs in that country. Second, this model emphasizes that a genuine dialogue that may produce social change is one that occurs only between two conflicting groups and not between individuals who happen to belong to groups in conflict. Third, the model is predicated on the assumption that only a genuine meeting between two confident, aware, and demarcated identities can lead to a constructive and mutually respectful coexistence between Jews and Arabs in Israel. This work aims to promote an encounter between secure identities. It represents an emphasis on interidentity dialogue about power and equality between Jews and Arabs, rather than a personal meeting between Jewish and Arab individuals or a simple airing of the contents of the intergroup conflict. Finally, although the work that is described in this book focuses on Israeli Jews and Arabs, its implications extend to other intergroup dialogues. The central assertion here—that amelioration of intergroup conflicts involves a dialogue between defined and demarcated social identities that discuss their relative power and inequality—is true of any intergroup dialogue.

2

JEWISH-PALESTINIAN RELATIONS IN ISRAEL

The Planned Encounter
as a Microcosm

RAMZI SULEIMAN

Planned group encounters between Jewish and Palestinian Israelis have been the object of considerable attention by researchers. Some have focused on the empirical study of variables involved in the encounter, such as prejudice (Bizman 1978) and readiness for relations (Amir 1976). Other studies have taken a holistic-theoretical approach in an attempt to analyze the interaction processes that take place in the encounter (e.g., Katz and Kahanov 1990; Sonnenschein, Halabi, and Friedman 1998).

A satisfactory classification of the types of encounters held between groups in prolonged conflicts was suggested by Katz and Kahanov (1990). According to this classification, planned encounters may fall into one of three categories: (1) workshops in the spirit of the "human relations" tradition; (2) workshops emphasizing cross-cultural learning; and (3) workshops based on a conflict-resolution approach.

Workshops that emphasize the human relations approach are typically characterized by a focus on the here-and-now psychological aspects of the encounter experience. Facilitators of groups of this type encourage participants to freely express their thoughts and feelings about other group members and about the group as a whole. Psychological methods and techniques employed in moderating group dynamics are frequently used to "reflect" and analyze the intra- and interpersonal process. The emphasis in such meetings is on personal and interpersonal processes. Their primary goals are to raise awareness of and sensitivity to the personal experiences of outgroup members and to encourage empathy toward them. The facilitators of these groups tend to emphasize commonalities between members of the conflicting groups and to shunt aside "problematic" political issues in the hope that this may lead to a humanization of the other—a member of the rival group—and to a weakening of stereotyped attitudes toward him or her. The expectations are that such change may encourage participants to develop trust in outgroup members and to improve their relations with them and that these positive changes will be generalized to other outgroup members.

The second approach mentioned above emphasizes cross-cultural learning as a means of helping individuals to understand the influence that culture has on perceptions of the self and of the other (Triandis 1983). According to this approach, intergroup tensions in many cases are the result of cultural differences in norms of behavior. Understanding the cultural characteristics of the other group and exposure to them should bring members of the two groups closer together (cf. Brislin 1981; Argule 1982).

The third approach is based on conflict resolution and conflict management. It assumes that the conflict between two groups is mainly a realistic one (Levine and Campbell 1972) and that ameliorating conflict requires searching for ways to bridge differences between the goals of the two groups. The emphasis here is more on seeing the participants as representatives of their groups and less on their psychological world or on their interpersonal relations. Jewish-Arab encounters using this approach have usually been simulation games in which participants from the two groups represent their respective group's interests.

Another typology was proposed by Ben-Ari and Amir (1988), who classified the encounters in accordance with three different models: the contact model, the information model, and the psychodynamic model. The contact model contends that the meeting, or contact, in itself is sufficient to generate a positive change in the attitudes toward the outgroup members and to improve the relations between the two groups. This assumption is in fact refuted by a number of studies showing that under certain conditions the contact can worsen relations instead of improving them (Amir 1969; Cook 1978). According to the contact hypothesis, the encounter between group members must meet certain conditions in order for positive outcomes to be achieved. These conditions include giving an opportunity for interpersonal and intimate contacts between members of the two groups, equality in status between the groups, institutional support for the meetings, and setting common goals for members of the two groups (Amir 1969).

The information model has characteristics in common with cross-cultural learning. It assumes that the development of stereotypes and prejudice arises from insufficient information or from misinformation regarding the outgroup and its members. According to this model, the encounter provides an appropriate opportunity for clarifying faulty preconceived stereotypes and modifying them in light of more accurate information. This model ignores the motivational-functional component of stereotyping. It focuses on the stereotypes per se instead of viewing them as an additional cognitive structure that supports a whole complex of attitudes, intentions, and behaviors. Moreover, contrary to the model's assumption that unmediated exposure to information has the power to reduce stereotypes, empirical evidence shows that the opposite may also occur—new information is likely to get a twisted and slanted interpretation in a manner that is consonant with existing stereotypes (Darley and Gross 1983).

The psychodynamic model assumes that the individual's negative attitudes toward the outgroup and its members are loaded with projective contents and may often reflect his or her intrapsychic world. Improvement in these attitudes, according to the model, is contingent on raising the individual's awareness of his or her own deep emotional problems and improving ways of coping with them.

In evaluating group encounters between individuals from different ethnic groups in Israel, Ben-Ari and Amir (1988) note that "the quality and scientific merit of this work are far from satisfactory. Many programs for 'change' have been designed, but in most of them the goals have not been well defined, and their theoretical foundations are not always clear" (50). I may add that a flawed characterization of the goals and a faulty understanding of the processes that took place in the group and of what is necessary for generating the desired changes have all led to irrelevant considerations in determining the nature of the group and the facilitation style. Because most encounter programs have been run within the framework of the educational system, conventional educational views have influenced the goals set for these meetings and the style of intervention. Moreover, in the absence of other methods and styles of facilitation, psychological facilitation has predominated. In fact, this was a natural outcome because most facilitators have been psychologists, consultants, social workers, and educators with a background in psychology. The process of adapting the facilitation style to the specific characteristics of encounter between ethnic groups was developed quite slowly, through trial and error. Hence, one may contend that this process was not comprehensive and that sufficient effort has not been made to transfer accumulating experience to new facilitators.

Another factor that has significantly affected the nature of the encounter groups relates to the fact that virtually all the initiatives and funding for these encounters have come from state institutions, such as the Ministry of Education, or from nongovernmental Jewish organizations. This fact invariably had a decisive influence on setting the boundaries between what was permissible and what was not permissible within the group and clearly slanted the objectives to meet the expectations and needs of the Jewish participants. Michelovitch (1986) has similarly noted that because these encounters were mainly a Jewish effort, potential "blind spots" may have been created, given the limited ability of a particular group to respond to the needs and sensitivities of members of a different group.

The hegemony of the psychological facilitation style, which emphasizes personal experiences and interpersonal communication in the here-and-now, mandates a symmetrical view of the relations between members of the two groups. This implies, among other things, an expectation of similar behaviors on the part of the Jewish and Palestinian participants. In addition, the characteristics of the structure and the process of a group created according to a psychological model are more suited to patterns of personal and interpersonal behavior and less suited to political and intergroup behavior. Hence a basic contradiction exists between the structure of the encounter group and its potential for advancing intergroup contents and processes.

Nevertheless, the "squeezing" of most encounters into a psychological and interpersonal model has not prevented intergroup processes from occurring. The purposeful playing down of political and intergroup components by facilitators has not been successful in suppressing such processes. One might say that despite the existence of a variety of goals and styles of facilitation, the encounter groups have always been a microcosm in which salient intergroup processes have indeed occurred, along with intra- and interpersonal ones.

In the remainder of this chapter I shall utilize a number of theoretical ideas derived from Social Identity Theory (SIT) in order to better understand common intergroup processes that take place in Jewish-Palestinian encounter groups. This theory, proposed by Henry Tajfel (Tajfel 1981; Tajfel and Turner 1986), views the group itself as an entity that is qualitatively different from the sum total of all the individuals constituting it. The basic unit of analysis according to SIT is the group and not its individual members. Rather than discussing various hypotheses that can be derived from SIT concerning intergroup relations, I shall focus here on two aspects related to the theory and utilize them to analyze common interpersonal and intergroup processes in group encounters. These two aspects are the dimensions of the interaction and the asymmetry in power between the groups that are involved in the encounter.

DIMENSIONS OF THE INTERACTION

Researchers and facilitators working with Jewish-Palestinian group encounters in Israel distinguish between interactions occurring on an interpersonal level and interactions occurring on an intergroup level (e.g., Hoffman and Najar 1986; Amir and Ben-Ari 1987; Katz and Kahanov 1990). Katz and Kahanov contend that the tension between these two levels reveals one of the central dilemmas in Jewish-Arab encounters. They describe this dilemma as "the tension between the outlook of 'the political man' and that of 'the psychological man'" (36). The continuum hypothesis proposed by Tajfel and his colleagues (Tajfel 1979; Tajfel and Turner 1986) provides a fruitful theoretical framework for understanding these two dimensions of interaction. Based on this hypothesis, one may view any interaction between two or more individuals as if it were taking place along a continuum: at one end the entire interaction is determined by interpersonal relations and individual traits and is not influenced by the social groups or categories to which the individuals belong, while at the other end interaction between two or more individuals (or between groups of individuals) is determined entirely by the affiliation of the individuals to various social groups and categories and is not influenced by personal or interpersonal relations (Tajfel and Turner 1986, 8).

The importance of the continuum hypothesis is that it provides a model encompassing the two levels of interaction and allows one to hypothesize about different variables involved in group interactions. For example, Tajfel hypothesized that in situations of conflict the two groups will operate closer to the intergroup pole. Moreover, he assumed that under such conditions, intergroup relations will be characterized by two qualities: (1) members of the outgroup will be perceived as resembling one another or, in Tajfel's terms, as "unidentified elements within a unified social category" (1981, 243); and (2) ingroup members will show a high degree of uniformity in their attitudes and behaviors toward members of the outgroup. In Tajfel's view, phenomena like depersonalization, dehumanization, and stereotyping are particular cases of the more general phenomenon of "nondifferentiation."

Encounter groups between Jewish and Palestinian Israelis provide almost laboratory conditions for examining the continuum hypothesis and predictions derived from it. Given the intensity of political conflict between the two groups, one may predict that individuals from both groups will tend to operate near the intergroup pole. This prediction does not accord with experience in various encounter groups in which Palestinian participants prefer to shift the interaction to the intergroup level, while Jewish participants prefer to shift it to the level of interpersonal communication. Following the warm-up stage in the first meetings, the Palestinian participants usually try to raise issues of a collective and political nature, like discrimination against Palestinian citizens of Israel, expropriation of land, Israel's occupation policies. Often, a Palestinian participant will turn to a Jewish participant or to the group as a whole with a question such as "Why don't you expropriate land from Jews for development purposes in the Arab sector?" or "Why can't I live in Carmiel in the framework of a government settlement policy?" It would seem that with queries like these, and many similar ones, the Palestinian questioner is relating to his or her Jewish colleague or to the Jewish group as a whole as a "representative" of the ruling majority group or even of the establishment. However, in their responses Jewish participants generally reject attempts to provoke a political dialogue in an effort to keep the group focused on personal and interpersonal experiences. These experiences are typically related to occasional meetings with Israeli Palestinians ("the worker who came to paint my house," "the student who sat next to me in class"), some of which have been positive, but most of which have been laden with anxiety. For the Jewish participants these personal experiences evoke thoughts and emotions linked to basic feelings of trust and mistrust.

The main point here is that while the Palestinian participants relate to the Jewish participants as representing the Jews in general, the Jewish participants prefer to relate to their Palestinian colleagues as exceptions and to focus mainly on the here-and-now interpersonal encounter with them:

> But I have a problem. . . . Not that I'm saying that there aren't two identities here, or two groups, but . . . the dichotomous division into two groups, all the time repeated, I have a problem [with that], and I remember this song all the time . . . , "Don't Call Me a People." Why . . . push it in this direction of two identities [when] maybe

that's really what we don't want to end up reaching. Maybe there's something that's kind of shared, maybe universal.

Similar observations are presented by Katz and Kahanov (1990), Amir and Ben-Ari (1987), and Sonnenschein, Halabi, and Friedman (1998). Katz and Kahanov note that they found a greater tendency among Arab participants toward a political-group emphasis, along with a relative avoidance of exposing differences of opinion within their camp. In contrast, they found that personal self-disclosure, confession of weakness, and admission of doubt were much more common among Jewish participants (34).

In light of the above observations, two remarks—one theoretical and the other pragmatic—seem in order. On the theoretical level, the validity of the continuum hypothesis in relation to situations of asymmetry, such as encounters between members of a majority and of a minority, may be challenged. As originally formulated, the continuum hypothesis is a symmetrical argument. It does not distinguish between the responses of members of the respective groups. It seems that this hypothesis needs to be modified to take into account the characteristics of asymmetry embedded in interactions between minority and majority members. The preceding observations suggest a possibility—not accounted for by the continuum hypothesis—that the two groups engaged in an interaction need not operate around the same point on the interpersonal-intergroup continuum. For example, in a given interaction, most members of one group might operate near the intergroup end of the continuum, while most members of the other group—during the same interaction—might operate near the interpersonal end. Moreover, the findings of Levy and Guttman (1976) and of Adar and Adler (1965)—regarding the absence of a correlation between the attitudes of Jewish youth on interpersonal subjects and their attitudes on national-political subjects—raise the possibility of an additional extension according to which the interpersonal and the intergroup levels of an interaction need not be diametrically opposed. A modified model of the continuum hypothesis might assume that the two levels of interaction are represented by two bipolar and orthogonal dimensions. An individual could have an interaction with an outgroup member that is positive on both dimensions, negative on both, or positive on one and negative on the other, and at different degrees of intensity of positivity and negativity.

Another theoretical weakness of the continuum hypothesis lies in its ambiguous definition of the nature of the interaction. Specifically, the hypothesis—as originally stated—does not distinguish between individuals' perceptions of the situation (evaluative dimension), their behavioral intentions (intentional dimension), and their actual behavior (behavioral dimension). The distinction between the evaluative dimension and the intentional and behavioral dimensions throws light on situations in which individuals choose actions that do not reflect their real thoughts and feelings. Such situations are fairly common in the behavioral repertoire of Jewish participants in encounter groups, who will nearly always prefer to shift the interaction away from the intergroup level and toward the interpersonal level. The possibility for a disjunction between the individual's perception of the level of interaction (interpersonal/intergroup) and his or her behavior enables individuals who so desire to avoid political questions and difficulties raised by individuals from the other group and to emphasize personal and interpersonal experiences. Katz and Kahanov (1990) give validity to this analysis in stating that, "according to the advocates of the political model, the psychological model is manipulative. As if to say that when there is a reality involving a horse and rider, it is the rider who will say, 'No politics!'" (43).

Thus far I have mainly addressed the theoretical aspects of the relationship between the interpersonal and intergroup levels of communication. Another problem, pragmatic in nature, relates to the degree to which the group-dynamics format of encounters is suitable for generating a process that enables a productive "flow" between the two levels of interaction. In their comparative evaluation of the "political-man" conception as against the "psychological-man" conception, Katz and Kahanov (1990, 34) point out that "the transition from the level of personal relations (the psychological model) to that of intergroup relations (the political model) can be very instructive concerning external social processes, but is also liable to seriously impede the resolution of dilemmas raised by them. The moment the speakers become spokespersons for their groups, the possibility for the creation of a common denominator is diminished."

Similarly, Amir and Ben-Ari (1987) rely on the findings of Levy and Guttman (1976) and of Adar and Adler (1965) concerning the lack of correlation between personal attitudes and political-national attitudes to conclude that "the interpersonal aspects at the micro level of intergroup conflict may be addressed, without necessarily addressing intergroup aspects on the macro level"; they immediately add (313):

> This is, in fact, the source of hope for successful encounters between Jewish and Arab youth in Israel. It must be understood that in whatever concerns Jewish-Arab relations, action on the micro level is a

tangible possibility. In contrast, action on the macro level is simply not under our control. Moreover, structured techniques and psychological approaches are likely to bear fruit in working with problems and conflicts the source of which is psychological. But on the macro level, other factors—political, economic, religious and cultural—are likely to be the basis of the conflict, and thus to limit the effectiveness of the psychological tools in solving problems.

Although I concur with the contention of the authors that "structured techniques and psychological approaches are likely to bear fruit in working with problems and conflicts the source of which is psychological," I disagree with their conclusion that the source of hope for successful encounters lies in addressing interpersonal aspects and not intergroup aspects. My nearly opposite conclusion is that because most issues addressed in these encounters are essentially not psychological, the effectiveness of encounter groups in addressing such issues is bound to be limited. Put differently, I contend that the psychological nature of the encounter group limits its ability to cope with conflict problems and contents related to intergroup aspects.

The deflection of focus arising from the psychological character of these groups, in favor of interpersonal relations, is clear and self-evident. In the absence of other rules, it is the prerogative of any individual (not less so any group) to strictly clarify that he or she is not prepared to discuss political issues and thereby to set the boundaries of what is permitted and what is not in the encounter. The Jewish participants in such groups can demand (as they usually do) that the Arabs relate to their emotional pain and distress as a condition for continuing the encounter. The road to intergroup content is evidently by way of interpersonal paths, and Arab participants who are interested in the continuation, and success, of the encounter are prone to be responsive to this type of demand. It follows that the symmetrical nature of a psychologically oriented group is likely to be the source of an asymmetry that inclines the group in a psychological and interpersonal direction, far away from the political and intergroup dimensions.

ASYMMETRY IN POWER

Interestingly, the research on Jewish-Palestinian encounter groups in Israel has almost entirely disregarded the power dimension of the encounter. No serious regard has been given to the fact that the majority and minority groups participating in such encounters differ significantly in their social status. The organizers of such groups invest considerable organizational effort in neutralizing status variables, usually by nominating two facilitators, a Palestinian and a Jew, and by securing numerical parity between participants from the two national groups. One might contend that understanding the social process of majority-minority relations is essential for making inferences about the intra- and interpersonal processes, as well as the intergroup processes, that take place in Jewish-Palestinian encounter groups. This is especially true given the fact that the dialogue in these groups is focused on the relations between the majority and minority groups to which the participants in the meetings belong.

In this section I attempt to pinpoint different psychological responses on the part of majority- and minority-group members within the encounter group. Before doing so I wish to emphasize two principal characteristics of the asymmetrical relations between majority and minority. First, the majority (the high-status group) holds most of the material resources common to the two groups and thus holds the reins of power and control in the state. This implies that, whereas the majority can discriminate against the minority—and indeed it does so extensively—the minority cannot practice substantive discrimination against the majority. Second, the majority is represented by a wide range of governmental and nongovernmental institutions through which it enforces its control over common resources, and it acts in various ways against any tendency on the part of the minority to change the discriminatory status quo. In contrast, the minority's own institutions and organizations are of limited effectiveness.

The gap between the two groups on the level of institutional organization dictates that individuals from the respective groups will have different modes of "conflict-oriented behaviors." Although members of the majority can rely on many institutions to address matters related to the conflict, members of the minority cannot. This asymmetry obliges minority members to have a greater degree of involvement in issues related to the intergroup conflict. As a substitute for institutional activity, the minority must base its struggle on noninstitutionalized, grass-roots activities. This requires a highly salient group identity and the enlistment of people's emotions to bolster the group's unity and increase individuals' readiness to involve themselves in behaviors relating to the conflict. This asymmetry implies a difference between minority- and majority-group members concerning the relation between attitudes and behavior vis-à-vis the conflict. The minority's noninstitutional organization and action and the need for a high degree of involvement on the part of minority-group members render a stronger attitudinal-behavioral link more crucial for the minority than for members of the majority. This asymmetry likewise implies that members of the two groups will have different perceptions of the degree of centrality and importance of their group identities. One might conjecture that members of an unorganized minority would tend to ascribe more weight to their collective identity, given its focal role for group cohesion.

As stated before, despite the importance of power and status differences in determining individual and group responses in situations of intergroup contact, these variables have not earned the attention they deserve in the research on encounter groups or in the broader research on intergroup relations. An important contribution in this regard is provided by SIT, especially the ideas proposed by Turner and Brown (1978) concerning the social and psychological responses of minority- and majority-group members in asymmetrical interactions. According to Turner and Brown, the responses of members of the high-status and the low-status groups are dictated, among other things, by their perceptions and evaluations of the conflict on two central dimensions: the degree of stability of the status quo and its degree of legitimacy. Combining these two factors as dichotomous variables yields four theoretical possibilities: legitimate-stable, legitimate-unstable, illegitimate-stable, and illegitimate-unstable. For the sake of brevity, I will not discuss all four possibilities. Instead, I shall focus only on those that seem most relevant to the case at hand.

Regarding members of the Palestinian minority (low-status) group, one may contend that, in general, they will evaluate the status quo as illegitimate and will try to narrow the "social distance" between themselves and the majority (high-status) group. It follows that minority members will perceive the situation as unstable in addition to evaluating it as illegitimate. The main prediction made by Turner and Brown regarding this situation is that minority members will act in one of three possible ways: (1) they might try to cross borders—as individuals—and "pass" to the high-status group (i.e., by individual mobility); (2) they might use cognitive styles characterized by social creativity, either by changing their value system so that negative comparisons become positive or, alternatively, by changing their referent outgroup and engaging in downward—rather than upward—comparisons; or (3) they might challenge the status quo by competing, as a collective, with the outgroup (i.e., through social competition with the outgroup).

Although actual mobility is not a real option in planned encounters, some behaviors on the part of Palestinian participants in such encounters may be interpreted as attempts to close the social distance between themselves and the majority group or even to "cross boundaries" (Sonnenschein, Halabi, and Friedman 1998). Examples of such behaviors are expressions of "understanding," on the part of the Palestinian participants, of the Jewish majority's reasons for oppressing the minority. Sonnenschein, Halabi, and Friedman (1998) quote cases in which Palestinian participants expressed some "understanding" of the fact that Palestinian travelers are obliged to undergo strict security checks at Ben-Gurion Airport and even of the cries "Death to the Arabs!" sometimes heard on the Jewish street. The authors point out, based on their observations, that the Jewish group usually expresses great interest in Palestinians who attempt to cross borders in manners similar to the ones described above.

Other responses by Palestinians participating in encounter groups may be classified as "creative" ways of enhancing their own group's esteem (for example, by emphasizing their pride in the richness of the Arabic language and traditions): "I want to speak Arabic. When I speak Hebrew, they take it as weakness on my part. I am an Arab [woman] so I have to express myself in Arabic; they are Jews, they speak Hebrew. I represent the Arabs here and I have to represent them in every aspect, and language is one of the important things in that identity. It makes me proud to speak my own language." But for the most part minority members' responses to intergroup contact are characterized by an increase in ethnocentrism and in intergroup tension. A clear expression of this tension is the attempt of minority members to focus the group discussions on political issues, while avoiding intimate conversations of an interpersonal nature. The typical process in these encounters is a relatively rapid transition from the stage of "good intentions" (in which the group—under pressure from the Jewish participants—settles into a pleasant atmosphere with an emphasis on what the two groups have in common) to the stage of intergroup confrontation: "In high school, I participated in a workshop at Neve Shalom. At first we only talked and got to know each other, and we had fun. After that, everything blew up, and we couldn't stand each other. It wasn't easy, especially after a few days of being friends and feeling close. We went home, each of us with his burden, but not as friends." The process of consolidation as two national groups and the pressure to divert the dialogue toward the intergroup course are always initiated by the Palestinian participants (Sonnenschein, Halabi, and Friedman 1998).

Alongside the overwhelming majority of Palestinians in Israel who see the status quo as illegitimate and unstable, a small minority among them see it as illegitimate but stable. The general characteristics of this fraction resemble those of the "assimilating" group in the typology proposed by Smooha (1980). The need to diminish the cognitive dissonance experienced by such individuals can cause them to justify the discrimination against their own group, which they see no way of changing.

Applying the typology offered by Turner and Brown to the majority group seems more interesting. One could contend that in general the majority would evaluate the status quo as stable or at least as stable enough to render the minority group unlikely to seriously change it. Under this assumption, the alternatives proposed by Turner and Brown are reduced to two: that majority members will evaluate the status quo as legitimate and stable, and that they will evaluate it as illegitimate and stable. Turner and Brown do not formulate a clear prediction regarding the first possibility, although one might suppose that majority members who perceive the status quo as legitimate and stable will continue to discriminate against the minority and will not demonstrate sufficient sensitivity concerning the existence of such discrimination. The prediction made by Turner and Brown concerning the second possibility is quite interesting. They posit that majority members who perceive the existing situation as stable but illegitimate will engage in discriminatory behavior toward the minority but, at the same time, will attempt to justify their behavior by utilizing cognitive strategies that are self-confirmatory. As the theory of dissonance posits, majority members who experience the cognitive dissonance between the discriminatory behavior of their group and their sense of the injustice being done will try to reduce this dissonance by changing their attitude toward the minority-group members in a manner that justifies the discrimination against them.

The range of justifications expressed by majority-group members in Jewish-Palestinian encounters is quite broad. They may be simple and overt or complicated and covert. Three types of justifications that are common in such encounters are stereotyping, rationalization, and delegitimization. The use of negative stereotyping is a simple and direct tactic for justifying discrimination toward members of the Palestinian minority. Claims like "Arabs are not capable of adopting Western technologies" or "educational problems in the Arab sector are mainly an outcome of cultural differences" are examples of commonly used justifications.

Rationalization in the present context refers to the use of pseudo-rational arguments to justify discrimination. A common claim in this category is the justification of denying full rights for Palestinian Israelis by arguing that they do not fulfill their obligations as citizens of the state: "I am bothered by the issue of not serving in the army. I'm interested in hearing your response. It bothers me that every time something about national security comes up . . . maybe you feel a divided loyalty. The sense of oppression comes from obstacles that were always there and that will remain. We have to get to a situation of assimilation and not two separate groups."

Finally, delegitimizing the minority group is often used as a rationale for justifying discriminatory actions toward its members. A common claim made in encounters to delegitimize the Palestinian minority is that "this is a Jewish state and so it is natural that Arabs can't have equal rights." Another related example holds that "this is the only state we [the Jews] have, whereas you [the Arabs] have more than twenty states." Yet another example is the claim that "if you define yourselves as Palestinian, you can't also be Israelis."

These three strategies do not exhaust the possibilities, nor are they necessarily mutually exclusive. For example, majority members sometimes try to delegitimize minority members by means of negative stereotyping. Stigmatizing Arabs as "primitive" or reiterating that they lack a democratic tradition are common examples of how negative stereotyping is used to increase the social distance from the minority as a way of delegitimizing its members: "The problem is your leaders. They're extremists. They're demagogues and instead of moderating the situation, they inflame it. The anger and all those things are a product of education and leaders who want to get political power for themselves at the expense of this thing. All this kind of stuff, that fans the flames of these things."

Throughout the preceding discussion I assumed that the groups involved in the interaction behave as unified and coherent entities. But this assumption does not hold in all cases. In fact, accumulated experience with encounter groups reveals that intergroup processes are often utilized for achieving intragroup goals. An outstanding example is the excessive extremism shown by members of disadvantaged subgroups within the majority (e.g., Jews of Sephardic origin). By widening the distance between themselves and members of the Palestinian minority, some Sephardic Jews seek to narrow their own social distance from other members of their own group.

CONCLUDING REMARKS

In this chapter I used a number of theoretical ideas from the realm of social psychology to analyze common processes that take place in planned encounters between Jewish and Palestinian Israelis. In the distinction made between the interpersonal and the intergroup dimensions of interaction, I emphasized the existence of a clear bias toward interpersonal communication. This bias, arising from the psychological character of the encounter, has greatly limited its capacity to address political issues. It also creates another difficulty in that it forces a symmetrical structure onto the encounter; as a result the relations of dominance between the majority and minority are ignored, and the ability to cope with the various ramifications of the asymmetry embedded in these relations is limited. The theoretical analysis in the final section highlighted some aspects of the differential responses of minority and majority based on the differences in their respective power and relative status. An important difference, worth emphasizing here, is the centrality of national identity for members of the Palestinian minority and its importance for increasing group cohesion and mobilizing the group for collective activities. The same does not hold for members of the majority, who can rely fairly well on the existence of an organized institutional infrastructure designed to control and manage the conflict with the minority.

The asymmetry in majority-minority relations produces different responses from majority and minority members. The analysis provided in the previous section underlined a number of different behavioral and attitudinal responses by members of each group. As described, these differences are determined mainly by the power relations between majority and minority and by the perceived stability and legitimacy of these relations.

Can planned encounters—despite their structural bias toward psychological and interpersonal communication—serve as a platform for political dialogue between Jews and Palestinians? Rather than attempting to provide a definitive answer to this question, I prefer to emphasize two elements the existence of which seems necessary if encounter groups are to be applied effectively for political interventions.

First, the encounters must be managed in a way that ensures that interpersonal communication will be invested in favor of cultivating intergroup dialogue. Maintaining the intergroup dimension at the center requires that facilitators not yield to pressure coming from Jewish participants who try to impose a "veto" on political and conflictive aspects. It also requires the development of facilitation techniques that are suitable for group interactions that are political in nature and the encouragement of expressions of group cohesiveness and group identity. The technique recommended by Sonnenschein, Halabi, and Friedman (1998), in which separate group meetings are held, appears to be effective in encouraging group members to assert their collective identities and in legitimizing these identities in the eyes of outgroup members. This is especially important for members of the Palestinian minority, who have a greater need to assert their national identity.

Second, group members should be provided with relevant historical and political information and informed about the research literature on groups of differing status. The sociological research on majority-minority relations and the social- psychological research on the effects of status and power differences on intergroup relations are especially relevant for this purpose. Basic knowledge of this research, along with appropriate facilitation approaches, can improve the participants' understanding of their own attitudes and behaviors, as well as of those of other ingroup and outgroup members. This, in turn, can improve the effectiveness of encounter groups in achieving their objectives.

3

AWARENESS, IDENTITY, AND REALITY

The School for Peace Approach

RABAH HALABI AND
NAVA SONNENSCHEIN

Before we present the approach we have adopted in our work at the School for Peace, we will give a brief overview of the various working models that exist in this field around the world. (A more thorough survey may be found in Chapters One and Two; here we refer only to highlights).

The theoretical and practical approaches to work involving meetings between groups in conflict are characterized by two major axes.

Individual Orientation	*Group Orientation*
Continuum 1: human relations . . . . . conflict resolution	
Continuum 2: contact hypothesis . . . intergroup encounter	

The first of these is a continuum defined by workshops in human relations at one end and workshops in conflict resolution at the other. In human relations workshops, the main emphasis is on the psychological aspects of the encounter experience. The goal of this approach is to emphasize what participants have in common and to relegate conflictive subjects to the sidelines. Conflict-resolution workshops, in comparison, assume that there is a basis in reality for the conflict between the two groups and that resolving it requires a search for ways to build bridges between the disparate goals of the two groups. This approach emphasizes seeing the participants as representatives of their respective groups, with less emphasis on their inner psychological world and on their interpersonal relations (Abu Nimer 1999).

The second major axis generally addressed in studies of groups in conflict is a continuum defined by the contact-hypothesis approach at one end and the intergroup approach at the other. The contact-hypothesis model assumes that simply bringing together people who belong to groups that are in conflict and creating interaction between them on a personal basis, when they are cut off from their group affiliations, can reduce both their hatred for one another and the preexisting stereotypes they have about one another. The assumptions of this approach are that interpersonal conflicts are the outcome of a lack of information on the part of one group about another group and that a personal connection can correct the distortions and regularize the relations. The intergroup approach, by comparison, contends that the encounter will be useful and will reduce stereotypes not when the group identity of the participants is minimized but rather when it is emphasized and when the interactions taking place are primarily of a group nature. Only in such a case, according to this approach, may one generalize from the personal experience in the encounter to the external reality as it is lived outside the group (see Chapter One).

The two continua are similar in that each of them, at one pole, relies on deconstructing the group dimension in favor of individual contact, while at the other pole each relies on strengthening the group dimension and on intergroup interaction. The approach we use at the School for Peace is close to the second pole—that is, our emphasis is on the encounter between Jews and Arabs, on the conflict, and we relate to the participants as representatives of their groups. But our approach is not exactly identical to any of those described above. We have developed our model over a number of years through trial and error, and only in hindsight, and sometimes even during work in progress, have we formalized its basis in a number of theories that we will discuss in detail below.

As our point of departure, we began working from the other end of both continua, from the human relations and contact-hypothesis end. This kind of model, imported from the United States, was the only one that was known and available in our field at that time in Israel. The goals we set for the meetings we conducted back then were to develop individual and group awareness in the Jewish-Arab context, to decrease stereotyping, and to encourage development of empathy for the other. The encounter was constructed on an individual rather than a group basis. We stressed that participants spoke for themselves and not in the name of a group and that they should direct what they said to someone specific within the group. When a participant spoke in the first-person plural ("We . . . "), we corrected him or her, noting that he/she was not the spokesperson of a group.

Because encouraging good communication between the participants was important, we employed a variety of interpersonal communication techniques. The meetings revolved mainly around the expression of feelings, and the maxim of the facilitation was that there is no arguing with feelings, that one may try only to understand. Thus, for example, when a Jew said that he was afraid of Arabs, the Arabs were supposed to understand this fear and empathize with it. We came to see over time, however, that this approach made it difficult to get to the roots of the fear and the reasons behind it and to try to argue with the conception of reality that underlay it.

Both participants and facilitators, especially the Arabs, were frustrated and dissatisfied with this model. They experienced the meetings as artificial and inauthentic on the one hand and as representing the interests of the Jewish participants on the other. This impelled the staff of the School for Peace to undertake an ongoing quest to improve and perfect our model for encounter. The changes were dictated above all else by our own instincts and our own thinking. Only later did we become acquainted with theories relevant to the approach we had developed in our work, theories on which we can now base our model and by means of which we can also conceptualize and describe this model.

THE GOAL OF THE ENCOUNTER

In our work, the vision of a humane, egalitarian, and just society is always present in our mind's eye. Our goal for the encounters we facilitate is to develop the awareness of the participants about the conflict and their role in it, as well as to enable them to explore and evolve their identity through interaction with the other. Awareness gives people the option to choose their path according to their understanding and consciousness; having a clear and mature identity equips a person to build reciprocal and egalitarian relationships (Phinney 1990; Helms 1990a). In pursuit of this common goal, the task of each of the groups is a little different because the reality in which they live is asymmetrical. The Arabs must deal with being the controlled, the minority group, with all the ramifications of that. And the Jews must deal with being the rulers, the majority group. Meanwhile both groups need to investigate the oppressive patterns in which they are caught and move toward liberation from these patterns through the search for their humanity (Freire 1972).

Our main assumption is that the conflict between Arabs and Jews is between two peoples, two national identities, and not between individuals. Hence we think that the goal of the encounter can be achieved only by sharpening these identities and by facing up to the reality of the conflict between the two peoples as it is reflected in the two groups engaging in the encounter (Wilder 1984; Stephan and Stephan 1984; Tajfel 1978b). Thus we treat the encounter as an intergroup meeting—both structurally and in the world-view that informs the work of the facilitators.

THE STRUCTURE OF THE MEETING

The encounter takes place in small groups of fourteen to sixteen participants. We try to have an equal number of Jews and Arabs in each group. Each small group works with two facilitators, one Arab and one Jewish. Discussions within the group take place in two forums: one is the full binational setting, and the other is the uninational forum, during which the Arab group sits with the Arab facilitator, and the Jewish group sits with the Jewish facilitator. As well, the two languages, Arabic and Hebrew, are official languages of the meeting, and we encourage each group to speak in its own language, with the facilitators offering translations.

In this manner, the message is conveyed to the participants that the encounter is between two groups, two peoples, two identities. This makes possible a dialogue between these two identities; a discussion of all the aspects of the overall conflict, including the political; and the clarification of the most difficult and most painful issues that stand between the two groups. Interventions by the facilitators complement this structure and flow from the same premise.

BASES OF FACILITATOR INTERVENTIONS

The role of the facilitators is to help the participants achieve the goal of the encounter. They do this by analyzing and clarifying the processes occurring between the two groups and by linking these processes to reality, through ongoing dialogue with the participants. Four basic assumptions are always at the forefront of their awareness and their understanding of the relations between Jews and Arabs.

First, the conceptions and beliefs on which a person's identity and behavior are constructed are stable and deep-seated. We are generally unaware of them, and they are generally resistant to change. Statements, opinions, and stereotypes are only the outward indications of these conceptions. Thus we aspire in the encounter to enable the participants to behave freely, as closely as possible in line with reality, so that through this behavior they can examine and comprehend their deeply held conceptions and attempt to deal with them (Bion 1961; Burton 1991). One of the principal conceptions is a feeling of superiority or inferiority, both of which flow from the asymmetrical reality influencing our thinking and behavior within the conflict (Libkind 1992; Tajfel 1978b).

Thus, for example, during the meeting a Jewish participant may declare that the interaction with the Arabs has made him a nationalist and an extremist, while outside he is a total leftist. We will interpret this to mean that the meeting has caused him to encounter his feeling of superiority, which he doesn't like to see in himself and which he has worked hard outside the encounter to suppress in order to be seen as liberal and enlightened. And so he is angry at the Arab, who is serving as his mirror, about what he sees within himself.

Second, the encounter is between two national groups and not between individuals. We see the group as essential, as more than the sum of the individuals who constitute it; and we believe that the interactions between individuals are shaped by their national affiliation and that they relate to themselves and to others as representatives of these groups. Hence we treat individuals as spokespersons for the national groups to which they belong, and we treat the group as representing the collective unconscious of its members (Bion 1961; Tajfel and Turner 1986; Brown and Hewstone 1986).

For example, when there is an argument between Jews and Arabs over the subject to be discussed, and two of the eight Arabs support a political discussion, we treat that as the stance of the Arab group. Sometimes when only one participant from a group expresses a particular opinion, we treat it as the position of the group. Our assumption is that when a position is expressed in the group and no one challenges it, the group sees that position as representative. Because the people are sitting in a group and talking, a great many personal interactions occur among participants. From our point of view these interactions are outside the target area, and we treat them as "noise in the system." As facilitators we are focused on what happens between the two groups as it relates to the conflict, and that is where we try to concentrate the attention of the participants.

Third, the group is a microcosm of reality—despite the fact that the encounter takes place in small groups and between single individuals from each people. We also assume that all the elements existing in the larger society may be found in some form within each one of us (Yalom 1975; Lewin 1948). Thus, for example, regardless of the actual numbers of Arab and Jewish participants in the meeting (even if there are more Arabs than Jews), the phenomena of majority and minority groups are manifested intact.

Hence, for instance, the Jewish group—at least at the outset of the meeting—demonstrates openness, and a variety of opinions are expressed by its members, whereas the Arab group offers a united opinion and does not allow itself the luxury of pluralism. We relate this to the sociopolitical structure in the outside reality and assume that for the Arab group, as the minority, it is important to be united and thereby gain strength; in contrast, the Jewish group, as the majority group and the stronger group in the room, can permit itself to be pluralistic and to express diverse opinions.

Likewise from what happens in the meeting we try to make deductions about reality and sometimes to observe what perhaps could happen in reality in the future. Consider the power relations within the meeting, for example. Over the years we have seen that these tend to change only when the Arab group becomes stronger and forces the Jewish group to change accordingly. We therefore conclude, likewise, that the asymmetrical relations on the outside will be prone to change only if and when the Arabs in Israel become stronger and force these changes to take place.

Fourth, we treat the participants in the meeting as an open group that is linked to—that comes from and returns to—external reality (Lewin 1951). Thus we try to understand what goes on in the group in the context of events happening outside, and we hope that the changes we observe in the participants during the meeting may later influence their surroundings and the society in which they live. When a report reaches the group, for example, that one side or the other has suffered a violent incident involving injury and death, the dialogue in the room becomes more moderate, turns softer, and shows consideration for the side on which there were victims.

When toward the end of the meeting the Arab participants become pessimistic, they report feelings of despair and sense a lack of utility in the encounter. We try to understand what they say not only in the context of what has happened in the meeting itself but also in relation to the fact that the participants will be parting soon and the Arabs will be left to face the difficult reality outside—which has not changed in the smallest measure during their encounter at the School for Peace.

Although the interactions and the processes we are investigating in the meeting are at the group level, the changes in the end are individual and occur within individuals in the group as a result of what happens in the group and between the groups. From this standpoint each group acts as a mirror for the other group. Thus each may see itself rightly, standing face to face with its truth and obliged to cope with that truth, and even to change accordingly if the individual has an inclination and a willingness to change. Because reality is asymmetrical, however, the change is not the same, not identical, for everyone. The Jews, as the dominant majority group, must cope throughout this encounter with being the rulers, with their feelings of superiority, with their patronizing attitudes—as against their desire to be liberal and egalitarian and humane. The Arabs, as the weaker group, must cope throughout the encounter with being oppressed, with their feelings of inferiority, with the internalization of their oppression—as against their desire to be free of that oppression and their aspiration for full equality. It would seem that everyone must change, if in a different direction; indeed the changing must be shared by both sides if they are to break free of the situation of oppression in which both are partners, albeit from different sides of the barricade.

Generally the Jews report on the changes that happen to them during the encounter. Typically they are proud of these changes and see making them as a courageous act deserving of recognition by the Arab group. They even expect that those in the Arab group will change in the same way and demand that they do. The Arab group tends not to report on the changes it undergoes; generally it even reports a complete absence of change. Maybe the Arabs' sense is that to change would signify weakness, or perhaps they feel that in the situation as it stands the group that should change itself and thereby change reality is the Jewish group, the strong group. In these circumstances, the facilitators must be alert and must direct the attention of the participants to the different space occupied by the two groups, a difference that causes them to respond differently.

The Jewish group generally opposes our approach, especially at the start of the process. Whereas we see the facilitation as relating to the Jews as a group, its members demand to be treated as individuals because each is a separate human being. They likewise resist the facilitation approach that contends that the group is a microcosm of Israel. The Jewish participants see themselves as liberal and leftist and believe that the racist Jews are elsewhere, on the outside. By contrast, the Arab group accepts our approach, even behaves supportively toward the facilitation, and urges a political discussion by the group.

Despite the differences between the two groups, at least on the level of declarations, we think that both want a political discussion, as do any two groups that find themselves in a situation of conflict (Tajfel 1981). But the Jews try to steer things in another direction once they begin feeling distress, as they stand facing reality and find that their humanity is called into question and their hegemony as a group is in jeopardy. Indeed, avoidance of conflict is known to be one of the strategies employed by the majority group in cases like this to perpetuate its control of the situation (Lukes 1974). Then, toward the end, the situation is reversed as the group returns to everyday reality. The Jewish group at that point feels less threatened; it feels pride in the changes it has undergone and thinks that it has done so for the sake of equality. The Arab group sometimes feels frustrated and disappointed because reality has not changed. On the contrary, reality is now perhaps worse, given the changed awareness of the Arab group toward it. An Arab participant expressed this quite clearly when he said, "That means that the encounter makes possible the creation of a slightly different reality from outside, making it possible to protest against the way things are and against the status quo. The Jewish group doesn't like this situation, and so things are very hard for it in the meeting. But, for the Arabs, things are better within the meeting than in the reality outside." And, in truth, that is the reality, with all its complexity and all that is so insufferable about it. These meetings cannot, and are not intended to, change reality. What they can and do change is the participants' awareness of the conflict and their social and political identity. From the Arabs' point of view, this change is insufficient; what truly cries out for change is the oppressive and discriminatory reality in which they live day after day.

DILEMMAS AND CHALLENGES

All of the foregoing calls into question the effectiveness of bringing these groups together: Is it, or is it not, right and worthwhile to do so? This is a legitimate question, especially against the backdrop of the reality that we are living through in these times. But if an encounter is going to be held, our model seems to us to provide a professional and profound approach—given that it treats reality as a whole, addresses the differing needs of the two groups, and gives all the participants the opportunity to take a look at themselves, to open up their awareness, to look at their ethnic identity. This is not to say, however, that we have found the optimal model—that we have reached our goal and can rest on our laurels. The work is constantly giving rise to dilemmas and problems, and we are always working on changing and improving. To conclude the chapter, then, we will address some of the dilemmas with which this working model of ours presents us.

The first and principal dilemma relates to the very act of bringing groups together and the degree to which doing so is effective, an issue already mentioned in passing. To this dilemma there is no quick and easy resolution. At the School for Peace, among our goals are to raise consciousness and to promote the development of identity. Through the encounters we conduct, these objectives are achievable, and indeed are achieved, with respect to both the Arab and the Jewish participants. But if we view the subject more broadly in light of the external reality and of the different aspirations and goals of our participants, the dilemma is not simple and in any case cannot be resolved at the School for Peace.

Encounter, any encounter, does not in and of itself change reality. In the best case it may alter the insight of the participants and thereby change the way they experience reality. The Arabs as a minority group often aspire to change the oppressive reality in which they live, and indeed in many cases that may well be the primary motivation for their participation in meetings of this kind. As we have already noted, such a goal is not realistic and cannot be achieved in any such meeting, regardless of the approach taken. Hence, the disappointment and frustration of the Arab group in the encounter are a result of the asymmetry of reality and of the fact that they are the weaker group in the conflict. In addition, the more authentic the encounter and the more it exposes the participants to an unblinking confrontation with their reality, the greater will be the frustration felt by the Arabs. In contrast, meetings that attempt to blur reality, to prettify it, could probably reduce those feelings of frustration by encouraging participants to stay cocooned in their illusions. That, obviously, is not our mission. In any case the most effective path to changing reality is social and political action. The encounter we conduct is an educational activity and as such is limited in its ability to change the face of society.

The second dilemma comes from the approach we use in our work. With our model, we concentrate on the relations between two groups and on the conflict that exists between them. In this context, the national voices of the two sides are the most authentic voices within the group. This is doubly reinforced because the participants themselves pay more attention to their comrades who speak in this voice. As one Jewish woman said in one of the meetings, "I respected the militant side more; although it was hard, it was more authentic. This is not an issue of opinions because there wasn't a lot of difference in the positions, but rather it concerns the ability to go all the way with things, to bring up the hard things that are unpleasant to say and unpleasant to cope with." In this situation the legitimacy of other voices in the group is likely to be negated, and a further complication arises if the personal gets mixed up with the national, as it sometimes does. Participants who need attention, who have to be at the center of the discussion, sometimes seize on this principle of the primacy of the national voice: they adopt the "appropriate positions" that will bring them to center stage. Given that our goal in a meeting is to investigate the totality of existing relations between Jews and Arabs, the facilitators must be alert to this trap—which is not simple to spot—and try to cope with it. The subject is further complicated when we take into account that in general the facilitators, like the participants, tend to have more respect for the national voice.

The third dilemma lies on the continuum between the individual and the group. In our work we focus on intergroup interactions and processes. We do not relate to interpersonal interactions, and at times we even see them as interfering in the attempt to gain a better understanding of the relations between the two groups. Sensing this, participants may feel that the facilitation is not respectful of individual differences and does not give them expression but instead uses these differences as an instrument in the service of a goal that, at least at the outset, seems veiled and unclear. And this feeling can intensify in the wake of the pain and distress participants experience during the encounter.

The goal of the facilitation is not to abuse the participants or to manipulate them or their feelings for any reason whatsoever; this is a potential unwelcome byproduct of the collective focus. We remain convinced that the advantages of our approach far outweigh its disadvantages. Tajfel (1978b) related to this dichotomy between individual and group when he said, "The point of departure (and of arrival) was, however, firmly kept in the arena of intergroup relations because of my conviction that it is only when this is explicitly done (at some risk of neglect of other issues) that we have, as social psychologists, a good chance of making a contribution to the understanding of social processes at large."

We close with two additional comments. First, we are in a continual process of learning and experimenting so as to improve our working model. Dilemmas and challenges keep us open as long as we remain prepared to deal with them and to make changes. And, second, we have evidently chosen for ourselves the hardest and most complicated way of working on the Jewish-Arab conflict. Our path requires of participants that they confront the conflict courageously and in depth, an approach that involves pain and frustration and disappointment. These feelings are projected onto the facilitators and onto the entire staff at the School for

Peace, and they themselves become discouraged and feel burned out even though at the same time they get profound satisfaction from doing serious work. We could be holding fun encounters that would lift the spirits of the participants and the facilitators alike. But that would be a sin against truth, perpetrated by us in collusion with the participants. We know full well that a heightened awareness of the hard reality in which we are living brings people to a far-from-easy confrontation with themselves and with the larger situation; it disturbs their peace of mind and the sense of comfort that hiding one's head in the sand can bring. Between these two options, the path we ought to follow is absolutely clear. In awareness, however painful, is embodied one of the most important human values: the right to have a choice and the option to change and to be changed.

4

LIBERATE THE OPPRESSED AND THEIR OPPRESSORS

Encounters between University Students

RABAH HALABI, NAVA SONNENSCHEIN, AND ARIELLA FRIEDMAN

In 1990, we introduced a year-long course as a joint project of the School for Peace and the Department of Social Psychology of Tel-Aviv University. The course is intended for students in the master's degree program in the department of psychology and other departments in the social sciences, and it ideally has an equal number of Jews and Arabs participating. The goal of the course is to learn about groups in conflict through study of the Jewish-Arab conflict.

The program combines experiential learning and lectures about theory. In the experiential part, participants are brought together for a series of Jewish-Arab meetings to learn about the nature of the conflict and the processes that characterize it. This part of the course is led by two facilitators (an Arab and a Jew) from the School for Peace, while the instructors for the theoretical part observe the process through a one-way mirror. The other segment comprises theoretical lectures about group process, social identity, and especially groups in conflict. The significant challenge in this part is to tie participants' experience from the first part to the insights of theory. Over the years, we tried to deal with this challenge in a number of ways without success. We came to the conclusion that aspiring to integrate traditional lectures with group processes and personal experiences is overly ambitious. The course in its present format is an experiential workshop throughout the year, with every fourth meeting beginning with a theoretical component. The hope is that the students will use the theoretical material they are exposed to during the course to work through and enrich what they are experiencing.

The style of group facilitation is open; participants are asked to discuss any subject they find interesting or troublesome that relates to the Jewish-Arab conflict. The facilitators attempt to point out or bring into sharper focus the processes occurring between the two groups in the room. The discussion is carried out mostly in a binational forum, although the first hour of every third meeting is devoted to a uninational forum. This uninational format divides the group in two; the Jewish students continue their discussion with the Jewish facilitator, and the Arab group has a separate discussion led by the Arab facilitator.

The theoretical component includes the following lectures (subject to changes and additions as the need arises):

> Group conflict: concepts, terms, and models
>
> Stages in group process
>
> Individual and social identity
>
> Stereotypes
>
> Cognitive maps of conflict
>
> Theories of the development of ethnic identity

We began a similar course at Ben-Gurion University in Beersheva in 1994, another at the Hebrew University in Jerusalem in 1996, and another at the University of Haifa in 1997.

This course, in its various venues, provides a unique and innovative study of conflict in an academic setting in that it creates a link between experiential, hands-on learning and theory. This integration is successful both for the students who participate in this enriching and unusual (according to reports) experience and for the instructional staff, for whom the integration of professionals specializing in Jewish-Arab encounter with academics dealing with theories of groups in conflict creates a rewarding cross-fertilization.

Since 1997, we have added to the program a joint workshop for all the students in the various university-level courses offered by the School for Peace. At this workshop, held at Neve Shalom/Wahat al Salam for two days, all the students who are enrolled in these courses meet together and continue their dialogue. These discussions open up new options for understanding the conflict because the much larger size of the group enables participants to play different roles than those they have been accustomed to in their own class meetings during the year.

THE COURSE AT TEL-AVIV UNIVERSITY IN 1996–97

The 1996–97 course at Tel-Aviv University was the sixth such course we have offered since 1991. The course was documented (verbatim) in writing by observers who had taken a similar course the previous year. Below we describe and analyze what took place in this course, attempting to utilize it to understand the processes typical of encounters for adults that we offer at the School for Peace, particularly the university-level courses. The course had sixteen participants—eight Arabs and eight Jews. In the Jewish group, six were from the department of psychology, one from the program for excellence in B.A. studies, and one from the law school. In the Arab group, four were social-work students, two were from the law school, and two were psychology students.

The group met for the entire academic year; there were twenty-two meetings of three hours each. The group also participated in the two-day, interuniversity Jewish-Arab meeting (mentioned above) toward the end of the year. Names used in the descriptions that follow are not the real names of the participants.

The first meeting opened with a presentation of the method of facilitation, the world-view behind it, and its concrete characteristics. After this explanation there was a brief round of introductions, and then the group embarked on an open dialogue that continued for the entire academic year.

An analysis of the written documentation on this group, as well as our accumulated experience working with Jewish-Arab encounters, points to a dialogue between two identities as being the central characteristic of the dialogue between the two groups. The encounter develops as a conflict between two identities until the point at which each identity acknowledges the existence of the other, in mutual acceptance. Or, more precisely, the Arab identity struggles for its existence as an equal identity, given that it is the weaker of the two and hence its existence may not be taken for granted.

At the beginning of the process, the Jewish group had trouble accepting the Arab identity, of which it had no awareness before the meeting, although in the end this approach changed and the Arab identity received legitimacy in the room. Acceptance of the Arab identity and conscious recognition of its existence enabled the beginning of a dialogue of equality.

The process in reality is more complicated and dialectical than can be conveyed in this chapter. The meeting creates interaction and reciprocal influence between the two identities. The intergroup struggle has its ups and downs over the course of the encounter, with different participants finding themselves at different life stages of the group. The changing character of the group process is manifest both in content (conveyed by means of verbal "language") and in behavior ("language" in its nonverbal sense).

For the purpose of recounting the process here, we simplify by subdividing the description of one particular group's meetings over two semesters into five distinct phases that are typical of many Jewish and Arab groups in the encounters we have run. The five phases are:

> Initial explorations and declarations of intent
>
> Strengthening of the Arab group
>
> Resumption of power by the Jewish group
>
> Impasse
>
> A different dialogue

All the direct quotes are excerpts from the documentation of this group and appear here, in translation, exactly as recorded. This kind of partial portrait cannot wholly convey, in all its complexity, what takes place in reality; but we believe this is the only way to enable the reader, in a reasonably brief and orderly fashion, to get a sense of the spirit of what happens in the group.

Phase One: Initial Explorations and Declarations of Intent

The first phase for this group extends over three meetings, more or less, and is characterized by caution, politeness, and an attempt to check out the rules of the game in the group. The boundaries between the two national groups are not clear yet, either from the standpoint of the discussion or in seating patterns, which are mixed. Identity does not receive a full and clear emphasis. Individuals from the Jewish and from the Arab group identify with stands taken by the opposing group while neglecting to present their own attitudes and identities. Participants at this stage discuss mainly the nature of the encounter and to what degree it is connected to reality.

At first the discussion is about the nature and character of the group. The Arab participants contend that the group is artificial and doesn't allow for real dialogue. One Arab participant, a man, says: "It's impossible to get to a real situation in which everyone talks and says what he thinks; the group is artificial." An Arab woman adds: "The question is whether this reflects what is on the outside; the manner of sitting is artificial; the question is whether it's possible to go beyond that; in the beginning it will surely be artificial."

The Jewish group thinks that it will be possible to hold a real dialogue although they agree with the Arabs that the group as a whole does not reflect the external reality. A Jewish man says: "I disagree, we came with the goal of talking. The arguments will be realistic because that's how we are. On the outside they are usually different; it is impossible to generalize from dozens to hundreds to thousands. The goal of generalizing from groups to people is mistaken." A Jewish woman supports that argument, adding: "The question is whether we can be a microcosm."

Thus, the Jewish group tries to narrow the dialogue to the framework of the group itself, irrespective of any implications for or influence on the reality outside; by contrast, the Arab group describes this as a fake dialogue, shrunk to the boundaries of the group—not significant or valuable, artificial. The meaning of the term *real dialogue* turns out to be different for the Jewish group and the Arab group. For the Arabs, the dialogue is real only if it is representative and hence has wider implications; for the Jews, the dialogue is real even if it does not represent reality as long as the participants bring to it realistic arguments.

From this point, a negotiation develops between the two national groups over the content of the group dialogue.

JEWISH WOMAN: It bothers me that this is an intergroup rather than an interpersonal dialogue. That is, like, almost impossible. It's insoluble. The best chance for talking is at the personal level.

ARAB MAN: I have a friend who is a Likudnik; that solves something?

JEWISH WOMAN: Our level is the interpersonal level, to move beyond slogans.

ARAB WOMAN: On the personal level, everyone can connect. The conflict is between groups and the personal level cannot solve it.

JEWISH WOMAN: The question is, what do we want? I have no pretensions about solving the conflict. I want to clarify my feelings and my attitudes.

ARAB WOMAN: I am new at this university, I came here as Nasreen, now when I go out for a break or when I go home, I go as an Arab [woman]. From a personal standpoint there are differences between me and the rest of the Arab group here. But I already feel that I am part of the group and not alone here.

ARAB WOMAN: We experience the conflict on different levels apparently; I, since I belong to a minority, live my identity as an Arab woman every day and every minute. I cannot turn it off.

We see here a vast and significant difference between the expectations and needs of the respective groups. The Arab group as a minority wants a national, political discussion and hopes for concrete results. The Jewish group as the majority is, at this stage, still not making the connection with its group identity. There is a diversity of expression on the part of its members, and they do not speak in the name of the group (although, for the sake of highlighting the disagreement between the two groups, the Jewish statements we have quoted thus far have been fairly uniform). It is our contention that the Jewish group's desire to avoid the political dimension and the intergroup conflict and their preference for talking on the personal level come from an unconscious wish to continue to protect the overall status quo as it exists in microcosm in the majority group— that is, to protect the dominance of the Jewish group.

At this stage reference is made to political issues in the discussion but in only a superficial way, as in headlines: a Jewish state versus a democratic state, service by Arabs in the Israeli army, benefits given to army veterans, the Arab identity in Israel, the language to be spoken at the meeting, land confiscation. There is rapid transition from one subject to another; and no in-depth, basic clarification of these issues develops. These indeed are the heart of the conflict but, at this stage, they are glossed over quickly as if they constitute an abstract of the tale yet to be written by the participants over the course of their encounter.

Phase Two: The Strengthening of the Arab Group

After the stage of courtesy and exploration, the Arab group begins to solidify and to unite around an emergent leadership that takes it through a series of measured steps. This process happens slowly and continues over a number of meetings; it demands of the Arab group effort, courage, and

inner strength. During the initial meetings about half the Arab participants have not joined in the discussion, and the talking is done by two or
three spokespersons.

As the dialogue progresses, additional Arab participants take courage and begin expressing themselves: "I felt strong in this meeting, in spite
of my frustration and powerlessness on account of the situation; I was able
to talk and express my difficulty and my anger." The Arab participants
draw this security and strength from one another, mainly during the uninational meetings: "In the uninational meeting, I felt safe. The meeting
was very fruitful. I felt very included, very much that I belonged, . . . with
the hope that maybe if we are united we can change things." And indeed
the Arab group has unified and its members are expressing similar ideas
and attitudes, leaving their differences to be thoroughly clarified in the
uninational meetings rather than bringing them up in the presence of the
Jewish group. The Arab group's uniting around strategic leadership has
strengthened the group; its positions are now being expressed sharply and
clearly, and it is setting an agenda that deals with the issues that are in
conflict. The group has done this in the knowledge that political dialogue
has the potential to change reality by changing the balance of power between the two groups.

During the next several meetings, beginning with the fourth, the
Arabs express their identity clearly and unequivocally, knowing that a
blurring of identities only weakens their standing in the room. The change
is also expressed by the way the participants are now sitting: in two groupings, one Jewish and one Arab, with the facilitators in-between.

> ARAB WOMAN: What is troubling is that the State of Israel is the state of the
> Jewish people and not the state of all its citizens; that's where the prob-
> lem arises. I define myself as a Palestinian Arab with an Israeli identity
> card—formally, a citizen. I don't feel myself to be an Israeli. I don't in-
> clude myself in the category of Israeli, don't identify with the Israeli
> team. In the recent incidents at the Tomb of Joseph [in Nablus], my first
> identification was with the Palestinians. I am a part of that people. I
> don't at all feel the Israeli part within me. And the state doesn't let me
> feel a part of it.

The issue of the State of Israel as a Jewish state, as this defines the identity of the Arabs in Israel, becomes the focus of the discussion in the group
throughout the year. The two groups hold a lengthy negotiation over the
options for changing the definition of the state so that it will be the state
of all its citizens and thus enable the Arabs to be included in it.

Another subject by means of which the Arab group expresses its identity in the room is discrimination.

> ARAB WOMAN: In Israel, 20 percent are not Jews. Their home, their identity is not Jewish; they have an identity, and they have a culture. If you go to a village in the Triangle [an Arab area in Israel] or in the Galilee, citizens of the State of Israel are living there and you see streets from the previous century. That's how people are living in Israel. And there are the unrecognized villages. People who have no running water, no electricity, they are not recognized by the government. There's no point in talking on the theoretical level; let's talk about the situation now.

> ARAB MAN: Why does an Ethiopian Jew have the right to come here, yet an Arab who was here in 1948, living here and making his living here, why doesn't he have the right of return? That is a lack of equality that bothers me.

The Arab identity comes also from the suffering that was the lot of the Arabs as a people and as a nation, as a result of the founding of the State of Israel.

> ARAB WOMAN: In the massacre at Kufr Kassem, soldiers shot at civilians. The problem is, how to reach a point where it is possible to live in equality. The option of living in humiliation is like death.

And arguments are made concerning the Palestinians in the occupied territories and the Palestinian diaspora: "To place a closure on an entire people, this is humiliating and tramples the honor of another people. Each day of the closure is house arrest. How would you feel if someone came and put a closure on you, so you are forbidden to come out of the house to get food. A humiliating situation, disgraceful, one that makes it impossible to understand any ambivalence or guilt feelings on your part."

These arguments come mostly from a few participants. At this stage the Arab group is uniting, and they express themselves in a firm and assertive manner, as a demand for rights to which they are entitled and not as a request or in supplication. This gives a lot of stature and power to the Arabs in the room, and there is a feeling that they are becoming the dominant group, dictating the dialogue and the agenda. The Jewish group finds the experience of this power difficult, as we shall see further on, because this is a situation that the Jews are not familiar with in their day-to-day lives.

At first the Jewish group accepts the arguments of the Arab group and supports the contention that they are entitled to absolute equality of rights, so that for a moment is appears as if there is no conflict at all between the two groups. As they proceed further it turns out that the situation is more complex.

After the Arab group raises the issue of discrimination and oppression, the Jewish group feels distress. This distress is expressed in various ways. The Jews have difficulty with the gap that has been revealed to them between their self-concept as liberals and their image as it is reflected in the way the Arabs perceive them. The Arab group serves as a mirror for the Jewish group, and the reflection the Jewish group sees does not accord with their view of their own image.

> JEWISH WOMAN: There is a gap between how I want to paint myself and what I am. I feel sentimental toward my grandfather and grandmother's generation, who were pioneers, but on the other hand [there is] the price paid by another group. I wouldn't want to know that I had caused this. This touches on my identity as a human being, as a state.

The Jewish group finds that it cannot run away to some tranquil place rather than face the criticisms of the Arab group.

> JEWISH MAN: I have a nice quiet world; I'm doing everything I can to run away. Yasmeen knocks on the door and puts a projector in front of me, and I want to ignore it.

The distress is so strong that it feels like an explosion. The Jews experience this loss of being on the side of justice and the loss of their power as the erasure of their identity.

> JEWISH WOMAN: They said "the Jewish people," and they expressed very hard attitudes toward the Jewish people. The way I see it my desire to be a people was trampled on here. I had a hard week after last week's meeting; what Ahmad did to me was very hard. What is going on in the room is the obverse of reality. Ahmad wiped out my identity in the room, and on the outside they are wiping out the Palestinian identity. I felt that I have to struggle; I usually fight people who are wiping out an identity.

The distress expressed by the Jewish group alarms the Arab group, who may also be frightened at the strength they themselves demonstrated, something unknown in reality. This evokes an internal dialogue among the Arabs and reflections as to whether they had exceeded the bounds of the permissible or of good taste.

ARAB MAN: I want to get the message across in a moderate way . . . after having been extreme in the first few meetings.

ARAB WOMAN: Extreme or not extreme is a relative thing. It depends on whom you are dealing with.

ARAB MAN: The framework here provides the opportunity for expressing one's opinion, . . . and I didn't think of wounding the other side.

These expressions of concern come up repeatedly among the Arab participants, mainly in the uninational meetings. The young people talk of an inner struggle over "whether to express yourself openly and authentically, given the price you are likely to pay for it," and between "whether to be yourself as a Palestinian Arab or to be an Arab as defined by the Jews."

Phase Three: Resumption of Power by the Jewish Group

The preexisting identity of the Jewish participants has been undermined: the Arab group has undermined the status quo that exists in the real world outside, and the Jews, as the dominant group, experience this as an eradication of their identity, a loss of control and a loss of power.

JEWISH WOMAN: It seems to me that the power game here is inverted; here the Arab group has the power. Here, to be right is to be strong. The weak side by definition is moral, and so, in the room, you are the strong ones.

The Arab group is perceived as strong in the room, a phenomenon that does not exist in reality, and the Jews do not know how to cope with it: "This is a little like arm-wrestling; it takes away the will to fight. They (the Arabs) are a very strong group; they have a lot of power. We tried to come to terms and they are always fighting us."

The Jewish group finds itself in distress and expresses feelings of frustration and even of despair.

JEWISH WOMAN: For me it is a feeling of frustration, pessimism. Maybe it's enough, I don't want to be here in this state, . . . but to leave here is not an option for me.

This may also be a message to the Arab group that the meeting has become unbearable, and the Jewish group expresses thoughts and reflec-

tions about leaving the course if the situation continues to be so frustrating. But the Jewish group emerges from this situation through a struggle
to bring back the prior situation and return control in the room to itself,
as is the case in reality. The group does this in all kinds of ways, the object of which is to undermine the situation that the Arab group has created and to thoroughly subvert the legitimacy of the Arab identity.

One method is to control the dialogue in the group and try to set the
agenda. The Jews demand that political subjects be put aside; they are to
be neglected in favor of talking about personal issues: "Sometimes things
have to be put aside. Maybe it's worthwhile to make this a meeting between human beings. Maybe we'll decide to agree with everything in order to put aside this endless dispute." And when this request finds no response from the Arabs, there is a more blunt and forceful demand: "Are
we going to talk for another twelve meetings about hunger in the [occu-
pied] territories? Nothing will come of this. I have the feeling that there
are human beings in this class who are just like parrots [parroting slo-
gans]. For sure everything exists, and we have to deal with identities. That
has to come up, but when that's all there is, then from my standpoint it's
an impasse." Attaching the label of *parrots* to the Arab participants is an
attempt to delegitimize the political arguments raised by the Arab group
during the meetings. The Arabs strenuously oppose this attempt and fight
a stormy battle to continue the political dialogue.

> ARAB WOMAN: I sympathize with you personally, but the problem is be-
> tween groups. Here we sit and talk, but then I go back to my village,
> and the sewage is running in the streets and the schools [buildings] are
> shacks. We can connect on the personal level, but this will not solve the
> conflict.

What the Jewish group doesn't succeed in doing in the group it suc-
ceeds in doing outside the group when the Jews are invited home by an
Arab participant for lunch. This event becomes significant for the group,
and in its wake the Jewish group is in a wonderful mood and the Arab
group is frustrated.

> ARAB WOMAN: I didn't like that; it's very much a stereotype. . . . Talking
> about Arab culture, no one thinks about going to a lecture by an Arab
> poet, what they think about is going to eat at an Arab's house. This
> whole discussion is like a game—as if we are playing at becoming closer.

The Arab group experiences this incident as an Arab participant's
unconscious collaboration with the Jewish group and is angry about it.

The group had aspired to a different relationship, knowing that to have a plate of hummus together doesn't change the relations between oppressor and oppressed. The Arabs feel they are shooting themselves in the foot and that the incident has served only to weaken the Arab position. The Jews by contrast feel that they have been strengthened and that relations are back to normal.

The Jewish group goes on with this task when it adopts two additional strategies, the first of which is to blur the distinction made by the Arab group between the good guys and the bad guys in the conflict by joining the Arabs in the position of the victim in the story: "Personally I am uncomfortable with the conflict, with the Jewish state, and so on, and with discrimination. We are not totally bad, unethical rulers. We also have a complicated stature here; it's not all black." And another Jewish participant offers a personal example to support this argument: "I was a pilot, and we did a lot of damage to the other side. This has cost and continues to cost highly in terms of health. . . . With you, there's no dialectic. . . . This is very strongly so for me. For you, the Jews are either good or bad. . . . The situation is much more complicated." This is the first time that this participant has mentioned that he is a pilot; this lends power to his position and that of the Jewish group.

At this point the Arab group feels weak; the Jewish group has taken over the dialogue in the group and continues to hit the Arabs where they are most vulnerable by alluding to the degree of sensitivity and humanity of the Arabs: "I ask myself, the pain over the soldiers who were killed this week, the soldiers at the Tomb of Joseph, the family that was murdered near Beit Shemesh—will the Arab side find room for this pain, will it be the same kind of pain for them?" A Jewish woman continues, bringing the point into sharper focus: "I don't identify with the terrorist, but I can understand his position; I don't see that kind of understanding toward the soldier on your part."

In fact the Jewish group is trying to portray the Arab group as lacking in sensitivity, and deficient in its ethical values, in contrast to the Jews who, according to them, have only the most noble values. This contention is rejected emphatically when the Arabs put the behaviors into the context of the conflict: "I can understand the difficulty you expressed about hearing how bad you are all the time, but it's also important to say that to ask the ruled to understand the pain of the ruler, who so thoroughly humiliates me, and to understand that he is doing this for reasons of security—that's just about impossible. You bring this up as if you understand us and we don't understand you. There is an asymmetry here, in the situation in reality, from my standpoint a humiliating asymmetry, so your argument is not relevant." The Jewish group does not concede this point and raises the argument of murder for the sake of family honor among the Arabs: "Murder 'for the sake of family honor' says something about attitudes toward human life. Damage to the honor of the family does not justify murder among Jews. With us, human life is the highest value."

This struggle over who is more humane is the second weapon generally utilized by the Jewish group to overwhelm the Arab group and win the struggle. Indeed at this stage the Arab group feels great distress. Their sense is that all their efforts have been for nothing, and that what has been is what will be. The Jewish group feels that it has regained power and control in the room.

Phase Four: Impasse

In this phase, during the course of a number of meetings, the dialogue is mired down; the reigning atmosphere in the room is one of exhaustion on both sides, especially in the Arab group, which expresses frustration and despair. The Arabs have concluded that the situation cannot be changed, that all the energy and all the talking they have invested to change the Jews and the situation have been in vain.

This situation emerges toward the end of the first semester and continues at the beginning of the second semester. The first meeting of the new term opens with an unequivocal announcement by one of the Arab women: "There is no point in continuing this dialogue; talking will not help. At most you can say that you understand us; what good will that do?" An Arab man expresses his disappointment in a different way: "For me, and I think for the rest of the Arab group, there has been no change in the group. In fact the change that has taken place in me has been a result of things that have happened outside the group." Another Arab woman gives voice to her despair and her sense of being detached from the situation: "Since the age of nineteen I have studied with Jews, and I see that I am not finding a place for myself—not because I don't want to, but because no place is left for me." There is disappointment and frustration because the Arabs are rejected and not accepted as citizens and as Israelis, although they have made a decision to be a part of that world: "I am really sick of proving my loyalty; you can see that the Arabs have long since done all they can; the Arabs have made their decision."

At this juncture, the atmosphere is difficult and depressing. The contentions of the Arabs meet with silence on the part of the Jews or, in the best case, with a comment to the effect that this is the way things are and not much can be done to change it. "I can't totally commit to changing; I have a need to talk in this room about my fear." The group feels that it has reached impasse, that it can no longer engage in discussion, that the dialogue has been wrung dry and that the course itself should have been limited to one semester. A Jewish woman expresses this feeling: "I don't see where this is going now, the dialogue between us; it doesn't appear that we can move on to anywhere." In these meetings there are a lot of absences and the feeling is of a physical disintegration of the group. An Arab man gives a metaphorical description of this sense of the group's end: "They say that at the end of the world there will be a bloodbath, and that will be it; that the Jews will be gathered in from all over the earth and that will cause a great conflagration and a terrible and devastating bloodbath. We can sit here and wait until it happens or we can do something to prevent the disaster."

This last comment gives expression to the transition from complete despair to action, from the disintegration of the group to the continuation of its existence. And indeed a transition takes place at this point from a lost-cause situation, in which the dialogue has completely broken down and everyone is talking about the end, to the beginning of a different dialogue. The change has come in the wake of movement on the part of the Jewish group away from its fortified position and its acceptance of the change in the balance of power that the Arab group had dictated earlier in the process.

Phase Five: A Different Dialogue

After both groups exhaust one another and after it seems impossible to move forward to anywhere at all, there is a breakthrough, and a different dialogue commences, one the group has not known thus far: this is a more egalitarian dialogue, with the talking taking place eye to eye and in mutual respect. This breakthrough is made possible by the Jewish group's acceptance of the new situation created by the Arab group: a situation that undermines the status quo so familiar outside the room, that of a dominating group and a dominated group. It happens when the Jewish group acknowledges the situation as it exists outside and takes responsibility for its part in that reality: "You talk about power. I take advantage of my power; I am in control, and I can ignore that. I can close the door and that's it. I am not being discriminated against; I am not under suspicion."

Other Jewish participants talked of the changes they experienced within the group:

> This is the first time that I am taking part in a meeting with Arabs, and during the vacation I thought about it and got some insight into what was happening in the meeting, and I want to share it with you. When the tragedy of the helicopters happened [in which Jewish soldiers died], I felt that there is hypocrisy on the Israeli side; in the media they allotted so much [time] to national mourning, compared to almost nothing when the tragedy of Kfar Kana happened [in which Lebanese civilians died]. It is hypocrisy not to feel sadness when Palestinian children are killed and in contrast to feel so much sadness when the soldiers were killed in the helicopter tragedy.

This revealing of their cards on the part of the Jewish group and their being willing to talk about themselves as rulers, as the strong group, and about the meaning of that open the dialogue afresh. The Arab group feels more comfortable, feels itself a partner in the dialogue and senses a new opening for the hope for change in the group and perhaps in reality. The Arabs begin to share what they have been experiencing and the insights they have had in the wake of the encounter: "I remember in the early meetings they said we were very strong, and the feeling was that the Arab group had power. Now I am laughing at myself a little; it's not clear to me where we got that feeling of power from. I am here as an Arab woman and despite that there are still power relations, relations of oppressor and oppressed, someone who has rights and someone whose rights are denied."

At this stage the dialogue flows; participants share the awareness they have reached. The struggle between the two groups is still there, but it is not central, as it was in the previous phase.

> Arab man: I want to be without feelings of humiliation and a sense of impotence. I want to exist and to belong, but I walk around with a terrible feeling of lack of honor, of fear, inferiority. . . . Not that I go around feeling resentment, a need for revenge, but it's inside me. Life is a kind of social game between a dwarf and a giant.

> Jewish man: I think that we here have given them that feeling because we behave toward them in a power-oriented way and in that sense we are responsible. . . . I and maybe all of us Jews are relating in a power-oriented way toward Arabs, and maybe the key to changing the situation

> is for us to acknowledge that. We are not the only ethical ones, and by putting responsibility on the other side we don't get ourselves anywhere.
>
> JEWISH MAN: After we acknowledge that, what is important is what we do because otherwise it's not a sensational discovery that we oppress [Arabs].

It is a sensational revelation for Jews to confess to being oppressors and to admit the significance of this control vis-à-vis the Arabs. It is especially meaningful to the Arab group, which has been struggling to hear this fact since the first meeting; but it is also significant for the Jewish group because this allows them to look at their identity as the group that is strong and in control.

Toward the end of the year, the dialogue returns to practical questions about how to live together and specifically about the nature of the state—Jewish or for all its citizens—a discussion that has been with the group throughout the year. But this time the dialogue is not argumentative; rather, it flows from a sincere desire to find a way to live together in equality and mutual respect.

> JEWISH WOMAN: It had seemed to me that I understood that if we concede on the Law of Return [an Israeli law granting automatic citizenship to immigrant Jews], you will concede on the right of return [the claim to the automatic right of Palestinians to return to Palestine/Israel]. There is a state that we are all living in and whoever is here has right of way over someone living elsewhere.
>
> ARAB WOMAN: The ideal and optimal solution is for two autonomous entities in the state because it is just not possible for this to be a state for all its citizens.
>
> JEWISH WOMAN: The question is whether or not this distinction will solve the problem. It is possible to go on hating Arabs in an autonomous entity as well. We need to build something in common. . . . The question is whether it is possible to build a social order that will end the matter of discrimination, of oppressor and oppressed, aside from the matter of national identity.
>
> ARAB WOMAN: I think that, as an oppressed minority within this state, I have no possibility of expressing myself within the collective, so I want autonomy in order to express myself.

At the start of the encounter the Arabs demand a state of all its citizens, and when they find that this is impossible and will not come about, they demand autonomy instead. Meanwhile some of the Jews, having agreed to a state of all its citizens, feel that this autonomy threatens the togetherness and the partnership.

This discussion and dialogue continue until the end of the year. Naturally the group does not arrive at a solution, but each person takes away something from this encounter. From the reports of participants one may infer the changes they underwent and sense how different these changes were for the Jewish group and for the Arab group. The Jews report insights into the complexity of the conflict and the difficult situation of the Arabs as a minority and about their own awareness of themselves as the majority: "At the start of the encounter, I wanted to prove that we aren't the bad guys and that no one is 'more right' in this conflict. After what I have heard from the Arab group, I understand now what it is to be an oppressed minority, twenty-four hours a day." Another Jewish participant adds: "There is something essential that is different between us, the struggle, the discrimination. . . . I feel that the conflict doesn't affect me as much as it does you; it becomes a part of your personality. At first I thought that we are alike, but I have reached the conclusion that we are not, and that frustrates me."

The Jews in fact are proud of the changes they have undergone and report this with a feeling of satisfaction, a good feeling. The Arabs are left with an ambivalent feeling and with questions as to the usefulness of this sort of meeting.

> ARAB WOMAN: "I live here with Jews and I have a lot of Jewish friends, and I get along with them great; and whenever the Arab participants in the group talked about discrimination, I didn't feel it. But now the more I am in this group, the more I begin to get in touch with the discrimination, and my Arab identity is strengthened.

> ARAB MAN: I feel that the encounter weakened me. It has made more tangible to me just how much I cannot behave as I like on the outside. Not that I lie on the outside; I say things that are more or less me, but I compromise. The group hasn't strengthened me but instead has weakened me; it has shown me my own weakness and has not helped me start to behave outside the way I behave in this group.

A Jewish woman aptly describes the distinctive influence this encounter exerts on Arabs and Jews when she says: "What in fact has happened to the Jews and to the Arabs is that they have become more aware, but the Jews are glad and proud of their awareness, whereas the Arabs have become fairly pessimistic in light of this awareness." This description hits the mark in expressing the asymmetry that exists between the two groups. After the meeting, each person returns to the respective reality from which he or she came. Reality has not changed in the wake of the encounter; what has changed is the awareness we have of it. Jewish participants feel proud of the awareness they have developed as a result of the meeting and of the changes they have undergone in this respect. This gives them a feeling of accomplishment, along with satisfaction. The Arab participants go home after the encounter to the same difficult reality, with an amplified awareness of that difficulty. Thus a new awareness does not, in and of itself, satisfy them—and may even frustrate them, further exposing them as it does to their weakness as Arabs and as part of a minority group in the face of the oppressive reality in the real world.

DISCUSSION

> While the problem of humanization has always been man's central problem, it now takes on the character of an inescapable concern. Concern for humanization leads at once to the recognition of dehumanization, not only as an ontological possibility, but as an historical reality. . . . Within history, in concrete, objective contexts, both humanization and dehumanization are possibilities for man as an uncompleted being conscious of his incompletion. But while both humanization and dehumanization are real alternatives, only the first is man's vocation. This vocation is constantly negated, yet it is affirmed by that very negation. It is thwarted by injustice, exploitation, oppression, and the violence of the oppressors: It is affirmed by the yearning of the oppressed for freedom and justice, and by their struggle to recover their lost humanity.

In Paolo Freire's *Pedagogy of the Oppressed* (1972), from which the quote above is taken, Freire discusses the nature of oppression and of freedom, the spiritual mechanisms of oppressor and oppressed, and the path to the liberation of humanity. His central contention is that a situation of dehumanization negates the humanity of the oppressor and the oppressed alike and that the task of liberation is laid on the shoulders of the oppressed: "This, then, is the great humanistic and historical task for the oppressed: to liberate themselves and their oppressors as well. The oppressors . . . cannot find . . . the strength to liberate either the oppressed or themselves. Only power that springs from the weakness of the oppressed will be sufficiently strong to free both. Any attempt to 'soften' the power of the oppressor in deference to the weakness of the oppressed almost always manifests itself in the form of false generosity."

According to Freire, *awareness* is the key word. As far as he is concerned, the key to change is through "praxis"—awareness and action intertwined with one another. Some will claim that the situation between Jews and Arabs does not resemble a state of oppression, but it is impossible to deny that in the Jewish-Arab conflict there is a ruler and a ruled; there are those who have rights and those whose rights have been partially denied them. What happened in the group whose story we have presented here in many respects resembles a process of liberation as Freire describes it: the Arab group gained strength and shed the pattern of internalizing its oppression; it came to express itself and its reality in a manner that was clear, sharp, and sometimes even assertive. The Arab group forced the Jewish group to confront that reality, a reality of oppression in which the Jews themselves have a part. Coping with this was difficult and painful and sometimes even intolerable for both sides in that it brought them out of their usual and familiar roles and upset the existing social order; on the road to building a new order, it created a feeling of anarchy. The Arab group grew stronger and more powerful but didn't wholly feel a connection to its newfound strength; sometimes it even drew back from this new situation, retreating to the cozier and more familiar refuge of being the weak and discriminated against. The Jewish group, meanwhile, felt that it was losing control and experienced the Arab group as dominant to the point of negating and wiping out the Jewish group's identity. This phenomenon is well-recognized in the literature. These effects are often observed as strongly in the "superior" group as in the "inferior" group, perhaps because destabilizing and delegitimating status relations present a threat to the higher-status group's identity and that group reacts with enhanced attempts to defend their now-fragile superiority. (See Branscombe et al. 1999.)

At that point in our group, the Jews' identity as powerful rulers was negated. That identity had been central for them, and they experienced its being challenged as a threat to their existence. Although it was an identity they may have disliked, it was also one that they had not rushed to relinquish voluntarily. Only under pressure from the Arab group was the Jewish group freed from the weight of this burdensome identity by their acknowledgment of their status as rulers and hence of having partially denied the Arabs their rights. The inexorability of this fact, for the Jews and for the Arabs, plus the Jews' assumption of responsibility for the situation, released the oppressors from their burden—liberating them from the need to be defensive about an identity in which they did not believe and that they did not want. Thus, according to Freire, the Arab group liberated itself and the Jews from a situation of dehumanization and replaced it with one of liberty and equality, which restored the humanity of both sides.

For the group we have been discussing, this description of reality fits as long as we see the four walls of their meeting room as the group's boundaries. In other words, liberation happened to these individuals among themselves and through their interaction with the other within the group. The situation is more complicated when we break through these boundaries to the reality outside the group, which is unchanged. Outside, the awareness of individuals and their internal liberation are caught fast in the unyielding bonds of an oppressive reality. Because we assumed that the group was a microcosm of reality, our hope was that what happened in the group symbolized what is to come in a changing of reality. That change, as we learned, will take place by means of the changing awareness of the Arab group; the Jewish group will be obliged in turn to become more aware and to let go of a little of their power for the sake of offering more equality and more humanity to both sides.

However, the situation is not at all simple, and, in particular, the process of change is not necessarily unidirectional. Strengthening the Arab minority is likely to cause the majority to become more extreme and more oppressive, as we saw with the group described in this chapter. Participants felt frustrated and disappointed, and reality is likely to intensify those feelings further. Awareness on the part of the minority group is a necessary but not sufficient condition for change because, for change to occur, both the minority group and the majority group must perceive the existing situation as not legitimate and not stable (Turner and Brown 1978). This situation apparently came about in our group. The question is whether a similar situation can come about in the larger reality. Outside our meeting room, the group involved is impressively more numerous than that of our sixteen participants, whose quest for dialogue arose out of their dissatisfaction with reality as it stands today.

5
RECONSTRUCTING IDENTITY THROUGH THE ENCOUNTER WITH THE OTHER

The Facilitators' Training Course

RABAH HALABI

At the School for Peace we have been conducting a yearly facilitators' training course since 1991, using a model developed by Nava Sonnenschein and me. Designed for university graduates in the social sciences and humanities who are interested in working in Jewish-Arab encounter, the course encompasses 160 hours and includes the following training components:

Experiential workshop: The initial workshop segment takes place over five weekends at the beginning of the course and brings the participants together for an encounter with themselves, among themselves. The assumption is that someone who intends to facilitate Jewish-Arab encounters must experience, in depth and exhaustively, an encounter of the same kind. Thus he or she learns by personal experience about the phenomena typifying such an encounter and can work through the experience inwardly so as to be ready subsequently, as a facilitator, to listen with complete and informed attention to the interactions of workshop participants.

Lectures: This segment includes lectures on well-known theories from the field of group facilitation, including W. R. Bion's, Focal Conflict, and T-groups, and theories relating to ethnic and social identity from the realm of social psychology. In working with Jewish-Arab encounter, the facilitator must be conversant with the inner mysteries of groups in general and also have an understanding of the dynamics of relations between groups in conflict.

Key issues: In order to enrich the participants' knowledge of the Jewish-Arab conflict specifically, faculty members systematically share with them the knowledge we have accumulated on the subject over the years. This is done via lectures on various subjects like facilitating with a partner, language in the meeting, encounters with youth, and working in the uninational forum.

Peer facilitation: In this segment, the course participants facilitate a group made up of their colleagues in the course. After each forty-five-minute facilitation session, the trainee facilitators, their peers in the group, and the senior course facilitators analyze what happened in that session and try to learn from one another's experience.

Supervised observation: Participants observe, by one-way mirror, a three-day encounter for young people. Two senior facilitators guide and supervise their observation and help them understand and analyze the phenomena and processes they are witnessing in the encounter.

Supervised facilitation: This is a practicum during which the trainees lead a three-day workshop for youth, with a senior facilitator as partner and guide. After this workshop, the course participants may themselves begin working as facilitators.

THE ENCOUNTER WORKSHOP

The faculty believe that a facilitator's primary resource is herself or himself—his or her personality, insights, and awareness. Hence our emphasis in facilitator training is not on the techniques and skills of facilitation but rather on shaping the facilitator's own identity and growth as a human being. This is accomplished primarily through in-depth self-scrutiny by participants, catalyzed by interaction with the other, during the first part of the course. To get a closer look at what happens to participants during the course and how this shapes them as they work to become skilled facilitators, I describe here the experience of two individual trainees, one Jewish and the other Arab, from the facilitators' training course in 1997. The course had eleven participants, five Arabs and six Jews. This description provides a sense of the inner world of two of the participants and the changes they underwent during the sequence of meetings—things they said both during the encounter and in analyzing the meeting in hindsight, a month after the close of the workshop, when they embarked on the second stage of their training.

The quotes cited here are selections from comments made by the two participants—Harel (a Jewish trainee) and Samir (an Arab trainee)—during discussions that took place in the group at various times. The quotes are arranged chronologically but are not continuous; each stands alone. I hope that the sequence of selections provided here will succeed in getting across the overall picture. All names are, of course, fictitious.

First Meeting

HAREL (*during a discussion of which language should be spoken in the group*): (*Turns to the Arabs.*) I don't mind if you speak only Arabic and someone translates; I think that is your right. Or maybe we should all speak English. It's just not fair that we should speak in a language that isn't yours.

Both sides have to relinquish something; we can find a solution; for instance, we could add something to the flag so that you will feel that it is also your flag.

There aren't too many democratic states in the region. Iran, Iraq, if they beat us, that will threaten our democracy. Although I wouldn't want to be an Arab in this state.

SAMIR (*during a discussion of which language should be spoken in the group*): There is a feeling that someone who knows Arabic is inferior. But it's not relevant to talk here in Arabic; we all understand Hebrew; it would be artificial. The state is not right, so it is threatened. The state has to fix itself and be just, and then you as Jews won't be afraid of us.

I feel Palestinian, without any connection to the Palestinian state. If a Palestinian state is established in the territories, it will belong to them.

The Palestinians in the territories have not suffered more than we have. Since there are 110,000 traitors there, they can't come to me with accusations. It's easier to connect with Jews than with Arabs from the territories.

Second Meeting

HAREL: I want complete equality. The only way to communicate properly with people is full equality, and what we have here is clearly not equality. There are big gaps between Arabs and Jews, but there are gaps everywhere, . . . We are creating an injustice, and this could boomerang on us. It's only logical that we will get what we deserve at the first opportunity.

We are looking for formulas to solve the problem. We are all human be-

SAMIR (*turns to a Jewish participant*): How can you come here, the conqueror of another people, and tell them that if only you weren't here, it would be better. I tell you that I do want you to be here.

The establishment is not interested in hearing us. Our leadership doesn't deal with the issues. We need another twenty years of education.

(*Turns to an Arab woman*): You're not objective [when you say that] you

ings, and we all want equal rights; that is clear to me. The stereotypes are only a shell. Underneath, we are all human beings.

can't travel from Jerusalem to your village with no problem. . . . So what if you are delayed five minutes being checked at a roadblock. I know a lot of people who show their ID cards to the police and go on through and that's that.

Third Meeting

HAREL: I feel a lack of communication between Arabs and Jews most of the time. The Jews can profit more when the Arabs become equal; we are wasting too much energy on how to control them. We have to look at the other, as a human being. . . . Even about Jerusalem, I think it has to belong to everyone, to Israel and to Palestine.

I want to go back to the question of language. I feel that this is a very important issue to you, that we will speak Arabic. I can understand and feel the great pain you feel in giving up your identity. But I think about myself at this moment, and I think that I am not going to study Arabic. I learned how important this is to you, but I feel the need to tell you this. This is the boundary for me right now.

There's something in that; it may be that language is about control. For me it would be convenient to speak English. I am ready to do without speaking Hebrew and speak English instead, but this isn't a solution from your standpoint. Language is something so significant and so strong and so total. It's not just a matter of what's convenient or inconvenient. It doesn't happen on that level.

SAMIR: I thought that here we would begin from a common starting point, Arabs and Jews, and would be more practical. Today I feel more with the extremist Arab side in the group. It's very hard for me to hear the things that some of the Jews are saying. I have a feeling that I'm more confused. (*In the uninational forum*): Before I came here, I didn't think that here we would deal with the points of the conflict as we do outside. I thought that we would sit down and enjoy being together. I have come to the conclusion that I can't change the world, and I thought we would forge a connection on a personal basis. But now I am confused; I am disappointed and frustrated.

I want to tell you something about democracy in Israel. I think that you are a primitive society; you relate to people according to their religion and nationality.

(*Turns to a Jewish participant*): I'm not sure now whether I want to be in contact, if you are going to have these attitudes.

Fourth Meeting

HAREL: I feel that we've reached the point of the real conflict and the real gap that can't be bridged. What we Jews want to happen and what the Arabs want—as you said, there is no difference among the Jews between the left and the right. Two groups have been created here, and the gap between them is great.

(*Turns to an Arab woman*): Just as you don't want to lie to yourself, we also cannot lie to ourselves. Most of the Jews cannot accept the idea of a binational state. I want the State of Israel to remain as it is with a Jewish majority, with the Hebrew language. On the other hand, there should be complete equality—that is, insofar as possible.

Why shouldn't you (*turning to the Arabs*) be Israeli? I think that the solution is that you should give up a little of your identity and at the same time be equal with us in terms of resources.

I think that I have undergone a process. At first I was looking for common areas for both of us; I saw us all as human beings. At a certain point I felt that I can't go with this all the way; I can't lie to myself. I don't represent only myself; I come here with my society. I come from the Labor Party and Meretz, and when I tell my friends what is going on here, they are rather surprised and scared.

SAMIR: It seems that war is the only solution . . . because of your approach. Your goal is not to reduce your fear but to control us.

I came to compromise with you (*turning to the Jews*), and you took advantage of my position [to seek] more concessions from our side; because of this we became more extremist. I'm sorry about that, but war is war. . . . We have been *freirim* [fools, patsies], always making concessions and doing what you want.

If the solution is to separate, with me leading my life, from my standpoint this is good; this is an optimal solution. I won't need to ask for my rights from anyone. . . . I don't believe you and you don't believe me; I don't want your charity.

I came here with an understanding of your side (*turning to a Jewish woman*). Now I don't care about that. I have come to the conclusion that either it's war, or we separate. You aren't capable of being reeducated. I can't live with you.

Fifth Meeting

HAREL: I don't know if I've changed. I didn't know that you have a Palestinian identity. . . . I thought you feel Israeli. I thought that there would be a Palestinian state, and that here we would all be Israelis; I didn't think that the Arabs inside Israel would be left with a strong feeling of Palestinian nationality. When I saw that your aspirations were so big, I wasn't ready to concede. . . . I didn't go from one extreme to the other; initially I evidently didn't understand what your intention was in a binational state.

(*In the uninational forum*): Their power let me see my power and understand that our power is different. I understood how we keep such a strong and clever grip on them so they won't feel their nationalistic feelings. To understand that, I had to go through a process, but in the end it is information. . . . It's true that it's different information when you get it straight from the people themselves. It's something living, a totality of things that influence you, that do something to you.

Now, I understand our control over you. I understand how this happens, and I understand that it's a very powerful and sophisticated setup. I understand control, and I understand the power in that control. Today I understand things that I suppressed and repressed so strongly. The control is so strong and so sophisticated, to the point where we don't know that it exists. Your message doesn't reach us, and that serves certain ends for us, things that are very real and convenient for us, things that we believe in.

SAMIR: I'm not sure that separation isn't good. Why did separation between France and Belgium not make them enemies?!

We can't build a leadership if you don't get off our necks. We are stuck here, and there are two choices: either we keep quiet, and that will be good for you, or we fight, and I'm not willing to concede.

I have gone through a process, and today I know that it's very important that we have ourselves together and have our national identity very clear. Today the situation is all or nothing. I can understand the thinking of my society, that we can't go on like this anymore. (*Turns to a Jewish participant*): I know that you are afraid of us, that we will explode. . . . It's worth your while to compromise with me.

You are living in a very violent country. (*Turning to a Jewish woman*): I am learning from you. You hang in there because you have power; you can be brought down only with power. (*Turns to a Jewish woman*): The morality that you are speaking of is not morality. I think that we Arabs came here so that we could bring you our pain to see. . . . The change in the way you think can't come about as the result of meetings like this; I expect more awareness. I believe that you will never help us to achieve our rights; only we shall help ourselves in that task. You cannot be relied on.

PARTICIPANTS' ANALYSIS OF THE ENCOUNTER

The trainee facilitators hold a discussion a month after the end of the initial workshop. Participants try to analyze and understand what has gone on thus far in the course in general and, in particular, what has happened to them individually. Below are the analyses offered by Harel and Samir.

HAREL: The meeting enabled me to get to know the conflict in a different way, a more realistic way. I want to say something here, something I didn't permit myself to say while the meeting was going on because there we were in a war. After I heard you *(turning to the Arab group)*, heard your demands and arguments, and I went back and thought them over, I found that I really cannot argue with you, and what you are asking for seems logical to me. This surprises me a little—after all the flareups and head-to-head confrontation in the meeting and how highly emotionally involved I was, that now I can come and say that after all I accept your position. . . . When I look back, I understand the phases I went through in the encounter. Initially I came here with some kind of universal message, a message of peace. But it was something that I never investigated and never confronted in reality. The nonstop pressure from the Arab group and their attack on us from a thousand angles and *(turning to the senior facilitators)* your stubbornness, that we would confront all of our feelings and thoughts and get to the root of the matter deep down . . . this made me understand that actually, at the real meeting place of Jewish-Arab encounter, stands this conflict. And then I also understood that in this conflict I cannot in any way make a concession about the state's being a Jewish state. That was something that so aggravated the Arab group, and we got totally stuck in the dialogue. . . .

  I don't think that the pressure from the group and from the facilitators made me return to my Jewishness, but rather they forced me to acknowledge what I really am. I just couldn't go on keeping my eyes closed or tell lies about my position on things I really believe in, and I couldn't run away from them. . . . The pressure made me go into a place that wasn't comfortable for me to be in and that's easy to run away from. Mostly, in the situation I was in here, there was nowhere to run to. So I had to look at the truth as it is, and then I could also say it in words and understand it better. What really is the truth of our reality is conflict, simply conflict. My worldview on the one hand says peace and on the other hand says a Jewish state, and I see that these don't go together. It's just a place that's hard to be in.

SAMIR: I came here on the assumption that I would come part way and so would you. I thought that everyone who came to the meeting would talk in terms of compromise. I was really surprised; I found that people think and talk very differently from me. I had to let go of the concepts and meanings I grew up with and brought to the meeting and adopt a different terminology in order to adjust to the situation and talk in your language. For example, I thought that everything in life has to be moral, and I found out that I was wrong and that power is what decides. I started to go back to my roots; I started looking for my roots and trying to understand why we Arabs have arrived at where we have. . . . I came to the conclusion that our situation in the state is terrible, not because the Jews are strong but because we are weak. We have no confidence in ourselves, although we have the ability. I found myself thinking and speaking in terms of power and using concepts of force and of threat. I think that the encounter turned me into more of an extremist than I was, and I became a pessimist concerning the option of living together. Because under the conditions you offer us, we won't ever be able to agree to live. . . .

There were moments in the meeting when I really felt despair and frustration; I was sure the Jewish group wasn't right, but I couldn't cope with that. I felt that I haven't the power to change that. I had an inward struggle with myself; I tried to find the power I have inside myself so I could face you as an equal and talk with you as an equal. That was hard and came as a surprise. In life I am able to live with myself and not cope with these things, and suddenly it hits me—boom!—right in the face. The person standing opposite me tells me, be the way I want you to, under my conditions, and if you lift up your head, I'll knock it down again for you. In my day-to-day life, I am in my own society, I know that there is discrimination against us, but I don't come up against these things in that way, so blatantly. I worked and studied with Jews for many years, but evidently in my daily life I adopted a kind of mechanism that enabled me to ignore the Jews and ignore the conflict because that was more comfortable for me. I usually see Jews for a short time during the day, and that's that. Here in this course there was an intensive encounter, and it was impossible to avoid coping with this. I was occupied with the subject all the time, even outside the meeting, and I began to think about how to stand tall and how to win out over them and even how to crush their pride a little. During these meetings, I went through a change, but I still haven't come to a coherent place inside myself about who I am, what I want to be, what I can do to contribute something with the conflict as it stands now. I'm confused. I don't exactly have answers to all the questions I have.

DISCUSSION AND ANALYSIS

The excerpts quoted are the words of only two individual participants, removed from their group context. Yet a picture nevertheless emerges that gives us a chance to understand the story told by these two individual participants and the process they underwent in the meeting. From the quotes, one gets the impression that there was a dialogue between these two people, although for the most part they were not speaking to one another and were even speaking at different times. This demonstrates how closely the group process and the individual process are connected; this connection may permit us to learn via the above "dialogue" about the experience of the group as a whole.

At first sight, the two participants' experience suggests that they became more extreme and that this process was consistent and reached its peak in the fourth meeting. In the fifth and final meeting, both relaxed somewhat, but they still left the encounter with hard feelings and harsh words. Many will claim that for these two participants, the meeting was a complete failure: not merely did the encounter not draw them closer, but it distanced them from one another and sowed dissension between them. We believe the matter is not that simple and requires in-depth study and assessment, especially because our goal is not to bring Jews and Arabs closer together but rather to raise participants' awareness of the conflict and foster the development of their national and political identity. (See Chapter Three.)

Theories of the Development of Ethnic Identity

To illuminate this case, I present here a short survey of relevant theories, and, in light of them, I trace what happened to the two participants in the meeting. When discussing identity, and certainly ethnic identity, many people tend to relate to it as something static, as given, to which one must adapt. This is called "the primordial approach." That approach sees ethnic identity as deep and primary, inborn, just like gender identity and skin color, and difficult to change (Isaacs 1989). More common approaches view ethnic identity as a dynamic process, as a product of the individual's interaction and negotiation with his or her sociocultural environment (Waters 1990; Padilla 1986; Barth 1969). Nagel (1994) described this process very well, comparing it to the way we go shopping in a supermarket. The boundaries of identity are fixed by the shape and size of the shopping cart we are using, and the content of identity is fixed by the choices we make to fill our cart from the totality of products offered. Hence, according to these approaches, identity is not given and fixed in advance. Rather, individuals have a degree of freedom in designing their ethnic identity within certain boundaries, which we will not go into here.

An approach has emerged that takes this one step further: not only is ethnic identity flexible and changing, but also that this change takes place in developmental phases, just as personal identity changes developmentally in the manner described by Erikson (1964, 1968). The contention is that ethnic identity, like a person's individual identity, develops from an initial and primitive stage to a higher, more mature, whole, desirable level. Today two distinct schools of thought deal with this subject. The first is represented by Phinney (1989, 1990; Phinney and Rosental 1992), who claims that a person's ethnic identity develops in the time dimension—the critical age being adolescence, during which the individual's ethnic identity is formed and crystallizes. The second approach, developed by Cross (1978) and continued by Helms (1989, 1990), claims that the principal factor in the development of ethnic identity is one's encounter with one's own identity via encounter with the other. Helms deals with ethnic identity in a racial context through the many studies she has conducted on the subject with blacks and whites in the United States. To help decipher and understand our present case, the models developed by Helms are more suitable because she deals with the development of identity through an encounter with the other, and this resembles what we do at the School for Peace. I will briefly outline here the models she offers in her book *Black and White Racial Identity* (1990a) and then apply them to an analysis of the case of our two participants.

Helms proposes two models, one for blacks and one for whites. She argues that blacks and whites live in different realities and hence need to be viewed through different lenses. Helms's models are developmental. Her assumption is that as one progresses from one stage to the next, one's identity grows healthier and stronger. She argues that the phased transition from stage to stage is a function of interaction with the environment and with the other. More specifically, in the context of her work with whites and blacks, it is a product of the encounter between the two groups.

Development of Ethnic Identity among Whites

Helms says that to be white in the United States is to be part of the ruling, dominant group. As such, white people enjoy the privileges of the majority group, even if they don't wish to do so. She adds that white people do not have to acknowledge their identity as white. Only in contacts with others (blacks) does the subject potentially come onto the agenda. Only when a black person's presence "penetrates and disturbs" a white person's environment and cannot be ignored does the white person have to confront the racist part of his identity. Helms proposes two consecutive tracks for the development of the ethnic identity of whites. The first ends at her third stage of development, and the second goes on to reach a sixth stage.

The first stage—contact—is the stage in which white people encounter the black identity as real and substantial. This stage is characterized by a naïve, universal view, and there is no awareness of the essence of white identity. The interest in blacks is still in the realm of intellectual curiosity.

At the second stage, white people reach an awareness that there are two racial groups—that is, they move beyond "we are all human beings." At this stage they begin dealing with moral dilemmas, caught between their aspiration to be liberal and egalitarian and the difficulty of accepting blacks as equal in every way.

In the third stage, a new order is created, and things are rearranged in such a way as to resolve the dissonance generated earlier. Rationales are found for inequality, for the white's superiority and the black's inferiority. People can get stuck here or can progress to the following stages if something significant that is relevant to the subject occurs to push them onward.

In the fourth stage, another look is taken at the assumption of superiority and inferiority. There is an acknowledgment of racism, and responsibility is taken for the individual's part in this racism. The white identity is now not negative, but a positive white identity has not yet been constructed. The thinking at this stage is how to help black people, from a paternalistic concern.

The fifth stage sees a redefinition of the white identity, leading to a feeling of euphoria and to an ability to deal with racism. The thinking here is about how to change the whites—that is, one's own side.

The sixth stage is the stage of internalization and actualization of the new identity, a positive white identity. At this stage there is no longer a need to oppress or to minimize the value of others based on their group affiliation.

Development of Ethnic Identity among Blacks

Helms claims that for black people, there are four stages in the development of ethnic identity. She adds that this is a developmental process, during which the person "becomes black"—black being defined either as a way of life and a way of thinking or as the attitude toward the black person and the affiliation with blacks as a group, not because of skin color. She describes this developmental process as follows:

In the first stage, there is an idealization of the white group and a devaluing of the black world. There is an adoption of the white terminology of an inner locus of control, meaning that the situation of individuals is fixed by their talents and the effort they make. The white group becomes the referential group. There is a great effort to be accepted by the white group.

The transition to the second stage happens by means of a significant encounter with racism directed toward blacks—whether encountered in a personal and frontal way or indirectly. At this stage, black people reach an awareness that reality cannot be denied and that they cannot in fact be part of the white group. They are disillusioned, and their entire world view is shattered. Helms describes this as being born again. There is much confusion and anxiety, beyond the search for a new identity. The person is not yet black but has decided to be black.

In the third stage the person goes from one extreme to the other, from denying the black identity to a totally black identity. The black identity is empowered at the expense of a personal identity. There is idealization of blacks and devaluation of anything that is white. This stage is characterized by anger: anger at oneself for having been naïve and part of the oppressive system for so long, anger at whites for being the oppressors, and anger at other blacks who have not yet developed and have been left behind.

A person in the fourth stage reaches a situation of equilibrium and internalization of a positive black identity. The affiliation is not coerced from without but is the outcome of an inward shift. Now with a stable and clear black identity, the black person can cope better with the world, from a position of confidence and strength. There is opposition to racism, but there is an option for cooperation on this issue with whites as individuals. There is an option to relate to white culture critically without completely negating it. And finally there is commitment to social and political activism.

The Development of Ethnic Identity in the Case Study

When we examine what happened to Samir and Harel in the facilitators course in light of Helms's theory, we see that the encounter caused both of them to scrutinize and develop their national-ethnic identity. The point of the encounter according to Helms is that there be a meaningful event that will thoroughly shake people up and lead them to confront their identity and struggle with it; this is not merely a routine, everyday meeting that we all, blacks and whites, Arabs and Jews, have all the time. Samir eloquently expresses the difference when he says: "I worked and studied with Jews for many years, but evidently in my daily life I adopted a kind of mechanism that enabled me to ignore the Jews and ignore the conflict because that was more comfortable for me. I usually see Jews for a short time during the day, and that's that. Here in this course there was an intensive encounter, and it was impossible to avoid coping with this."

Harel, too, testifies to having gone through a similar process: "I just couldn't go on keeping my eyes closed or tell lies about my position on things I really believe in, and I couldn't run away from them. . . . The pressure made me go into a place that wasn't comfortable for me to be in and that's easy to run away from. Mostly, in the situation I was in here, there was nowhere to run to." The encounter forced both participants (and, I assume, the other participants in the course as well) to stand facing their truth, facing their identity as it had been revealed by the other. And this enabled them to grow and take a step toward, in Helms's words, a healthy, desirable identity.

Here I will trace the process the two participants went through according to Helms's phased model. First, I examine what happened to Harel and then what happened to Samir, and finally I describe these processes in relation to each other.

Harel came into the encounter with good will, good intentions, and a liberal self-image like that of any other Israeli leftist, but he had never really confronted the issue: "Initially I came here with some kind of universal message, a message of peace. But it was something that I never investigated and never confronted in reality." The encounter with the Arab group, which was apparently a shock to him, did not allow him to continue to run away, inside himself, from the conflict and from the Arabs: "The nonstop pressure from the Arab group and their attack on us from a thousand angles . . . made me understand that actually, at the real meeting place of Jewish-Arab encounter, stands this conflict."

This presence of the Arabs, which penetrated into Harel's world and disturbed and confused him, in Helms's terms brought him to the (majority group member's) first stage, the stage of contact; this stage was evident mostly in the first two meetings, when he expressed a naïve universalistic view: "We are all human beings, and we all want equal rights; that is clear to me. The stereotypes are only a shell. Underneath, we are all human beings." At this stage, he also demonstrated a liberalism and nobility that later on would be seen to be exaggerated: "I don't mind if you speak only Arabic and someone translates; I think that is your right. Or maybe we should all speak English. It's just not fair that we should speak in a language that isn't yours."

Only in the third meeting does something finally click, and Harel reaches an awareness that the conflict is between two national groups and has to be addressed as such: "I feel that we've reached the point of the real conflict and the real gap that can't be bridged. . . . As you said, there is no difference among the Jews between the Left and the Right. Two groups have been created here, and the gap between them is great."

At this stage, he reaches an awareness that he, too, as an individual is part of the conflict; that he belongs to the Jewish side: "At a certain point I felt that I can't go with this all the way; I can't lie to myself. I don't represent only myself; I come here with my society." This awareness poses for Harel a moral dilemma. In contrast to his sweeping assent to speaking Arabic in the group in its first meeting, he changes his mind in the third meeting; he's no longer sure that he can accept Arabic as a legitimate language: "I want to go back to the question of language. I feel that this is a very important issue to you, that we will speak Arabic. I can understand and feel the great pain you feel in giving up your identity. But I think about myself at this moment, and I think that I am not going to study Arabic. I learned how important this is to you, but I feel the need to tell you this. This is the boundary for me right now." On the question of the nature of the state, as well, he expresses his ambivalence aloud: "Most of the Jews cannot accept the idea of a binational state. I want the State of Israel to remain as it is with a Jewish majority, with the Hebrew language. On the other hand, there should be complete equality—that is, insofar as possible." These reservations and dilemmas continue to be with Harel all through the meetings, and they constitute the central element of his experience in the encounter.

According to Helms, Harel should have moved on to the third stage in order to take care of the dissonance that had engulfed him and that is difficult to live with in the long term. If one looks closely, however, it would seem that, in his case, there was no third stage—perhaps because the matter of superiority is so unpleasant to acknowledge and declare or perhaps because the meeting, as an ongoing process, enabled him to move ahead and continue to deal with what was happening without passing through that intermediate stage. (Or it may be that our case is not an exact fit with the model.) In the fifth and last meeting, we see that Harel is already in Helms's fourth stage; he recognizes the superior position of the Jews as the majority and acknowledges the ways in which they protect their status as the ruling group: "I understood how we keep such a strong and clever grip on them so they won't feel their nationalistic feelings. To understand that, I had to go through a process." During that same meeting, he goes on to say: "Now, I understand our control over you. I understand how this happens, and I understand that it's a very powerful and sophisticated setup. I understand control, and I understand the power in that control. Today I understand things that I suppressed and repressed so strongly. The control is so strong and so sophisticated, to the point where we don't know that it exists." But in this stage, despite his awareness, he is still thinking of changing the Arabs because of a concern for them: "Why shouldn't you," turning to the Arabs, "be Israeli? I think that the solution is that you should give up a little of your identity and at the same time be equal with us in terms of resources."

A month after the workshop, in analyzing the experience he as an individual had undergone, Harel speaks with a good deal of awareness about the changes he has been through and about the deep insight he has, in light of that experience, about the conflict and his behavior within it. This indicates that he in fact is already at Helms's fourth stage, but we see that he still goes back and forth between this stage and the second stage. He still vacillates between moral dilemmas and taking responsibility for the situation: "What really is the truth of our reality is conflict, simply conflict. My world-view on the one hand says peace and on the other hand says a Jewish state, and I see that these don't go together. It's just a place that's hard to be in." Harel continued to struggle with the situation and continued to move ahead. Today he works at the School for Peace— but we'll get to that later.

Samir, as he reports in his analysis, has had many interactions with Jews. In fact he lives with and among Jews. But this is no guarantee of a confrontation with the subject. From what he says during the first two meetings, we see that he has come into the meeting at what Helms describes as the (minority group member's) first stage. He expresses an outlook that devalues his own group: "There is a feeling that someone who knows Arabic is inferior. But it's not relevant to talk here in Arabic; we all understand Hebrew; it would be artificial." He thus quickly relinquishes his language, a part of his identity, and perhaps to some degree would prefer the other language. And there is an inkling here of a yearning to belong to the Jewish group when he says that the Palestinians, "with 110,000 traitors, . . . can't come to me with accusations. It's easier to connect with Jews than with Arabs from the territories." It seems that he has adopted the terminology of the rulers and is even speaking with their voice, as when he turns to an Arab woman in the group and says: "You're not objective [when you say that] you can't travel from Jerusalem to your village with no problem. . . . So what if you are delayed five minutes being checked at a roadblock. I know a lot of people who show their ID cards to the police and go on through and that's that."

Only in the third meeting does he move on to Helms's second stage;

and he does so because of the positions he hears the Jewish participants taking, as he explains: "Today I feel more with the extremist Arab side in the group. It's very hard for me to hear the things that some of the Jews are saying. I have a feeling that I'm more confused." He has been living an illusion of being part of the (Jewish) society, and when this illusion is shattered before his eyes, he takes it very hard: "I thought that we would sit down and enjoy being together. . . . I thought we would forge a connection on a personal basis. But now I am confused; I am disappointed and frustrated." The shattering of his illusion effectively destroys the world-view he grew up with, and he must now build a new one; he has to build another identity. This is indeed, as Helms depicts it, a kind of rebirth: "I came here on the assumption that I would come part way and so would you. I thought that everyone who came to the meeting would talk in terms of compromise. I was really surprised; I found that people think and talk very differently from me. I had to let go of the concepts and meanings I grew up with and brought to the meeting and adopt a different terminology in order to adjust to the situation and talk in your language." After the rejection he experiences, he responds with anger and transitions sharply to his own group's side. This brings him to the third stage, as evidenced very clearly in the third meeting, when he turns to a Jewish participant and says: "I'm not sure now whether I want to be in contact, if you are going to have these attitudes." In other words, if you don't want me, I don't want you either; so be it.

Samir arrives at the extremism of which Helms speaks from an initial belief in dialogue; from initially seeking a solution through unity, he comes instead to seek a solution through separation and war. Turning to a Jewish woman, he says: "I came here with an understanding of your side. Now I don't care about that. I have come to the conclusion that either it's war, or we separate. You aren't capable of being reeducated. I can't live with you."

Samir also makes a drastic transition from idealizing Jewish society to totally negating it: "I want to tell you something about democracy in Israel. I think that you are a primitive society; you relate to people according to their religion and nationality." And he adds, "I am learning from you. You hang in there because you have power; you can be brought down only with power." He then turns to a Jewish woman and says: "The morality that you are speaking of is not morality." At the same time, he makes a total connection with his Arab identity and tries to magnify and glorify it: "I have gone through a process, and today I know that it's very important that we have our act together and have our national identity very clear. Today the situation is all or nothing. I can understand the thinking of my society, that we can't go on like this anymore." He returns to his roots, as he describes it in his analysis. He reaches the conclusion that only thus is there an option to change the situation: "I believe that you will never help us to achieve our rights; only we shall help ourselves in that task. You cannot be relied on."

But Samir's return to his roots and connection with the Arab identity is still in reaction to the trauma he underwent in the encounter with the Jews; this is not an identity internalized through personal choice, as happens in the fourth stage depicted by Helms. We see this clearly when Samir, in his analysis, speaks about his using the terminology of the majority: "I found myself thinking and speaking in terms of power and using concepts of force and of threat. I think that the encounter turned me into more of an extremist than I was, and I became a pessimist concerning the option of living together." There is still no adoption of an authentic Arab identity; instead there is the adoption of an Arab identity clothed in the concepts of the Jewish dialogue through adoption of a terminology and a manner of thought borrowed from the Jews. Thus Samir becomes confused and anxious, as he notes at the end of his self-analysis: "During these meetings, I went through a change, but I still haven't come to a coherent place inside myself about who I am, what I want to be, what I can do to contribute something, with the conflict as it stands now. I'm confused. I don't exactly have answers to all the questions I have." He has lots of confusion, and in its wake Samir also feels angry, at this stage. His confusion and anger will be exchanged later on for action, about which I have something to say shortly.

CONCLUSIONS

Helms built her theory around whites and blacks in the United States, yet we see that it is quite useful in our case involving Jews and Arabs. And if it is perhaps more suitable for examining the Arab (minority) side, that may simply be one more proof that people are closest to themselves, their identity, and their group. Helms, as a black scholar discussing white identity, makes a bold and welcome attempt that is worthy of admiration. Generally the situation is the reverse, and to question the accepted wisdom is a step in the right direction.

Worth noting and emphasizing yet again is Helms's contention that the development of an ethnic identity takes place through the encounter with the other. In our case, this has been proved true beyond any doubt. In addition, the changes that Harel and Samir underwent and their phased transitions were rather well synchronized from the standpoint of time. Thus, for example, the major turning point was in the third meeting, during which Harel moved into the second stage and Samir did too—a demonstration of how crucial the behavior of one side is in shaping the positions and views of the other. From this standpoint each served the other as a kind of mirror through which he could look himself straight in the eye and grapple with his truth.

The matter of extremism needs to be emphasized. We hear quite a lot about this in the context of encounters between Jews and Arabs; educators try to avoid it like the plague. For this reason they sometimes prefer an anemic meeting drained of purpose and direction, the main objective being that there should be no anger, and heaven forbid that someone should declare himself to have become more extremist.

In the case examined here, there was a lot of anger, pain, and frustration, especially on Samir's side, the Arab side. This anger, felt by all participants, is an obligatory part of the experience and embodies a difficult struggle that requires courage in order to build a new and healthy identity, as Helms would put it. Helms even describes this anger as something typifying the weaker group's third stage of development, an intermediate stage between loss of the existing identity and the building and internalizing of a new identity. This path to a new identity is indeed a difficult one, yet participants are obliged to walk along it in order to grow and develop. Both sides must grapple with this if they honestly want to escape from a naïve outlook that lacks commitment to reality and to the conflict. The struggle is real and profound. We will get nowhere by a blurring of identities. Only in bravely restructuring our identity, in refining it through talking as equals with the other side, is there hope for building a different reality.

Indeed, in the case here, both facilitator trainees, Harel and Samir, went past the stage of anger and frustration and "extremism," worked through them, and moved on. Today both are working here at the School for Peace as facilitators, and, I assure you, they do not take up arms against one another. Naturally their scrutiny of their identity and their struggle over the issues continues, through their work, to this day. This scrutiny is definitely an ongoing one, and we all struggle with it, even the senior facilitators. Harel and Samir, having gone through these first stages of coping, can now, with their more mature and healthier identities, lead others to confront the same struggle. Their own confrontation and struggle, in a sense, have turned into their primary tools in the work they are now doing with others.

6

THE COURAGE TO FACE
A COMPLEX REALITY

ENCOUNTERS FOR YOUTH

MICHAL ZAK, RABAH HALABI,
AND WAFA'A ZRIEK-SROUR

The youth project is the central program of the School for Peace and has been in existence since the school's inception. The program brings together Arab and Jewish eleventh-grade students for four days of meetings. The objects of the encounter for the participants are to get to know young people from the other group, especially their attitudes toward culture and politics, and to understand the complexity of the conflict and each person's role in it.

Over the years, nearly ten thousand Jews and ten thousand Arabs have participated in this program, about a thousand annually. We have worked with a number of schools for more than ten years, and each year new schools join the project. The Arab and Jewish students come from all over the country, from diverse socioeconomic backgrounds and lifestyles. The students choose to participate in the program and come to Neve Shalom / Wahat al Salam as a delegation under the auspices of their schools. The project has two directors, a Jewish woman and an Arab woman, and a staff of about fifteen Arab and Jewish facilitators trained specifically to lead encounters for young people in the School for Peace program.

We have chosen to work with students aged sixteen to seventeen because at that age young people are preoccupied in any case with shaping their social and political identity. Prior to that age, youngsters are involved in forming their personal and sexual identity, and hence an encounter revolving around questions of social identity is less effective and sometimes even destructive.

In contrast to our approach in working with adults, an approach based on an open dialogue between participants, in the model for young people the encounter is structured and preplanned, with activities known in advance. Coping with loaded situations is difficult at any age, but the difficulty intensifies at adolescence, and meetings between Jews and Arabs are charged in any case. The model we have created is an attempt to be responsive to these feelings. The structure of the encounter reduces anxiety and enables participants to cope more easily with the subjects that come up during the discussion.

We—the Arab and Jewish facilitators—have built our model of intervention together, based on our substantial experience in meetings between Arab and Jewish youth and giving due consideration to existing knowledge of group processes. The first part of the encounter, which takes place on the first day of every workshop, is devoted to getting acquainted and to building a cohesive and all-inclusive group; this is designed to create a supportive framework that subsequently will enable the participants to explore the painful and sensitive issues dividing the two national groups. The second phase, on the workshop's second day, is dedicated to a dialogue on subjects relating to culture and politics; the group, which on the first day came together, now splits and goes back to its original, divided, state. Boundaries are sharpened and conspicuous, and the fantasy that we are all human beings and therefore we will work it out begins to show cracks. The third phase, which takes place on the third day of the workshop, is devoted to negotiation between the two national groups. The negotiation revolves around the goal of finding a shared modus vivendi for the future and proceeds by means of a simulation game. The model of a formal negotiation creates new possibilities for dialogue between the two groups. The fourth and last part of the workshop, on its final day, aims to explore what participants have experienced and to prepare them for going home.

We describe here the sequence of events during an encounter, drawing on the processes that stand out most clearly from the many workshops we have run using this model. Each meeting, every group, and each individual are a world unto themselves, unique and special; although generalization is thus difficult, we believe that the processes we have selected for description in this chapter are so conspicuous and so typical for most of the groups that they can serve admirably to explain and instruct on the subject of Arab-Jewish encounter.

PREPARATION FOR THE MEETING

At the beginning of each year, we approach schools that participated in prior years as well as new schools that have expressed an interest in the program. Among Arab schools, many principals and teachers express a desire to have their school join the program, and there is a great deal of interest on the part of the students; hence a team of teachers presents the program to a single class, and the overwhelming majority of the students choose to participate. Fewer Jewish schools are interested, and the proportion of students in a given school who wish to attend is lower; thus in the Jewish schools the program is offered to an entire grade of some two hundred students and, of those, thirty students who want very much to attend are chosen to do so. The differences between majority and minority are already vast at this stage. Collectively, the minority is more highly motivated to meet the majority than vice versa. The teaching staff creates a group of about thirty students each of whom has expressed his or her wish to meet with young people from the other group. About two weeks before the meeting, an Arab facilitator from the School for Peace meets with the Arab group to prepare them for the encounter, and likewise a Jewish facilitator meets with the Jewish group.

The goal of the preparation with the group from each school is to provide the most possible information about the program, the encounter, details of the living arrangements, the form the discussion will take, the location of Neve Shalom / Wahat al Salam, and so on. Each national group is preoccupied with slightly different questions that arise from its respective place in the society and its respective attitude toward the conflict between the two groups.

In the preparatory meeting with the Jewish group, the students ask a lot of questions in an effort to find out "what they will be like." There is a lot of curiosity about the Arab group, some expressed delicately and politely—"Are they our age?" "Are they Israeli?"—and some necessarily concealing images of Arabs common in Jewish society—such as, for example, "Will they be dressed like us?" "Will they be extremists?"

Because Jewish society is sharply divided about everything touching on the issues to be addressed at the meeting, sometimes the discussion revolves around the question of presenting a variety of opinions versus presenting only one opinion when the Jewish students meet with the Arabs. The young people clarify for themselves what is going to take place, in which language the discussion is to be conducted, whether they will have to sleep in mixed rooms with the Arab young people or whether the housing will be separate, and what the security situation at Neve Shalom/Wahat al Salam is. (We house the students in separate rooms, rooms for Jews and rooms for Arabs; and we house the boys and the girls in separate rooms.) The Jewish young people are clearly torn between their desire to get to know the Arab participants as much as possible and their fears and sense of caution.

The Arab group, in its preparatory meeting, is preoccupied with the extent of its ability to express itself in the presence of the Jewish group. The participants generally worry that they don't know enough, at least not much as the Jews. They wonder how far they will be able to get into a discussion on political issues without ruining the positive atmosphere. And they are concerned about the matter of language. Although they are told explicitly that they can speak Arabic, they deliberate among themselves whether it is worthwhile speaking Arabic, whether the translating will disturb the dialogue, or whether perhaps it would be preferable to make the effort to speak Hebrew. (A fuller discussion of this question is found in Chapter Seven.) Another subject discussed at length is the attitude of the Jews toward the Arabs. The young people worry: "How will the Jews treat us?" "Are they ready and willing to meet with us?" "Are they also having this kind of preparation, and do they know whom they are going to meet?" This is a painful subject because it ties in with difficult experiences the young people have had with Jewish society.

THE ENCOUNTER AT NEVE SHALOM/WAHAT AL SALAM

Every encounter involves about sixty participants, half of whom are Arabs and half Jews. The meeting is conducted in small mixed groups of sixteen participants, and each group has two staff members, an Arab and a Jew, who serve as facilitators of the dialogue between the participants.

The First Day: Getting Acquainted

The young people gather in the clubhouse, with the chairs arranged in a circle. The two codirectors of the youth project welcome them and explain, in detail, the program in which they are about to participate. The Arab director speaks first, in Arabic, and after her the Jewish director speaks, in Hebrew. The staff purposely creates a reversal of the external reality found in Israeli society. We create this reversal in order to give a concrete example of the staff's belief that Arabic is to have equal standing with Hebrew in the encounter. During this welcome, the groups sit separately, looks are exchanged, whispering is heard, each group attempts to be seen at its best. The atmosphere is a little peculiar. There is the curiosity and apprehension that typify any meeting with strangers, but these are more pronounced and include a great deal of caution and nervousness. The members of each group try to hush the more vocal of their comrades so that the group will make a good impression. There is no contact or conversation between the two groups. Each group appears to be surveying the other according to the images and expectations with which it arrived. There is a feeling of relief, that help is finally at hand, when the directors at long last begin their ceremonial opening of the meeting. At the close of this plenum session, the participants divide up into groups of sixteen, Jews and Arabs, and disperse to the meeting rooms, each group accompanied by the pair of facilitators who will be with them for the duration of the encounter.

The entire first day is devoted to getting personally acquainted, with the goal being to create a comfortable atmosphere among the participants and to ease their anxieties about the meeting. The getting acquainted we offer begins in a lighter mode and gradually moves on to what is more weighty. In the first session, the young people learn the names of the members of their group, then proceed to a broader process revolving around subjects like school, home, home town, future plans. Finally, in pairs, participants get acquainted in more depth, recounting personal experiences to one another.

The games and activities at the beginning of the encounter break the ice and lower the initial barriers between the participants. The whole first day is characterized by openness and a great deal of good will. The positive atmosphere emerges after the initial surprise felt by the Jewish students that there are actually areas of commonality between the two groups—"They are dressed just like we are!!"—and that indeed they can be friends as long as everyone sticks to the interpersonal level. The Arab students come with a high degree of readiness to make friends with the Jews, and they too are surprised by the Jews' positive attitude and mainly by the interest shown by the Jews in the Arab group. Already, at the outset, the dominant language is Hebrew, and the Jewish group is a lot more vocal than the Arab group. But there is no mistaking that both groups respond out of their anxieties about the new situation.

There is an atmosphere of optimism in the group, optimism mixed with caution and curiosity. The caution typically manifests itself in the wish to touch on political subjects, on the one hand, and the reluctance to damage the atmosphere, on the other. Even in the early round devoted to learning one another's names, when each participant says his or her name and explains the meaning of the name, politics, with all its sensitiveness, does come up because some of the names have a national-political meaning (Golan, Palestine, Arafat, Nidal, Jihad, Yamit) and some of the participants were named in memory of family members who were killed in politically charged circumstances. But along with moments of embarrassment and tension, the atmosphere is also lightened by periodic bursts of laughter. The situation is somewhat reminiscent of relations between Arabs and Jews in Israeli society in general, in that everyone avoids talking about politics, and the power relationships—which are so crystal clear—remain.

In the evening, everyone gathers in the clubhouse and participates in a game. The object of the game is to strengthen the groups created during the getting-acquainted process. Each group sits in a circle on the floor and receives from the facilitators a large colorful placard bearing riddles that may be solved and assignments that may be completed only through cooperation between Arabs and Jews. When a group completes its placard, it takes another, different one and so on until the end. The group that correctly solves the most placards wins a prize. The placards are composed of short riddles and questions with clues supplied, such as:

Identify the personality: film actors/actresses, singers, and political figures from both societies.

Identify places in Israel and in the world.

Fill in the missing parts of the proverbs (from both societies, in both languages).

Identify cars, plants.

Identify holidays from the three religions (Islam, Christianity, and Judaism).

It is amazing to see how each mixed group sits together as a cohesive unit and works at solving the riddles. No one looks over at friends from the original (national) group. The mixed group is busy with its tasks, and the air of otherness has been instantly transformed into one of team competition. A great deal of cooperation is evidenced between Jews and Arabs; the feeling is cheerful and egalitarian.

The Second Day

Getting Acquainted Culturally

The morning of the second day is devoted to getting to know the culture of the other group. This is done in two stages. In the first stage, groups divide into quarters, with two Arabs and two Jews in each. Each quarter-group gets a card bearing a subject for discussion. When the quarter-group concludes its discussion of the subject, it receives another card with a new subject. The subjects are written on each card in Hebrew and in Arabic: "Relations between boys and girls in my society," "Relations between the generations," "Parents and children in my society," "Religious holidays and customs," "Beliefs and world-views," "Division of roles between the sexes in each society."

A discussion develops, and the participants quickly begin using phrases like "the way we do . . ." and "the way they do. . . ," phrases that were not heard the previous day. The dialogue takes on the character of a negotiation between two groups. The Jews report that they learned a lot from the discussions about Arab culture. In contrast, the Arabs report that they already knew what the Jews were telling them. This pronouncement creates an uncomfortable feeling among the Jews, who worked hard and spoke candidly and now are being told, "We knew all that."

The subject that generally emerges as the main subject for discussion is the relations between the genders in each society. In this kind of dialogue, the Jewish group feels itself to be occupying the high ground because it relates to itself as Western, whereas the Arab group relates to itself as (Middle) Eastern. Between these two poles, which emerge sharply in the discussion, Western culture is perceived as representing progress, freedom, and equality between the sexes, and Eastern culture as representing the primitive, the conservative, and the protection of a daughter's honor.

JEWISH BOY: Do you kiss each other in public?

ARAB GIRL: We marry young so we can have a properly arranged sex life and not the promiscuity that you have.

ARAB GIRL: For us the girl is like sacred. Her honor has to be protected, but we are not backward.

JEWISH BOY: Are marriages arranged?

ARAB GIRL: Yes, but not like it used to be. He [the father] recommends, but I decide, it's my life.

ARAB GIRL: I prefer feelings to be shown openly [not hidden, as is generally more customary among Arabs].

JEWISH BOY: Among us, things used to be done that way once upon a time.

JEWISH GIRL: We progressed and they didn't, that's all.

The tenor of the discussion is that if the two groups are to live together, the Arabs will have to change—because the Jews' outlook is preferable. Generally the Arab group also views itself as the group that must change. But sometimes, for argument's sake, the Arab group goes to the other extreme and takes a determined stand in defense of tradition, claiming that conservative values are good and that Western-style freedom leads to promiscuous behavior by Jewish girls. The Jewish group also tends to dig in, presenting their culture in an extreme fashion, as totally free and without boundaries. This extremism on the part of both groups is typical of conflict situations and reflects the acute transition from interpersonal dialogue to intergroup dialogue.

At this stage of the meeting, the participants are mainly experiencing the differences between the two groups and are coping with the images they have of the other and of themselves. The Arabs are coming face to face with the self-aggrandizement of the Jews and with the images of inferiority that they, the Arabs, have of themselves. The Jews are coming face to face with their own feelings of superiority and with the images they have of Arabs as inferior. This clarification is hard because it reveals to each group its own attitude toward itself and toward the other group and generally entails learning things that the participants would prefer not to deal with. The clarification is also difficult because it takes place right after the euphoria enjoyed by the participants on the first day.

After the discussion about cultures, there is a uninational meeting; each subgroup meets alone in a room with the facilitator who is from the same national group. The goal is for the group to understand and make sense of the experiences it has undergone, as a national group, inwardly. The switch to this forum is received gladly by the young people, who, at this stage, feel the need to calm down and, in a less intensive framework, to take a look at what has happened since they arrived.

In the Arabs' uninational session, the group is preoccupied with itself. The discussion focuses on the silence of some of the group's members. There is an attempt to clarify why people were silent during the joint discussion. The group recognizes the power that comes from active participation in the talking, for they saw the advantage the Jews had from the fact of their participation, and there is a demand made on the more silent ones to participate. Another subject that comes up has to do with the central issue of the dialogue, Arab culture. The young people have a trenchant discussion in which they are critical of their culture, although they do not allow themselves to verbalize this critique in the presence of the Jewish group. Often the discussion turns into an argument between the boys and the girls over the discrimination against and the suppression of women in Arab society. The encounter has brought to the surface disagreements within the group, and the uninational framework enables them to be discussed.

In its uninational meeting, the Jewish group clearly makes a transition from the stage of getting closer to and of having illusions about togetherness with the Arabs to the conflict stage. The group is occupied with the other (Arab) group and with its own (the Jewish group's) feeling of superiority vis-à-vis the Arab group. The most conspicuous feeling is anger that the good feelings of the evening before have been shattered along with the possibility, which had seemed so tangible, of developing relations on a personal basis. At this stage, the participants see the power of group affiliation as a crucial element in the relations between them and the Arabs. The discussion about culture and society sometimes evokes a trenchant internal dialogue between Jews of Western origin and Jews of Middle Eastern origin. This kind of discussion does not happen in the presence of the Arab group because there the internal differences are less relevant in comparison to the so sharply delineated other. In the separate framework there is the possibility of bringing up internal differences without losing "power." A penetrating dialogue ensues about the "superiority" of Western culture and the "inferiority" of Eastern culture and about resemblances between Eastern (Jewish) culture and Arab culture. "All in all maybe it's disgusting, but it's also complimentary that they copy us. . . . Our way is progressive. That inflates our ego and makes us behave in a way that disparages them, but it's also uncomfortable. There are also guilt feelings because they are willing to forego their own culture, but that is also a compliment, probably the Americans feel this way also." Toward the end of the meeting there is some anxiety about the coming discussion of political subjects. The participants express concerns that they will not be able to say what they really think—"because it will be hurtful and destructive"—and at the same time they are afraid of being attacked by the Arab group—"They have prepared for this moment, to really stick it to us."

Getting Acquainted Politically

We open this stage using a projective free-association technique called "photolongage" (based on a set of photos published by P. Babin, A. Babtiste, and C. Belisle in France). The facilitators spread a dark cloth on the floor. On top of it, they arrange black-and-white photographs showing situations in nature and in society in various places in the world. Each participant is asked to choose a picture and use it to describe how he or she feels as a Jew or an Arab in Israel; then there is a discussion of political issues. Subjects for discussion are raised by the participants, and the facilitators help the group to develop the dialogue. This political dialogue is perceived by the participants as a most important and critical one from the standpoint of the nature of the relations between them. They come to it tensely, watchfully, with curiosity and anxiety. They have high expectations of themselves. The Arabs expect themselves to stand up for what is theirs, to be adamant, and to change the Jews' minds. The Jews are expecting to hear what the Arabs are going to say to them, and at the same time are hoping that they won't have to hear too much. There is a kind of separation anxiety, a fear that the newly woven partnership is about to fall apart.

The discussion begins circumspectly. The Jews generally open the conversation and choose pictures that portray peace, comradeship, and the possibility of solving the situation or, alternatively, how complicated the situation is; in any case the pictures and explanations of the Jews are mostly general in nature. The Arabs choose pictures that portray destruction, despair, and grief. Some of the Arabs give voice bluntly to their anger and their pain in front of the Jews. The Jews, who "tried" to be gentle, feel they have been cheated.

The agenda is set by the Arabs. They tell of discrimination; the Jews reply with the issue of Arab violence. Each group chooses to talk about subjects in the arena in which it feels strong. The Arabs know that they are right and that they are entitled to their rights. They sense that the subject of discrimination and suppression is a bargaining card. The Jews evidently agree that justice is on the side of the Arabs on the matter of their rights, and hence they attack in the "moral" arena; in their eyes, the Arabs are less moral: they are violent and do not value human life. The discussion is heated. There is a feeling that the conflict is a conflict of the zero-sum type.

> JEWISH GIRL: We have one state in the entire world, so we are entitled to have all the rights.

> ARAB BOY: Why is there no Arab minister [in the government]?

> JEWISH BOY: Do you think we would let an Arab be Minister of Defense? This is still the State of Israel, and we are the majority.

> JEWISH BOY: Do you want there to be a Palestinian state?

> ARAB GIRL: Yes.

> JEWISH BOY: How do you expect me to put in a minister who identifies with another state? A minister has to be 100 percent Israeli, without a foreign passport.

> ARAB GIRL: In every Arab home there is someone in jail, someone who got killed, someone injured.

> JEWISH GIRL: That's our fault?

> ARAB GIRL: You don't think about whom you are killing.

> JEWISH GIRL: We don't kill anyone; we value human life. We don't go out in the street and kill.

> ARAB GIRL: A worker comes to a roadblock to go through; you put him in jail. He didn't do anything, just came to work.

> JEWISH GIRL: I agree that that is not okay.

The Arab group is adamant. They tire out the Jewish group, confronting it with reality. The Jews have difficulty ignoring the facts, which do not fit with the picture they had before of the world, of themselves, and of the Arabs; and the Jews persist in trying to hang on to the justifications and explanations they believe in. Each side is clearly struggling to justify its own narrative.

When the discussion turns to Israeli-Palestinian relations and the situation in the occupied territories, the subject of equal rights for and discrimination against the Arabs in Israel is neglected. Generally the Arab group becomes interested in raising it again.

> ARAB GIRL: I have to get something in order to reach equality. I was born here in Israel and not in the territories, and I am treated disparagingly.

> JEWISH GIRL: Maybe it sounds disgusting, but any rights that you people get I don't have to give you. It's a favor.

Uninational Summary Sessions

The last meeting of the day takes place in the uninational framework, which allows the participants to digest what they have experienced in the stormy sessions just concluded. The Arab group at this stage is disappointed and frustrated, and many things are said about how worthwhile the encounter and the dialogue actually are: "These discussions don't get us anywhere. We talked about the right, about the left, about the government—I don't think this will change anything; on the contrary, I feel we have gone backward." Some express nostalgia for the first day: "Yesterday it was nicer, the whole group from both sides was together." Some express a lack of self-confidence by suggesting that the Jewish group knows more and has more confidence in itself: "They are more confident than we are, they understand what they are talking about." The Arabs do not give equal weight to the knowledge that they bring to the discussion, much of it based on their own and their relatives' personal stories and day-to-day experiences. It is hard to stand up to the official information that the Jews bring from textbooks and from the establishment.

In the wake of this feeling of weakness, there is a demand on the part of the group members to unify their forces and strengthen themselves vis-à-vis the Jewish group. "We must not argue among ourselves; we have to be united and become a single unit. We haven't come here to solve our internal problems; we have come to talk about the problems between us and the Jews." "We Arabs, we have differences among ourselves but we have to bridge these gaps and be united, otherwise we won't be able to obtain our rights." At this point the Arab group vacillates between, on the one hand, disappointment and hopelessness, which are caused mostly by their failure to persuade the Jews, and, on the other hand, recognition of the need for unity, by means of which they can achieve more and change reality.

In the Jewish group, the talk at first focuses on the Arab group—"the way they were," "what they did to us": "Samakh [an Arab boy] really irritated me. He sounds as if he's trying to provoke us." "They went out of there with more confidence in themselves. They want equality." "It's aggravating when they put the facts right in your face. What can you say?"

The discussion gradually moves into an internal one relating to the group itself. Then the lack of trust and the fear emerge: "I am willing to bet that if we were the minority, they would treat us the way they do in those states where anyone who opposes the regime, they shoot him."

The confusion intensifies. It comes from the crisis in relations that began in the joint group — the move from closeness and friendship to tension and hostility. But at the same time it is a product of the encounter with the stories that were told with such force, anger, and determination by the Arab group: "We have an advantage; we are the majority, and that is a fact. But it has to be understood that in a democratic state they have to get the same thing." "I am prepared for full equality."

The group vacillates between the desire to protect the status quo and justify power relations as they are and the desire to establish an egalitarian society. The pendulum swings wildly from pole to pole. The retreat begins around the question of trust: "If there is a war, on whose side would they be?"

The Jewish participants end the second day of the encounter feeling angry and bewildered. This is the first time during the workshop and in their lives in general that they are encountering an Arab group that is adamantly demanding its due. It is also the first time they are being required to argue with the other side instead of among themselves, and suddenly the variations within the group become blurred because one of its most basic axioms has been shattered, namely that the Jews have more justice and morality on their side than do the Arabs. Things are less clear and less one-dimensional, hence the feelings of bewilderment.

This crisis for the Jews has without a doubt been engendered by the Arab group; thus the disappointment the Arabs feel with themselves, as expressed in their uninational meeting, is puzzling. It may be that they didn't live up to their own expectations of themselves, but there is no doubt that they have succeeded in confounding some of the basic axioms and beliefs of the Jews.

At the end of this hard day, no formal activity is scheduled for the evening hours. There is a clubhouse for participants' use where they are free to meet under the supervision of the teachers accompanying them, and indeed the groups generally take advantage of this evening for informal conversations, dancing, and social games.

The Third Day

The Simulation

The entire morning is devoted to a simulation game. All the workshop participants take part, and the game is run by the participants themselves, with the facilitators serving as advisors only.

All the participants gather in the clubhouse. The youth program directors explain the morning's task:

> Imagine that we are now fifty years in the future. There is a comprehensive peace between Israel and all the Arab countries, including the Palestinians. The situation of Palestinian Arabs in Israel has not changed in the wake of this peace agreement and remains more or less as it was in the past. The Arab population once again demands equal rights, but there is no response. A wave of protest develops that includes demonstrations and mass riots. The government meets to discuss the situation, and a decision is made to solve the problem of the Arabs within the state. To this end, the Prime Minister names a special minister to preside over the matter. The presiding minister invites the head of the Supreme Monitoring Committee (the committee that represents the Arabs in Israel) for a preliminary dialogue, after which he decides to divide the problem into four subjects: security, education, symbols and representation, and the character of the state. The minister deputizes someone to oversee each of the four subjects and invites the Arab Supreme Monitoring Committee members to hold discussions with the government-appointed members on the subjects that have been decided on.

After this description of the task, the participants are asked to divide into two groups in separate rooms, the Jews in one and the Arabs in the other. The Jewish group organizes itself—a presiding minister, four committees headed by deputy ministers—and prepares for negotiations. Concurrently, the Arab group organizes itself—a chairperson for the Supreme Arab Monitoring Committee, four delegations—and begins its own preparations. From here on, the Jewish minister and the Arab chairperson are in charge; they are advised by the facilitators, whose role is now to provide information on request and to propose strategies to further the negotiations.

The delegates do not meet on neutral ground. For the negotiations, the Arab delegations come to the government "offices" of the deputy ministers, which are arranged with suitable props including large conference tables and "Ministry" signs on the doors. Several rounds of negotiations ensue, with time out in-between for the delegates and committee members to consult among themselves; the exact timetable varies. When the negotiating groups finally reach an agreement, they put its main points in writing.

When the allotted time runs out and the negotiations end, the presiding minister and the chairperson of the Supreme Monitoring Committee host a ceremony, something like a press conference, in which they summarize the events of the morning and present to all the participants the achievements of the various delegations. Each pair of committee heads, Jewish and Arab, reports in Arabic and in Hebrew on the agreements they have reached and on the difficulties that delayed or prevented agreement.

Here are examples of agreements:

Agreement on Symbols and Representation

"Do not search for the way to peace; peace is the way." The national flag will have a brown background with two blue stripes; in the center will be a Star of David and, within it, a *sabra* [a plant]. The anthem stays the same, except for the word *Jewish*, which becomes *Israeli*. Regarding holidays: there will be mutual respect between Jews and Arabs; the national day of mourning will be a day of mourning for both peoples, followed by a day of celebration. There will be at least one Arab justice on the state's highest court. The Minister for Arab Affairs must be an Arab. Twenty percent of the nation's ambassadors will be Arabs, and they will be assigned all over the world.

Signed by the Jewish and Arab principals to the negotiations.

Agreement on the Future of Education

There will be both binational and uninational schools. . . . Parents and children will have the right to choose their schools for themselves. . . . The languages of instruction from kindergarten on will be Arabic and Hebrew. . . .

A binational school will have a five-day school week. . . . In elementary schools, each religion will have its own vacations. . . . In the upper schools, all the students will have all the holidays. . . .

All students will study history, literature, and citizenship. . . . Binational school students will study general history, history of the Arab people, and history of the Jewish people. In the uninational schools . . . the national history of the neighbor will be optional. Uninational schools will offer general literature and Hebrew/Arabic literature, . . . and binational schools, general, Arabic, and Hebrew literature. . . . All students will study citizenship in the same way. . . .

A Directorate for Arab Education will be established in the Ministry of Education, headed by an Arab, and Arab schools will have Arab supervisors. . . . The Arab sector and Arab students will have guaranteed representation at the universities. . . . Students who wish it will be examined and will submit papers in the language of their choice. There will be equality in the hiring of Arab lecturers.

All the schools will observe national education-sector ceremonies, including a memorial day for Arabs who have fallen as well
as for fallen Israeli Army soldiers.

The process that takes place during the simulation game is special
and moving; it gives participants an opportunity to organize themselves
in new groups when they choose the committees in which they will participate. The reorganized groupings enable each participant to get to
know additional people, but they serve mainly to create a framework that
enables the young people to debate, argue, and negotiate without affect-
ing the dynamic evolved in the previous day's small groups. And indeed
the participants take advantage of the negotiations to explore their views
and those of their partners candidly and to the last detail.

Another element that characterizes the simulation is that its objective is different from those set for the participants thus far. We emphasize
that participants must try to reach agreements. At this stage of the negotiations, the participants must take responsibility to move the process forward and achieve results. The great seriousness with which they assume
this role is astonishing. The young people enter into the negotiations and
forget they are playing a game. Their responses are sensitive; they insist
on certain points; they send delegations to persuade the opposing side;
and sometimes they even cry when they feel that they are losing. There is
hectic activity throughout the hours of the negotiations. The seriousness
is also evident in the way the participants relate to the presiding minister
and the chairperson of the Supreme Monitoring Committee. Their authority is accepted; people turn to them when there is a crisis in the negotiations and consult with them. The de facto autonomy inherent in this
activity is clearly tremendously meaningful to the young people.

The simulation is followed by a process of analysis and evaluation,
with each committee meeting first uninationally and then jointly. In these
two meetings, the facilitators return to their original roles as group leaders. They try to help the young people link the events of the simulation to
external events in Israeli society by stressing the power relationships between the various groups, the dynamic of conducting negotiations, and
how groups relate to internal minorities.

The Jewish group has a hard time if they have not arrived at agreements, but they have just as hard a time if they have reached agreements
because now they feel that perhaps they gave away too much: "We have
sold the state." Participants have difficulty arriving at compromises and
sharing the positions of power and the symbols of the state; and when

they are obliged to do so, they are worried about going home: What will people think of them? How will they be able to communicate what they have experienced to their friends back home who are skeptical, especially if they feel that they haven't stood firm in their role as "sentries at the gates"? Frequently, this pressure moves the Jews to declare that it was all just a game and that they were not in an actual negotiation.

Another feeling that emerges at this juncture is astonishment and anger, a feeling that the Arabs "want too much." "I felt that the request to change the anthem and the flag wasn't necessary because they are under Israeli citizenship." "Coexistence means that we will not be above them, aside from the anthem and the flag, . . . but this is a matter of principle." "The national anthem and the flag, that's too much." "They [the Arabs] came on as oppressed, totally without hope, and we responded considerately, and then they came with demands."

The Arab group comes out of the negotiations with mixed feelings. There were achievements, but they worked extremely hard all along the way: "I didn't expect them to agree to everything, but I feel that in the room there was an attempt by the Jewish group to control everything, and that was very hard." "Our demands come from reality. We want to change the existing situation. We want to get to a feeling that we have importance." "We don't want everything all at once."

The Arabs feel that the Jews played at negotiating, as if they didn't take the whole thing seriously. "They disparaged us all the way through the negotiations." This feeling comes from the gap they confront between what happened in the simulation and the realities of their lives. If they have reached agreements, then it was a game because it's a fact that in the outside world the Jews are not so eager to compromise; and if they haven't reached agreements, then the Jews weren't approaching the task with due seriousness.

The Final Evening

Each national group meets for an hour with its accompanying teacher to prepare a performance for the final evening. In the evening everyone gathers in the clubhouse; after each group presents its performance, the formal part of the evening is concluded, and the participants then usually organize dancing.

During the formal program the groups present songs, dances, or dramatic skits. The Jews usually seem to have more problems relating to the task. The Arab program generally includes a *debka* (folk dance) or a skit with a traditional Arab wedding. The Jews often sing a peace song. It seems to be easier for the Arab group to select something to present from Arab culture, whereas more than once a Jewish group has found the task embarrassing and confusing. It is unclear to us why this is sometimes the case.

After the formal segment, there is almost always a desire to continue in one another's company either to play or to dance. The participants try to dance together but get stuck in a "war of cassettes." Each group attempts to dictate the type of music, whether Arabic, Hebrew, or English. The tension between East and West is not verbal; it comes through in the different sounds and rhythms. When the Arabs put on Arabic music, only some of the Jews join in, and vice versa. Sometimes one group takes over, and the other moves to the fringes of the hall or leaves. Sometimes two disk jockeys are chosen, and a compromise is reached on the dance floor.

The Fourth Day

The last day is devoted to summing up and to farewells; we help the participants digest the tumultuous experience in which they have taken part. This process takes place during two meetings.

Concluding Dialogue

In the concluding discussion, the participants and the facilitators try to make sense of the process they have been through, and they take leave of one another. We have chosen a number of quotes from some of these final meetings as a brief sampling to convey the atmosphere as participants come to the end of their encounter.

> JEWISH GIRL: At the start I had a good feeling; then there were situations that were really unpleasant. I am glad that after we fought, we were able to join in singing together, and that's the goal we should have been looking for. The simulation game very much strengthened the feeling that there is really something to talk about and we didn't just come for nothing. The political stuff yesterday really made me angry; we calmed down only in the evening.

> JEWISH BOY: There were things that weren't pleasant. All in all we dealt with them, and we could have gone on longer in the evening social part. I personally learned that it is possible to listen right to the end. In the political discussions, it degenerated into shouting and personal exchanges, but all in all it was good.

ARAB BOY: Most of the responses of the Jews were to the political discussions, although there were lots more things in this meeting. I must tell you that although it caused discomfort and shouting sometimes, we cannot give way on politics because that is in fact the heart of the matter. We could have been nice to each other and had a good time together without serious arguments. But that would have been fake and inauthentic.

Despite the upheavals and the gap between the groups, there is an enormous desire on the part of everyone to make an effort to end in a positive atmosphere. The young people do their utmost to speak in a cordial manner, with respect and with great sensitivity.

"Letters"

Each small group gathers in its room. The facilitators distribute sheets of paper and pens and invite each participant to write a concluding letter of farewell to the members of his or her group—with thoughts, impressions, and experiences from the encounter. One quickly sees, under every tree and scattered about on the lawn, boys and girls sitting down and writing their impressions from the three days that have passed.

The facilitators collect these letters to be photocopied, collated, and distributed to each participant as a souvenir album at the meetings that will take place at their schools about a month later.

Here is an Arab boy's letter (written originally in Arabic):

The group was basically okay; there were moderate opinions, but to my great sorrow most of the opinions were extreme, especially on the part of the Jewish group, which expressed racist opinions. Evidently they don't know what peace is; on the one hand they want peace and equality with us, and on the other they aren't prepared to give us the most elementary rights. They claim that the fact of our existence in this state is an achievement, and I say to them that if that is the general idea among the Jews, it will bring disaster down on all of us in the end. I am filled with hope that this will not happen to us. I say to the Jews that we will not leave our land and our country and we are not going to Egypt and not to Jordan. The Jews see us as if we were another Jewish ethnic group, that we should assimilate and be part of them. They expect that we will abandon our language and our culture and adopt their language and their culture, but anyone who thinks that should be examined by a psychologist. People who want peace have to keep an open mind and be ready to make concessions and have to trust the other side.

[Here, he switched into Hebrew:]

Finally, I decided to write in Arabic, for two reasons: out of pride in our language and as a reply to those who claim that they don't have to study Arabic. Then how will they understand what I say? How can there be cooperation and peace between us that way?—With thanks, and farewell.

Here is a letter from a Jewish boy (written originally in Hebrew):

To all the members of "The Shining Dove" [group]: These four days that I have spent at Neve Shalom changed my entire point of view about values; I never thought I could live with them [Arabs] in peace, in fun, and that we could be friends. Every day I heard in the media, on the street, that there was another terrorist incident, another bus blown up, and it made me hate the Arabs more and more, and I didn't know that not all of them are that way, that not all are murderers and terrorists. I discovered also that there are children and young people my age who like to have fun, listen to music, play soccer and basketball, exactly the things I like to do. I discovered also that they have feelings and opinions, political and otherwise, and that they too have something to say and something to contribute and something to give to improve the situation as it exists today so that all of us can live together without everyone suffering every day, day after day of his life. I am not writing in this letter what we did, all the arguments, scars, differences of opinion, because on that subject there is no agreement between us. They want and they make demands, and sometimes they are even right. They are not demanding exaggerated things, but we cannot change anything; we just listened and tried to understand, and I really understood them. I don't know what I would do in their place. I don't know how I would be able to live and to put up with the conditions they have to live with. So in short I had a great time in these four days. I discovered new people, a new culture, a new world, and I hope that really they will be able to do something to improve their lives in Israel and not curse us, the Jews, every day of their lives.—Bye-bye.

The meeting concludes with everyone assembled together, as it began. The directors sum up in a few words and take leave of the young people. Then, each pair of facilitators in turn calls the names of the members of their small group and presents each one with a certificate of participation. The ceremony lends a formal dimension and gives recognition to the effort made by the participants. We end the workshop in the plenum so as to give a sense of power to the young people. The participants are clearly moved. Each time someone's name is called, there is tumultuous applause. Sometimes there is a funny remark or a line from a song as one of the names is called and the student accepts his or her certificate. It is quite obvious that a group entity has been created; there is warmth among the participants and a feeling of satisfaction that they have accomplished something together. The air is different from that of the opening meeting on the first day. The participants are sitting intermingled, the air is electric and full of energy. When the ceremony is over, they exchange addresses, have their photographs taken together, and accompany one another to the buses. Then they part, sixty young people who have spent four days together challenging, with such great courage and sensitivity, the separate realities to which they will now return.

7
LANGUAGE AS A BRIDGE
AND AN OBSTACLE

RABAH HALABI AND MICHAL ZAK

The matter of language in the School for Peace (SFP) has preoccupied our staff right from the beginning. During the early years, language was treated as merely a tool for communicating. We related to communication problems as to a burden, an obstacle that we needed to overcome by any means possible. During those same years, in the workshops for youth there were noticeable manifestations of dominance by the Jewish group in contrast to the passivity of the Arab group. Most of the talking by the Arab group was through one or two spokespersons, with the others remaining silent. The encounter, from beginning to end, re-created absolutely the patterns of relationships in the larger Israeli society, and at its conclusion both groups were left with a large measure of frustration. The Arab facilitators were not strict about speaking Arabic and translating from Arabic to Hebrew; the two languages had no official status one way or the other; and we did not make the use of language in the meetings a subject for research by means of which we could have been learning about the way the two groups related to one another. Over the years, with the development of our unique model of encounter (see Chapter Three), the subject of language became conspicuous in the encounter itself and turned into one of the important elements of conflict. The operational model that was developed is based among other things on the assumption that it is possible to make an ongoing connection between the events and processes of the group and the reality outside the group, and vice versa, on the understanding that the group is a microcosm of reality (Sonnenschein, Halabi, and Friedman 1998).

In this chapter, we try to arrive at an in-depth understanding of what happens between the two groups, Arab and Jewish, in relation to language. We begin by briefly surveying the literature on the subject in order to frame our case within the wider context. Then we describe the situation of the two languages in the State of Israel, at Neve Shalom/Wahat al Salam (NS/WAS), and in the School for Peace. Finally we analyze the principal processes that participants undergo at encounters run by the SFP in relation to the encounter between the two languages.

REVIEW OF THE LITERATURE

Language is a tool for communication between people, but it also expresses identity, culture, and tradition. Most studies of language have examined the first aspect, language as a means of communication. Little has been written about language as an expression of identity. "There is a need for comprehensive research to understand why philosophers chose to consider the area of language an object for understanding and not an instrument of action and power" (Bourdieu 1977). Bourdieu goes on to contend that language has a function not only as a communication tool but also as power. People speak so that they will be understood and also so that they will be believed, so that others will do as they want, respect them, and differentiate them from others. Bourdieu further contends that, on both the group and the individual level, language is valued according to how its speakers are valued because languages are equal from the linguistic standpoint but not from the social standpoint.

V. N. Voloshinov treats language as a linguistic act that creates meaning. This act is born, lives, and dies within a social context. In his view, the literal import of the words does not carry their linguistic meaning, but rather the relations between the speakers decide the meaning of the exchange of words (cited in Bukhurst 1990).

Amara and Kabaha (1996) continue that same line of analysis, holding that the function that language fulfills as a means of communication, while important, is not its only or its main function. Language conveys content and is itself content. The idea is that human beings do not convey or express with their language only thoughts, feelings, and expectations;

rather, with the use of language, we define for ourselves who we are and how we wish to be seen by others.

Billing (1995) adds another dimension to the description of what language is. He claims that in their search for security, people who speak the same language are involuntarily attracted to one another. Language has a positive role in forging nationality—that is, in creating modes of belief and behavior that cause social arrangements to appear natural or to be taken for granted.

Based on the foregoing, one may conclude that language is an important element in determining the identity of groups and of peoples and in the formation of relationships between them. Giles, Bourhis, and Taylor (1977) enumerate the elements necessary for a group's vitality. A vital group will have a high, positive self-image, and this is a prerequisite for intergroup relations of a more egalitarian nature. Control of one's own fate, a strong sense of self, pride in one's history, location in a particular territory, and representation of the group in the establishment—all of these are among the elements that forge a vital collective entity. To these are added the defining element of language and especially the use of the group's language in the activities of the establishment (Hamers and Blanc 1989).

Ng and Bradac (1993) add the element of conquest, which does not appear in the work of Giles, Bourhis, and Taylor. They contend that a change of language in a group is an outcome of a conquered group's becoming, in the best case, bilingual. Otherwise, when conditions are hard, the group is likely to lose its language altogether. In some cases, the new language is acquired but at the expense of one's own language, and, over time, the first language is lost. An emotional price is attached to this phenomenon because language is tied to identity. People who have lost their language lose their authentic sense of self by becoming speakers of a foreign tongue. In the extreme case, identification with the oppressor is also seen: the use of the foreign language does not have merely an instrumental motivation arising as a pragmatic response to the desire to obtain, via language, social recognition or economic advantage; rather, there is an integrative motivation catering to the desire to be a part of the dominant group. This desire involves identifying with the dominant group and its culture and, indeed, accepting the superiority of the dominant culture.

Because language is an important component of identity, it also is an important medium in relations among groups and peoples who speak different languages. In order to understand these relations and the conflicts that exist in the world, then, we must necessarily refer to the subject of language and its role in forming and shaping relations among different peoples.

Tarrow (1992) analyzes three communities in Europe: the Welsh in Britain, and the Basque and the Catalonian in Spain. She suggests that we may understand the situation of a multicultural community in one of three ways that also represent different ideologies: assimilation, adaptation, and multiculturalism. The first, the path of assimilation, allows for no pluralism in society, and there is inequality between groups that is accompanied by legislative remedies that to some extent meet the needs and values of the oppressed group. The intent is that in the end the oppressed group will assimilate into the dominant group.

The second path, that of adaptation, leaves room for the language and culture of the oppressed group along with the language and culture of the dominant group. There are programs of study about the culture and history of such minorities, and bilingualism arises, but all these relate solely to the oppressed group. In these societies, separate identities are conserved, and a common ideal of adaptation to the dominant society is shared by all.

The third path, that of multiculturalism, includes programs of study in the educational system for reducing racism and promoting human rights. There is cooperation and interaction between the societies; there is reciprocity, mutual dependence between groups, and the beginnings of a process of resolving the conflicts. Tarrow contends that societies undergo this development in stages but that, even in countries that have arrived at the last stage—the adoption of the multicultural approach—and that have affirmative-action and other programs to combat racism, all of that will be meaningless if not accompanied by structural changes in the power relationships between the dominant group and the oppressed groups.

HEBREW AND ARABIC IN ISRAEL

This analysis of the various approaches adopted by different societies takes us to the particular case of the society in Israel. Israel is at Tarrow's second stage and operates in the adaptation mode. We give a brief description of the situation in Israel here in order to make a connection between theories and the reality in which we live. Our hope is that this review, together with the theoretical material, will provide an understanding of the relations between Arabs and Jews in Israel, of the situation at NS/WAS, and especially of the fascinating dynamics in the relations between Arabs and Jews as these manifest themselves through speech—that so very human and basic way in which we make a connection with one another.

The Legal Status of Hebrew and Arabic

The situation in Israel is especially interesting because Hebrew is the language of this state only, a local language serving the six million citizens of Israel, while Arabic is the regional language, spoken by 181 million people, and the fifth most widely spoken language in the world (*Time*, 7 July 1997). Arabic is a minority language in Israel but the language of the majority throughout the Middle East.

In Israel, both Arabic and Hebrew are official languages because of historical circumstances rather than direct policy. During the period of the British Mandate, Hebrew, English, and Arabic were official languages by law (Mandate for Palestine, Article 22, 1922). With the declaration of independence of the State of Israel, the Knesset voided the status of English as an official language while Arabic and Hebrew retained their prior status. Actually Hebrew is the country's primary language both officially and in practice, and Arabic is completely marginal.

True, the Declaration of Independence states that there will be freedom of religion, conscience, language, education, and culture. But in practice, even in the law, there is a preference for Hebrew over Arabic. By way of example, a knowledge of Hebrew is one of the requirements for receiving certain government positions; the government seal is designed with only Hebrew text; and there is a requirement in the Law of Citizenship that one must know some Hebrew in order to receive citizenship. Hence it would not be exact to say that there is linguistic equality. Some people thought that Arabic ought to be granted the status of a national minority language throughout the state, not just in Arab areas, and that legislation should be passed to anchor this status in law (rather than in such Mandatory law as remains in effect). But the position that prevailed called for maintaining the status quo and preventing any arrangement that might have the effect of engraving a binational cast on the character of the state.

Linguistic Policy in the Educational System

The state educational system in Israel is divided. Jewish students study separately from Arab students, and each system functions in its own language. Although the Compulsory Education Law of 1949 does not mention the language of instruction in the Arab schools, in practice instruction is carried out in Arabic.

If we look at what takes place rather than at what the law says, there is in Israel one principal language, Hebrew, and it is used in all realms of life; then there is English, which is studied as a required language from the fourth grade and serves as the language of international communications (the *lingua franca*). High school students are required to study an additional language, Arabic or French: French because in the past it was the *lingua franca*, and Arabic because it is the language of the neighboring countries of the Middle East and the principal language of the largest minority in Israel (Shohamy 1995).

Linguistic policy in Israel derives from and is driven by ideology. This is perceptible if one looks at the centrality given to the Hebrew language as a component of the national renaissance of the Jewish people. There is no doubt that Hebrew is linked by a strong bond with Zionism. The intention was that Hebrew would serve as a unifying factor for the various groups of Jewish immigrants, and the success of this legacy became a test of the new state's power. Immigrants were required, sometimes even violently, to relinquish their language, but in practice the monolinguistic policy did not include Arabs and *haredim* ("ultra-Orthodox" Jews). What these two groups had in common was that neither of them was part of the Zionist consensus (Shohamy 1995).

In contrast, the educational system uses the Arabic language simply as a tool of communication. Arabic as taught in the Arab schools has different educational goals than those governing the teaching of Hebrew in the Jewish schools. "In the Arab schools, language study has been shrunk to the development of language skills, to expression and understanding during use. It appears that there is no value in Arabic literature, at least in the eyes of the planner. Jewish literature, in contrast, is seen as having value" (Mar'i 1978).

In the Media

In Israel there are daily and weekly newspapers and monthly periodicals in Hebrew and in Arabic. The Arab public is exposed to the Hebrew media, but the Jewish public has no contact with the media written in Arabic aside from a few articles translated into Hebrew. Thus an Arab cultural ghetto is formed with which the majority group has no contact whatsoever; and moreover the majority group is alienated from what is created in the culture of the largest minority group in the state, a group that is thereby transformed into a silent and silenced entity from the standpoint of the Jews. There is but one state television channel. This channel broadcasts a number of hours in Arabic but, in practice, the lion's share of the programming consists of programs purchased from Western stations. To portray the dominance of Hebrew, which is so taken for granted, the telephone company, which has a monopoly on communications in Israel, tells its customers in a recorded message (in Hebrew), "The English announcement will follow the Hebrew one"! Thus there are Jews living in Israel, for whom Arabic virtually does not come into their lives, and Arabs, for whom Arabic has become a private, personal language that in many cases does not enter the public sphere or the workplace.

LINGUISTIC BEHAVIOR AT NEVE SHALOM/WAHAT AL SALAM

There is an assumption that the village of Neve Shalom/Wahat al Salam is different than the Israeli reality because the village was founded to foster and continues to live on the basis of equality between Jews and Arabs. Here we examine the relationship between the two languages in the everyday reality of the village.

The village has an official name in Hebrew and in Arabic: Neve Shalom/Wahat al Salam, which is meant to convey the partnership between Arabs and Jews in the life of the community. In practice, when one is speaking Hebrew, the village is called "Neve Shalom"; when one is speaking Arabic it is sometimes called "Neve Shalom" and sometimes "Wahat al Salam." Only when the members of the village are speaking English or another third language, do they refer to the village by its full name in both languages—as if some distance is required in order to believe that partnership is possible, but with each in his or her own language, within the borders of his or her own community only.

On the bulletin board in the center of the village, official notices of the village Secretariat are posted in both languages. When an Arab member of the community posts a notice meant for everyone, it appears in both languages; a Jewish member will post a notice in Hebrew or ask an Arab resident to translate it into Arabic for him. Unofficial notices and messages are generally in Hebrew.

All the Arab residents of NS/WAS are fluent in Hebrew and Arabic. No Jewish resident of NS/WAS is fluent in Arabic, a few Jews know some basic Arabic. General meetings for discussing and making decisions about crucial matters pertaining to the management of the village are conducted in Hebrew. The minutes are recorded in Hebrew, although the secretary who types them after the meetings is an Arab woman. During the meetings, some people choose to express themselves in Arabic. Generally this happens in the heat of an argument or as a means of protest, but in any case this phenomenon is new. In the early years, when the great majority of community members were Jewish, Arabic was not heard at all in joint forums. As an Arab woman says, "I don't envision myself initiating a social or cultural activity in Arabic because this will be perceived as isolationist, whereas activities of that sort in Hebrew are perceived as belonging to all of us."

Linguistic Policy and Behavior in the Educational System

At NS/WAS, there is an elementary school, a kindergarten, and a nursery school, all of them binational and bilingual. "In the school, care is taken to use Hebrew and Arabic in a dual way as mother tongues so as to assure equal expression for both nationalities" (from a promotional brochure). Administration of the school is joint and is divided between an Arab general manager and an educational manager, a Jew. The staff has an equal number of Jewish and Arab members. Over the years there was first a majority of Jewish students and subsequently a majority of Arab students; in recent years the numerical gap has closed, creating numerical parity.

According to the model that was developed, teachers are to teach in their own language. Likewise, in the preschools, the kindergarten teacher and caregiver are supposed to speak with all the children, each in her own language. Publicity material about the schools is in both languages, and all letters from the administration to the parents are in both languages. In the kindergarten and the nursery schools, the staff are supposed to have equal standing, rather than that of a teacher and an assistant, but in practice not all the preschools have two certified teachers. In some of them the fact that there is a Jewish certified teacher and an Arab noncertified teacher has an impact on the respective degree of involvement of the two.

The number of teaching hours in Hebrew and Arabic is much greater than is normally the case in the educational system in Israel. The children learn to read and write and speak both languages from the first grade. The number of class hours in the school per pupil is larger than normal, mainly as a consequence of the extra investment in language study on the various levels. At the same time, the number of hours that Jewish students are exposed to Arabic, that is to say to speech in Arabic, in the various disciplines is seven, and their exposure to Hebrew is twenty hours. The number of hours that Arab students are exposed to Arabic is twelve, and to Hebrew, sixteen. (The example is from the schedule for the fourth grade in 1997.)

Each teacher gives instruction in his or her own language, and the class is supposed to adapt to the language of instruction. Textbooks also fit this model and are in both languages. The English teacher, for example, is Jewish, the class is mixed, and the textbook is bilingual in Arabic and Hebrew. In history the teacher is Jewish, the textbook is in Hebrew, and there is an Arabic translation of it. The nature-studies teacher is an Arab, and she uses a text in Arabic for the Arab students and a similar compilation of material in Hebrew for the Jewish students. All the books are published by the Ministry of Education. All the Arab teachers, with one exception, are completely fluent in Hebrew. None of the Jewish teachers is fluent in Arabic, two read and write Arabic, and some have limited comprehension and speaking skills.

In practice, Hebrew is dominant. At the conclusion of their studies at NS/WAS, the Arab students are fluent in both languages. The Jewish students, on concluding their studies, read and write Arabic with difficulty; they understand Arabic when spoken to but barely speak it. In most of the classes taught by Arab teachers, there is broad use of Hebrew to make it easier for the Jewish students. In the preschools, some of the Arab caregivers translate what they are saying when conversing with the Jewish children. In one of the preschools, the Jewish caregiver understands Arabic, whereas the Arab caregiver speaks little Hebrew, and this enables Arabic to be spoken in that preschool more than usual. In the kindergarten, the Arab kindergarten teacher consistently does not speak Hebrew with the children, but because her communication with the Jewish teacher is in Hebrew, the Arab children from a young age get the message that when interacting with Jews it is possible and preferable to switch to Hebrew, and the Jewish children get the message that they don't have to work too hard to learn Arabic. All the interactions between the children when they are playing in a mixed group are in Hebrew, even if most of the children playing at a given moment are Arab. Often Arab children speak Arabic among themselves and switch to Hebrew for the benefit of the Jewish children. In recent years, the school has offered a program of Arabic language study for the benefit of teachers and parents.

Linguistic Behavior and Policy in the School for Peace

The SFP is managed in rotation by an Arab and a Jew. The staff has both Arab and Jewish members. The staff's ideology is based on equality and on giving maximal expression to Arab identity and to Jewish identity. In all the activities of the SFP, both languages are official languages. The promotional material of the institution appears in both languages. Correspondence is mainly in Hebrew, and once in a while letters also go out in Arabic.

In practice there is a large gap between the proclaimed policy and the actual situation. The Jewish facilitators who are members of the staff do not know Arabic. All the meetings that take place in mixed forums are conducted in Hebrew. Only some of the material passed out to participants in the courses and seminars is in both languages. Workshops that bring together Arab and Jewish adults are conducted in Hebrew. In the workshops for young people, the option of speaking in Arabic is not available to the Jewish youth because they do not know Arabic. And the Arab participants mostly do not exploit their right to speak Arabic, despite the fact that talking in Hebrew is hard for them. Only recently has the staff decided that the facilitators working in the SFP must know how to speak Arabic. To that end, a course in spoken Arabic has been started for the Jewish staff members.

THE LANGUAGE OF ENCOUNTER

In this section, we describe the processes that manifest themselves in workshop encounters between Jewish and Arab participants with respect to language. We focus on meetings between young people; in them the phenomena are more conspicuous because there is no one language with which both groups are comfortable. We describe the interactions that take place when the Arab group or members from that group speak in Arabic. We then cover the subject in the context of adult groups. We do not describe other dynamics, such as when only Hebrew is used or when the Arab group members are silent.

Meetings of Young People

The subject of language occupies the young people from the first moment they become interested in coming to an encounter. During preparatory meetings at schools, the question arises as to the mode of communication between the participants. In both groups, the students wonder how the Jewish and Arab young people will work out the communication, in Hebrew and Arabic, between them.

The Jewish young people usually ask, "Do they [the Arab students] know Hebrew?—because we don't know Arabic." A brief discussion ensues on the subject, during the course of which the group hears from the facilitator that both languages are languages in the meeting and that it will be interesting to see how they will cope with this new situation. The responses are divided: some understand the situation, and some express disappointment that translation will make dialogue cumbersome and will hamper the direct connection they would like to forge. At this stage the group accepts the arrangement recommended, that both languages are legitimate in the meeting.

The Arab group, at the preparatory meeting, lingers over the subject of language, devoting a great deal of time to it. The declaration of the facilitator that both languages are languages of the meeting provokes a discussion of the use of Arabic in the company of Jews. This behavior is unique: it is more than likely that these students have not previously experienced a discussion involving Jews in which they themselves spoke Arabic. The dilemma is between the desire to be clear in expressing both the substance of what is said and their identity versus the desire to communicate directly and according to the accepted rules of the society— that is, in Hebrew.

> A GIRL: The only thing we have left from our identity is the language. It is inconceivable that we should give up that as well; we must speak in Arabic.

> A BOY: Language after all is an instrument of expression. The main thing is that they should understand us and that we should express ourselves clearly.

Sometimes a group ends its preparatory meeting with a decision to speak Arabic, but, as will be made clear below, persevering in this decision is difficult.

Day 1: The Getting-Acquainted Stage

Encounters at NS/WAS open with a meeting of all participants. Arabic is heard before Hebrew as the staff opens the workshop with an official ceremony. Hebrew is heard as a translation for the Jewish participants. This formal opening contains a clear message from the SFP. The message is conveyed in behavior rather than by talking about it; in the preparatory stage, it was conveyed only by means of talking about the language issue. Through this message a situation is created that is the obverse of the

Israeli reality wherein Hebrew is heard alone or as a primary language and Arabic, when heard at all, is heard as a translation "for those who do not understand" or "for the weaker participants." This opening in Arabic creates among the Jews in the hall conspicuous unease, which arises from the novel situation in which they find themselves: a situation in which they do not understand what is being said. Sometimes laughter is heard from members of the Arab group at a joke to which the Jewish members are not privy. The greetings and explanations continue for about five minutes, without a break, and the translation comes afterward. Sometimes there is a need to hush the Jewish participants, to calm them down and assure them that their turn will come, that they should be tolerant. The inversion of presentation of the languages also has an impact on the Arab participants: they are relaxed, sometimes they make jokes in Arabic during the explanations, and their presence as a group in the hall is perceptible.

After the opening session, the participants divide up into mixed groups of sixteen, Jews and Arabs. Each group has two facilitators. The Arab facilitator opens in Arabic, and the Jewish facilitator, in Hebrew. The mode is formal, as in the assembly session, but also to the point: the staff wants to create a situation in which speaking Arabic is a legitimate option. Generally this does not happen at this stage of beginning to get acquainted. Most of the talking is in Hebrew. Now and then someone introduces himself or herself in Arabic, and the Arab facilitator translates. It is clear that that particular Arab participant is weak in Hebrew and therefore is speaking Arabic. Doing so is acceptable to the Jews in the group; they are tolerant of someone who does not know Hebrew. A good atmosphere develops and is maintained throughout the first day, the day for getting to know one another as individuals.

At the start, through interventions, the Arab facilitator explores whether there is a need to speak Arabic so that the Arabs will understand or whether the use of Arabic is symbolic. This groping for clarity is important in order to find out to what degree translation is necessary and to what extent the use of Arabic is critical for communication. Because the use of Arabic is perceived both by the facilitators and by the group as cumbersome, if there is no need for translation to assure comprehension, generally the facilitator defers on this issue and does not speak Arabic.

Throughout the first day, in parallel with the social atmosphere in the group, Hebrew reigns.

> JEWISH GIRL: The Jews who come, come with the goal of talking, and the Arabs don't talk, except for a few.

ARAB BOY (in Arabic): Maybe I don't talk because your education is that people talk all together, and you don't let me talk.

It is easy to see that the experience of the Arabs is different from that of the Jews. The Arabs are preoccupied with the effort to communicate; they hesitate over whether to speak in Arabic, to speak in Hebrew, or maybe just to keep quiet. It appears that they experience themselves as less present in the group compared with the Jews—a hard and frustrating experience.

Day 2: The Stage of Conflict

On the second day of the meeting, the program calls for intergroup interaction even more than on the first day. In the intergroup situation, competition between the groups tends to sharpen, and each group works to unify itself and tends to present itself as homogeneous. The languages are enlisted in the service of both these tendencies, and we witness some marked phenomena.

The more the subjects brought forward for discussion deal with the differences between the groups—that is to say the more that questions arise concerning society, culture, and politics—the more the use of Arabic increases. This happens after the groups divide, for the first time, into national groups, in which the Jews and the Arabs discuss their feelings separately and try to understand the encounter thus far.

Generally during its uninational meeting the Arab group is preoccupied with language and with its ability to express itself. Without any Jews present, the discussion is held in Arabic, and this in and of itself gives a feeling of empowerment and highlights the price the Arab participants have paid thus far in the encounter.

BOY: I will speak to them in Hebrew because he [the Jew] doesn't understand Arabic. It's as if I were talking to a small child. I have to speak in his language because he doesn't understand the language of adults.

GIRL: We give up our right to talk Arabic in order to send them a message, but they don't get it. We have to convey to them that we are giving this up for the sake of the dialogue.

Sometimes the Arab group decides to go back to the meeting and speak Arabic—to enable everyone to participate and not embarrass those who speak Arabic from lack of choice, but mainly to insist on their rights.

Such a decision is generally arrived at under intense pressure from those who do not speak Hebrew fluently.

> BOY: I am not willing to speak Arabic if some are speaking Hebrew. What will they think of me?
>
> GIRL: What's the problem? Talk in Arabic. We will help you, and the facilitator can also translate for you. Why shouldn't I talk Hebrew when I know the language?

Usually the negotiations on this subject are not simple, and only sometimes is there a consensus that the entire group will begin speaking Arabic, with all that that entails. Most of the time, the Arab participants will not speak Arabic in the meeting or will limit their speech in Arabic during most of the encounter, despite their difficulties in expressing themselves in Hebrew. The shame of not knowing Hebrew takes precedence over the chance to express oneself.

One young woman who was at an encounter as a schoolgirl is now participating in a course we teach at the university. Years after the original experience, she reports that she joined the current course because in the meeting during high school she was unable to express herself in Hebrew and preferred to keep silent. That failure is still with her; now she wants to repair the negative experience she had back then. We assume that many of the Arab participants experience this same difficulty and remain in the meetings as passive onlookers, giving up the possibility of speaking and expressing themselves—which is to say, the possibility of speaking in Arabic. In the meeting they become "present absentees." (This is the term used to describe Palestinians in what became Israel who were refugees at the time of the 1948 postwar census and thus absent from their homes; on their subsequent return, they found that they no longer had any citizenship status in the eyes of the official institutions of the new State of Israel: physically they were there, but officially they were elsewhere.) Here, likewise, we shall regretfully refrain from addressing further the experience and the silence of the present absentees in the meeting room because our subject is dialogue. We shall proceed to consider those who did speak in Arabic and especially the instances in which the Arab group as a whole exercised its right to speak Arabic. This turning point creates a not inconsiderable upheaval in a meeting and leads to a new relationship between the two groups.

The agenda moves on, and we come to the stage of talking politics. The Jews experience the presence of the Arab identity in the group as a threat to their own identity because the Arabs are talking more now and in Arabic. The Jews attach great significance to this behavior. At times they see that a statement is being made, that the use of Arabic goes beyond self-expression for the sake of communication; in that moment, for the first time, use of the language becomes a tactic and a political statement. The Arabs appear to be in the right no less than the Jews, and this situation surprises the Jews. The palpable presence of Arabic along with the powerful substance of what is said changes the power relations between the two groups. In many cases the Jews delegitimize Arabic. They are angry, and they accuse the Arab facilitator, who is translating, of distorting or rendering imprecisely what is being said; there is a feeling of lack of trust. Actually the two groups are carrying on a trenchant negotiation. The atmosphere created is that of a zero-sum game, as if in another minute the tools will be shattered. It is unclear what will happen. Has someone gone out of the room? Will the Arabs "break" and stop being "present" with their whole identity to please the Jews? This is a critical stage. Amazingly the groups, from a sense of responsibility, continue the negotiating between them, despite the tension and the unpleasant atmosphere.

Each group is in fact coping initially with a situation that is new for it: the Arabs, with demonstrating the reality of their Palestinian identity in the presence of the Jews, even at the cost of provoking the Jews' anger; and the Jews, with a sense of loss and of assessing the degree of their own tolerance when confronted with this Arab identity's claiming room for itself in the space they had thought was theirs alone and that is gradually becoming shared.

JEWISH GIRL: I just couldn't get Arabic; I just couldn't get it.

JEWISH BOY: We study four years, that's enough. . . . If you don't learn Hebrew, it will be very hard for you to manage.

ARAB BOY: So let's talk in English, not in Hebrew and not in Arabic.

JEWISH BOY: But we need a language of our own, a Jewish state; the language of Jews is Hebrew. If we were living in your state, we would speak Arabic. It's to your advantage.

JEWISH BOY: If I were the Minister of Education, I would require the Jews to study Arabic. (All the Jews jump on him.)

JEWISH BOY: Why are you speaking Arabic? We are trying to talk here. (Arabic is now being spoken in the room.)

ARAB GIRL (in Arabic): You said you don't need Arabic; now you see that to understand us you do need it. *(The Arab facilitator translates this statement into Hebrew.)*

ARAB GIRL: I didn't think this would bother you. This is my language; I feel more comfortable and express myself better in it.

JEWISH GIRL: It interferes because we want to hear you, without a translation.

ARAB GIRL (in Arabic): She said that deep down she doesn't want to learn Arabic. That makes me angry. I liked learning Hebrew. *(Followed by Hebrew translation.)*

Day 3: Negotiation about the Future Relations between Jews and Arabs in Israel

Another day goes by, and Arabic gains ground and is heard more. On this day there is a simulation game. The groups are gathered together in the hall, and the young people are asked to conduct a negotiation between them and arrive at agreements on various subjects relating to the relations between the two groups in Israel. The discussions involve participation of Arabs in the government, integration of the two cultures, changing the symbols of the state, and school curricula. The entire day is run as a simulation. The students take on official roles and assume certain ways of behaving that are a little different than in the open dialogues. (The Arab participants assume the role of representatives of the Arabs in Israel, and the Jewish participants take on the role of members of the government, Jews.)

The new roles enable the young people to experience new ways of behaving: the use of Arabic by the Arab representatives in the negotiations, for example. In some instances they arrive at the negotiating table and open the discussion in Arabic. The representatives chosen by the Arab group are not necessarily those who do not know Hebrew well. On the contrary, sometimes they are precisely the students who were conspicuous in the discussion during the earlier sessions, in Hebrew. Their official standing as representatives gives them legitimacy to speak Arabic, and for the first time Arabic is transformed into a resource: nothing is more useful in a negotiation than having a "secret language."

The Jews are furious at this attempt to speak Arabic, despite the fact that a moment earlier, in their own prior discussion on the subject of linguistic rights, they expressed, among themselves, support for the official standing of Arabic in Israel. Usually they capitulate to the Arab dictate and conduct the negotiating via an interpreter. The combination of the translation process and the negotiating character of the discussion puts the whole dialogue on a more equal basis compared with that of the previous day. In moments of stress, the Jews become furious with the translator on the grounds that the translation is not reliable. This lack of trust may arise from the difficulty of sitting in a room together and carrying on a negotiation over the future of the society, a negotiation from which the Arabs can only profit, relative to their present situation, and in which the Jews will be required to give things up. The content of the talks at this point is conflictive, and the manner of talking—that of delegates in a negotiation—is more formal. Hence there is a kind of reciprocal synergy between the content and the manner of speaking. This juncture—in which the intergroup focus is at its most intense, mirroring external reality—is crucial.

Two examples illustrate the process that the participants go through. In a discussion taking place in one of the Jewish groups after the simulation, while attempting to analyze the processes that occurred during the negotiations, one of the Jewish boys says angrily, "And along with everything else, the Arab facilitator didn't translate them properly [otherwise we would have concluded agreements with them]." But another Jewish boy adds, to the astonishment of the group: "That's not so; he translated okay. I understand Arabic." The possibility of a Jew's mentioning that he or she understands Arabic is extremely low, and this boy's doing so bears witness to a different balance that has been created within the group vis-à-vis the Arabs, Arab culture, and the Arabic language, and hence also, for some of the Jews (from Arabic-speaking backgrounds), vis-à-vis themselves. That same boy had sat for three days in the mixed group and not let on that he understood Arabic; he didn't regard it as an asset in which to take pride.

Another example is from the ceremony at the conclusion of the simulation, during which the agreements reached by the various committees are presented. These agreements have been written in both Hebrew and Arabic. When the committee heads report on the agreements to all the participants, the Arab representative reads the agreement in Arabic, and the Jewish representative reads the agreement in Hebrew (with the Arab generally speaking before the Jew). Most of the Jewish group is respectful of granting this stature to the Arabic language in contrast to the stressful and uneasy atmosphere in the assembly held on the first day. In one of the workshops, the heads of the committee dealing with symbols and ceremonies decided not only to read their agreement but also to illustrate a decision they had arrived at: that in the State of Israel there would be two anthems, "Hatikva" ("The Hope"—the national anthem, which has a Jewish character and Jewish symbols) and "Biladi, Biladi" ("My Land, My Land"—an Arab national song). They asked all the participants to stand, and everyone did so; the Jews sang "Hatikva" and after them the Arabs sang "Biladi, Biladi" while the Jews continued to stand. It was a rare and moving moment in which both languages, and indeed both national identities, coexisted in the same space. This event was undoubtedly an outcome of the process the participants had undergone during the three days of the workshop.

Encounters between Jewish and Arab Adults

To round out the picture, we look now at what happens with language in meetings involving adults. In these encounters, the Arab participants are quite fluent in Hebrew and express themselves without difficulty. Hence language as an expression of collective presence is much less evident in the dialogue. Nonetheless language does appear as a subject for discussion, and some Arabic is spoken. Both the content and the speech represent part of the group's dialogue and support the conjecture that language is not merely an instrument of communication.

Usually in the first meeting of long-term groups (those that will meet over several months), it is the Jewish participants who bring up the matter of language and suggest the possibility of speaking in another language aside from Hebrew.

JEWISH MAN: Doesn't it bother you that everything here is in Hebrew?

ARAB WOMAN: That's part of communicating. It is annoying. Most Jews don't know Arabic. In order to know one another it is necessary to speak Hebrew. . . . It's a part of life.

ARAB MAN: We always have to make the effort, ever since we were little.

ARAB MAN: There is this feeling that the person who knows Arabic is inferior, it's a lower-class language. This is a general feeling; it has to be changed.

JEWISH WOMAN: I wouldn't mind if you speak only Arabic and someone translates.

ARAB WOMAN: I am not going to talk Arabic, and I won't pretend that the situation is that way and I accept it.

This is a strange conversation, with the Jews worrying whether Arabic will be represented and the Arabs insisting on speaking Hebrew. Is this possible? But the real situation is a bit different. For now, this is a theoretical conversation about principles, but when the Arab participants do talk Arabic among themselves, even if only in the coffee breaks, it evokes an immediate response. A Jewish woman says: "You are speaking outside among yourselves in Arabic, and that bothers me; I feel excluded."

When the Arabs speak Arabic in the group, it puts pressure on the Jewish group and provokes a strong reaction from some of the participants. They demand an immediate translation of everything that has been said. Hooks (1994) suggests that the need of white people (in the United States) to understand everything, right this minute, can be viewed as a type of control. She suggests that white people in a situation of encounter can exploit the space created, the space of not understanding, in order to pay attention without judging. "This type of lesson for whites in a multicultural society is mandatory so long as there is white superiority."

In one of the groups, two Arab participants were talking together in Arabic about a personal matter that had nothing to do with the group. The Jewish group demanded a translation, but none was given. This became a significant incident in the life of that group and tinged the dialogue in the meeting for many hours. The Jewish group felt a lack of control and possibly also a sense of impotence.

> JEWISH MAN: We don't know what you are talking about; I don't know whether you are laughing at me.

> JEWISH MAN: In refusing to translate, you are conveying that you don't want us to understand, so evidently you have something to hide.

In another incident, in a course for facilitators, in the first meeting a Jewish participant showed what seemed to be a lot of tolerance and was in favor of talking in both languages: "I don't care if you speak only Arabic and I have no need for control through speaking Hebrew." In the third meeting the same man, at the beginning of the meeting, took the floor in an assertive manner and said, "I would like to go back to the matter of language. I see from talking with you, during the breaks, that it is very important to you that we speak Arabic and that our language for you is like a surrender. At this point I know that I am not going to study Arabic. . . . I don't need the language." And in response to the discussion that ensued on the subject, the same man went on to say: "There is a question of control here. We want the language to be Hebrew. I am willing to concede about the Hebrew in favor of English, but not in favor of Arabic."

Language is such a significant thing and so strong and total; it's a very big thing with a lot of power, influence, and force. This is not about what I find comfortable or uncomfortable; it's not on a technical level; it's a matter of principal."

We see that even when from a technical standpoint language does not present a problem for communication between Arabs and Jews, it still is a focus for discussion between the two groups in their encounter. And through language reality intrudes into the meeting; language symbolizes the control and the dominance of the Jewish group vis-à-vis the Arab group.

DISCUSSION AND CONCLUSION

Because each group has its own language and at any given moment only one language may be spoken, a fertile ground is created for conflict over the language to be spoken in the room. This potential will not be actualized if the Arab group gives up its right to talk in its own language. The conflict will emerge if the existing order, according to which only Hebrew is spoken, is disturbed and the Arab group insists on speaking its own tongue.

As we have seen, most of the time the Arab participants work hard at speaking in Hebrew, even when it is difficult for them, because the Jews don't know Arabic, and the Arab group very much wants the dialogue. But this also expresses a majority-minority relationship between the groups, an asymmetry that also manifests itself with regard to the two languages. Hebrew is perceived by the Arabs as a more modern language, one that facilitates social mobility. Hence someone who is fluent in Hebrew, among the Arabs, is perceived as smarter and also tends to be given a leadership role in the encounter. Those who are not fluent in Hebrew prefer to remain silent rather than speak in Arabic, which is perceived as an inferior language. This situation changes when the Arab group gets stronger; the Arab participants stop being embarrassed to speak Arabic and stop regarding their language as inferior.

The Jewish group takes it for granted that everyone will speak Hebrew. The Jewish participants are prepared to allow speaking in Arabic, especially at the beginning of the encounter, when the Arab group is weak and when language is treated as merely a tool for communicating. Once the Arab group becomes stronger and decides to speak Arabic as part of the expression of its identity, the "liberal" declarations by the Jews turn out to have no substance. Speaking in Arabic is perceived as a change in the status quo and as a loss of control by the Jews in the room, as participants note at the end of the meeting:

> JEWISH GIRL: I got aggravated when they talked Arabic because suddenly I felt I wasn't in control.
>
> JEWISH BOY: When they spoke Arabic, I felt, like, small.

The Jews show marked impatience toward Arabic and demand that every single word spoken in the room be translated, even when uttered by Arabs talking among themselves. The demand is usually directed to the Arab facilitators, and in this way the Jewish group neutralizes them in their principal role, that of facilitator. Sometimes they go so far as to call into question the facilitators' authority and reliability, suspecting that the facilitators are distorting what they translate. Even Arabic spoken during the coffee breaks is sometimes perceived as not legitimate. The Arab participants who insist on speaking Arabic are perceived as extremist and threatening. The Jews experience them as if they are trying to sabotage the encounter and the communication between the two groups. Rosi Braidotti best describes the process the Jews undergo when he writes that "the feeling of crisis of our time is the crisis of the dominant group, those who had secure hegemony and now find it challenged. For those who for a long time were quiet, this period is one of challenge and of hope" (quoted in Sampson 1993).

Contrary to logic, carrying on a dialogue in two languages is not an advantage for the Arabs in the meeting; instead, it turns into a disadvantage. On the one hand, when the Arab participants give up their right to talk in their own language and speak instead in the language of the Jews "for the sake of the success of the meeting," they express themselves less well. Some in the group remain silent because they cannot speak Hebrew well, and sometimes the Jewish group accuses them of being passive. On the other hand, when the Arabs decide to talk in their own language, the better to express themselves and their identity, they are accused of extremism.

Paradoxically, the two languages have more or less equal standing only when the Arab participants do not know how to speak Hebrew. This happens in encounters between Jews and Palestinians from the Palestinian Autonomous Area. In these meetings, most of the Palestinians do not speak Hebrew and hence a situation is created that is different from that described thus far. The talking is done in both languages, Arabic and

Hebrew, or else in English. In one such meeting held at the SFP, Palestinian attorneys from the Palestinian Autonomous Area met with Jewish Israeli attorneys. The discussion took place in English. Two of the Palestinians did not know English well and asked that the talking be in Arabic and Hebrew. The members of the group were responsive to their request, but the Jewish group clearly had difficulty giving up talking in English. After repeated requests by the facilitators and the participants, the Jews relinquished English, except for one participant who continued to speak English throughout the meeting, despite being the least fluent of anyone there. That same participant also expressed the most nationalistic position of all the Jewish participants. Our assumption is that the Jewish group had trouble accepting the egalitarian situation manifested through the use of both languages in the room. That single Jewish participant insisted on speaking English because English was perceived as the language of the West and hence "the language of progress"—in other words, I can't accept you as equals, even at the cost of having to mumble my way through in English.

In conclusion, we have shown that language is in fact not merely a tool for communication; it is first and foremost a symbol of identity and culture. A three-year-old Arab girl from NS/WAS expressed this well when she was playing with her Jewish friend and in a moment of closeness said, "Too bad you're not in my language." Language, in the Jewish-Arab encounter, represents a space for power struggles between the two groups. Given that the conflict between them in real life has not yet been resolved, the dialogue between the two groups over language and over the actual use of this or that language in a specific instance is still at its height. In our innocence, we at SFP have tried over the years to overcome the difficulty surrounding this subject of language with a variety of technical approaches, some very unusual—but in vain. As the Arab saying goes: "We cannot straighten out a man's shadow when the man himself is bent."

8

COFACILITATION

A SYMMETRICAL DIALOGUE
IN AN ASYMMETRICAL REALITY

MICHAL ZAK AND RABAH HALABI

Facilitating groups with a partner is a complicated craft requiring much skill and practice. How much more so, then, when facilitating an encounter between two national groups in conflict. Elsewhere in the world it is customary to run such meetings with a third-party facilitator who serves as a kind of mediator and arbitrator, the assumption being that this type of facilitating is more objective because it is external and hence immune to the pressure of special interests. Our contention is that there is no such thing as objectivity when intervening in any type of group. Moreover we think that objectivity is not crucial in leading Jewish-Arab encounters, which strive to raise awareness rather than to reach agreements or provide solutions to problems. In fact, the facilitators' involvement in, knowledge of, and insight concerning the conflict can only help; these characteristics support rather than impede progress toward the goals of the encounter.

Given these considerations, we at the School for Peace have chosen to facilitate these encounters ourselves; and, moreover, we have chosen the option of cofacilitation: an Arab and a Jewish facilitator working together in every situation that requires the involvement of a facilitator and in every group, large or small. We think that Arab-Jewish cofacilitation is important and possibly even indispensable for several reasons, principally:

141

Each side is limited in its ability to understand the other side; hence a single facilitator for the encounter would leave blind areas in understanding what goes on in the group.

Both an Arab and a Jewish facilitator are needed in order to allow work to be done by each group in a uninational framework.

Our approach allows for a process of transference by all the participants with the facilitators, through whom they can learn about and come to understand their own behavior.

By creating technical equality, we allow the participants the space they need to explore in depth the relations between them.

The facilitators who work at the School for Peace go through an intensive, specially designed training course as well as a continuing course of in-service training and supervision and guidance while they are working. This is to enable ongoing monitoring and critiques of their work and to provide them with a framework for dealing with their reservations and with the dilemmas they find themselves confronting with the groups they facilitate.

We think that the best way to give you, the reader, a vivid sense of the facilitation model with which we work is to present a dialogue between the two of us dealing with what we do and how. We hope this will give you a sense of sharing in the experiences and the dilemmas we face as partners in facilitation. We want to emphasize that the dialogue is based on our own past and continuing work in facilitation, on experiences related to us by facilitators we supervise, and on the insights of colleagues with whom we work.

MICHAL: In the beginning of this chapter, we noted that facilitating with a partner expresses a technical equality, the appearance of equality. I think this demands fuller and deeper explanation. Is it your opinion that the equality we achieve by having two facilitators working together is no more than symbolic?

RABAH: The equality, as we said, is technical. Although it is not merely symbolic, neither does it transform the encounter into one that is essentially equal. That both sides are represented in the facilitation and have an equal number of participants does not transform the encounter into one of equality because reality penetrates into the meeting and dictates the interaction between the participants and the nature of their encounter.

M: I think this shows vividly how much the reality both outside the group and within the group is not a reality of equality. We have supposedly built a model that is egalitarian: two facilitators sit with the group and there are an equal number of participants in the meeting from both the national groups. This structure neutralizes the possibility that someone will say, "Well, the dialogue is not equal because there is only one facilitator here," because there is a tendency on the part of participants to project the lack of equality onto the framework. But our need for this model also demonstrates that despite all the processes we have undergone as a staff and despite all the insights we have and all that we agree on politically, there is still room for two facilitators because our experiences are so different.

R: Well, that seems self-evident and won't change, even if we go through another hundred years together. We will still be who we are—an Arab will still be an Arab and a Jew will remain a Jew, even with all the insights we have. Our affiliations are not going to change with time or with awareness, but our identity can expand and deepen following the encounter, within the bonds of affiliation.

M: I didn't think it was going to change, but I wanted to make this point clearly because some people think that we are supposed to be beyond the conflict and that we are a kind of third party in this whole thing. I want to emphasize that we are in no way beyond it, not from the standpoint of our identities and not from the standpoint of the manner in which we analyze and experience what goes on in the group.

R: It seems to me that the question of our not being a third party is important, and we should stop and deal with that. I think that in general we are expected to be objective, as if the Jewish facilitator could be both a Jew and an Arab, and the Arab could also be a Jew. Participants, in fact, seem to have two expectations of us: that each facilitator will take the side of his own, and they will both be objective.

I don't think it is possible to be objective; hence we don't have to pretend to be objective. What we do have to be is fair. In other words, the Arab facilitator comes with perceptions and feelings and knowledge and insights as an Arab, and the same for the Jewish facilitator, but they are supposed to be fair in that they do not use the group for their own needs and don't use their authority to put this group in a corner or help that group. There is a difference between objectivity and fairness. The Arab facilitator should not help the Arab group; the Jewish facilitator should not help his group. They should help both groups arrive at insights about what is happening to them in the encounter.

M: I don't think the impossibility of arriving at objectivity is the basis on which we ought not profess objectivity. I think that even if it were possible to be objective, objectivity would weaken our contribution to the group. We are working on the fault line between our professional roles as facilitators and our social and political responsibility as facilitators. In my opinion, it is not necessary that we be objective, but it is important that this be clear to the participants so that we don't use our power in a manipulative way.

R: Concerning the other expectation—that each of us should be on his own side—maybe something needs to be said about this as well. It seems to me that this expectation is what drives us. I don't know how it is for you, but this was obvious in my experience, at least in the beginning. The perception common among the general public regarding encounters between Jews and Arabs was that the goal was to bring people together by blurring identities and weakening the bonds of national affiliation. Hence Arab facilitators who work in these meetings (even if they run meetings with an altogether different orientation) are in a defensive posture and are continually obliged to prove their loyalty to their Arabness in various ways. I remember myself helping the Arab group during the breaks and even during the facilitating in order to prove my Arabness and be accepted by the Arab group.

I felt this need less and less as time went on, but it still exists, even today, although in different circumstances—for example, when it is necessary to confront the Arab group. I notice in such situations that, consciously or unconsciously, I make allowances, perhaps I am coming from that same place of the need to be nice to the Arab group in order to be accepted by it.

M: For me, the process was different. Looking back to when I first began facilitating, it was important to me, as you described, to be accepted by the Arab group, not for the reason you mentioned, obviously; rather I needed them to accept me as a Jew who was supportive enough, a leftist and all that that implies. I remember the first time I facilitated, at the end of the workshop I got positive feedback from an Arab girl; I don't even remember if I got such positive feedback from Jewish participants, but I remember how happy this made me and how important it was to me that the Arabs told me that I was okay.

The process I went through was to break free of the experience of wanting approval from the Arabs and to begin to worry about what you described, about my place in the Jewish group, for two reasons. First, I see that I don't have to exert myself with the Arab group; I am already marked as "a good Jew" in their eyes. The harder work is with the Jewish group because often, precisely because I am close to and have ties to the Jews, I feel angry with and disappointed in them. It took me a long time—and the process is still going on—to support them, to understand them, to not attack them, to challenge them as someone who is part of them and a lot like them and not as someone who is on a higher plane than they are.

R: You say that the Arab group accepts you because you do this work and be-cause of your being a leftist. I would ask whether the Arab group accepts Jewish facilitators because they are in a position of authority, and it doesn't matter how they facilitate or what their political positions are. The Jewish group also accepts the authority of the Jewish facilitator despite the fact that sometimes the Jews are more critical of the facilitators.

M: How we are perceived as authoritative, that is a crucial subject. The ques-tion must be asked whether the pair of facilitators represents one unit be-cause what you are saying is that this isn't so. I have no basis of comparison for knowing whether they accept me only because I am an authority figure, but it seems to me that this certainly plays a role.

R: My experience is that, as an Arab facilitator, I have to work three times as hard to receive the same recognition as the Jewish man or woman who fa-cilitates with me. Not only that, but I have to go on working hard all the time in order to prove myself over and over again; I can't rest on my laurels in this respect. Generally the group perceives the Jewish facilitator as an authority, even if that person is inexperienced. In contrast, the Arab facilitator is al-ways being tested even if he or she is the more senior facilitator.

I remember once that an intern facilitator, a Jew who was observing me at work, behaved as if he were in charge of the group, even took over the technical things like the collection of the pencils and markers. Usually the group directs technical questions to the Jewish facilitator; their doing so gives me the feeling that they turn to him or her as the authority, and this creates a problematic feeling for me.

Once I was facilitating with a woman who left the group a quarter of an hour before the end, and the group began laughing and goofing around as if there were no facilitators in the room, despite the fact that I was still there. Once we tried to clarify to what extent the group was accepting of the facilitation, and it became clear that the Jewish group didn't perceive me, the Arab facilitator, all that much as the facilitator of the whole group, whereas the Arab group did perceive the Jewish facilitator as the facilitator of the whole group. So, all the participants accepted the Jewish facilitator as a pro-fessional authority, and at least half the group was testing my authority. When this happens, it has no connection to how I facilitate or what level of professionalism I have. It is clear to me that some of this feeling is subjective, but it is built on truth at its foundation.

Sometimes during clarifications with Jewish partners in facilitation, it turns out that they feel the opposite—in other words, that I am the dom-inant one and they are on the sidelines. Despite the fact that today I some-times feel that way myself, still my authority is tested at every moment, something that is not demanded of the Jewish facilitator.

M: That's rather surprising because other factors ought to have come into the relationship between the facilitators and between them and the group, such as seniority, professionalism, and gender; but what you describe, especially the part about the intern, says that national identities are more primary.

I am familiar with this problem, but the opposite has happened with me. I am thinking all the time about whether I am taking over, trespassing on the other facilitator. This has often hampered me in working—maybe because, in order to be egalitarian, I was exerting the same effort that you say you have to make in order to retain authority. This was mainly something I experienced at the beginning of my work as a facilitator, and, as you described, for me also this reality has changed but is still in my consciousness.

The Jewish and Arab participants ask me all kinds of questions relating to technical aspects of the meetings. You claim that they turn to me because they perceive me as the primary facilitator. I, however, experience these situations differently. In my view, they come to me with technical issues because I am a woman, and arranging things is less a professional role than that of a mother. I am offended when participants create this kind of division between us.

R: Your description is interesting, but in a certain sense it is also problematical. First, in order to create a situation of equality between the two facilitators I don't think that a facilitator has to hold back. That is not a healthy situation and may even be patronizing. Second, I don't experience in our partnership that there is a need for some kind of holding back on your part in order to create an egalitarian situation. Sometimes, in fact, there is an opposite problem when our presence as Arab facilitators is conspicuous. In the last meeting we did with the university students, for example, there was a sense that you as Jewish facilitators felt threatened, and you described us as controlling. It is interesting to ask, where are you getting the feeling that you have to make yourselves smaller? Gender is an interesting issue that hasn't been given enough attention until now, but for whatever reason this has been secondary in my experience as opposed to the national divide.

M: Undoubtedly we have to go deeper into the question of gender relations between us as facilitators and in the group. To me it is clear that my identity as a woman affects my role as a facilitator. If I had to rank my identities, then my identity as a Jew in the meeting is more central—but maybe we oughtn't to rank them but rather to examine how our different identities affect us as facilitators.

To return to the subject of equality between us, I have to agree with you that there is something patronizing in this phenomenon of holding back. I think that this is part of a process that sort of moves around. It's not good to hold back. In a good situation the quality of relations between the facilitators would change, would be fluid. I remember, for example, that when I began to facilitate, I didn't rely on and didn't trust the Arab facilitator. I didn't think he knew what I knew or that he could control the situation in the group well, and of course I never thought he could be better than me. You mentioned the opposite phenomenon, in which the Jewish facilitators feel threatened when the Arabs take control. Perhaps this seems like the inverse of the phenomenon of holding back, but we are talking about the other side of the same coin. For Jewish facilitators the feeling of threat comes from our lack of ability to share the hegemony. The situation you described fascinated me because I really did feel bad in that meeting, as did other women facilitating there, not because I thought that the Arab facilitators were leading the group to a bad place, but because I wasn't present as a Jewish facilitator. It was as if my voice had been silenced for the moment.

R: I think we've exhausted the question of authority. With your permission I want to move on to talk about the essence of the facilitation role. Sometimes it seems that the facilitators are going easy on the Arab group because it is the weaker group, and the facilitators are trying to help it express its victimization so as to highlight the justice of its grievances. However, they try to educate the Jewish group and help it to see the light. So it seems as if both facilitators are attacking and confronting the Jewish group and helping the Arab group.

     Still, the situation is not simple because the two groups are not equal and their situation is not symmetrical; nevertheless, it seems that this is an incorrect interpretation of our role as facilitators. I think that our role as facilitators must be to guide each group to understand its place in the relationship between the groups and how it functions in the conflict. Our role is not to help one group against the other but to help each of them to cope with its situation: to enable the Jewish group to cope with the fact of being the dominant group, the one in control, with everything that flows from that, and to enable the Arab group to cope with the fact of its being the weaker group, the one controlled, with all that that entails.

M: Initially you said that it's not necessary to strengthen the legitimacy of the Arabs or help them bring out the truth. I think that, in many groups, the experience of the Arabs has been that bringing justice or truth before the Jewish group is not a matter of course—it doesn't happen on the outside.

     We sit today, the day after Land Day, and all I heard yesterday on the radio was that the police spoke with Arab notables to ensure that there would not be disturbances, and then they interviewed Azmi Bishara [a Knesset member and one of the most prominent leaders of the Palestinians in Israel] and asked him what would happen. He scarcely spoke about the issue of land; he said only that "we are sure that the day will pass without incident." He was busy appeasing the Jews and responding to the agenda of the Jews. So, for the Arab group, I think that just expressing these things, saying them even if this annoys and angers the Jews—that's a lot. It seems to me that sometimes they can't talk without the presence of the Arab facilitator, who helps them and shows them that he or she also challenges the Jewish group, even if that makes the Jewish group angry—in short, providing a model.

R: Certainly the presence of a strong Arab facilitator provides a model for the Arab group, and from that standpoint it is important that the Arab facilitator has a presence in the group, but it doesn't seem to me that the Arab facilitator has to help them say things. There are two risks there. First, when Arab facilitators help the Arab group express themselves, they generally do it by speaking in their stead, and then they actually silence the Arab group. Second, such help comes from egotistical considerations and not from what is good for the group because weak Arab groups that aren't able to express themselves project onto the Arab facilitators and they connect with the facilitators' own weaknesses in the situation and get upset. Then the facilitators try to resolve their distress through the Arab group and save them from facing up to the situation. The Arab facilitators' role in these instances is to work things out so that the Arab group expresses its difficulty, to understand what brings the group to speak or to be silent, for awareness is a necessary precondition for change.

M: You are leading up to the thought that one has to enable each group to express its difficulties or to be aware of its behavior. Maybe it's not a coincidence that for me it is important that the Arab group make its voice heard— that is, that it tell its stories of oppression in an aggressive way. Maybe indirectly it's easier for me to hear the claims of oppression when the Arab group is strong and demanding; when the Arab group mainly describes its weakness—or, as one of the participants said, when it describes how much its head is bowed—I find this intolerable to hear because, in the bright spotlight that is created, I am the oppressor.

In addition, there is also a big gap in knowledge between the two groups. We see this, and I think that this is the point at which we Jews begin to be spared, and have spared ourselves, recognition of the reality and of the stories and the facts. This does not allow for really coping with the situation because it's easy for the Jewish group to say, "Sure you deserve equal rights, and sure we are for equality." We see that the liberal statements are made rather quickly and sincerely because they have never been put to a real test. Never have the Jews heard the demands of, never have they confronted the anger of, the other group. Possibly it's unfair to demand that this should happen in the meeting, and maybe I am using the Arab group to put the Jewish group through a process. It's hard for me to let go of this because in a meeting with a strong group there is a lot of power.

R: It seems to me here that you are driven by a personal need of yours for the Arab group to be a successful mirror for the Jewish group so that the Jews will face up to the gaps between what they say and how they behave. You want a strong Arab group so that you can confront the Jews with the reality of their being rulers and oppressors. As you said, it's not comfortable for you to be part of the oppressor group, and you want the Arab group to do your work for you. The Arab group as an oppressed group has enough to do by itself, for itself. It has to deal with its own weakness; it isn't obliged to provide the goods—not for the Jewish group and not for the Jewish facilitator. Both groups have to cope, each with its situation, and with what comes out of their interaction with one another.

M: Yes, I agree with this goal. I also have personal interests, and it is important to be aware of them and to separate them from the group process. You say that they must cope with what comes out in the meeting. But it is important to remember that generally in practice what comes out in the meeting is that the Arab group holds up a mirror, so to speak, to the Jewish group, making visible the gap between our declarations and our feelings and even our behavior. We have to be cautious about using our power as facilitators to try to make the group behave in a certain way.

R: That's true—that the Arab group represents a mirror that reflects reality as it is and not as we wish it were. Sometimes I feel that Jewish facilitators want to teach the Jews that they are not liberal and also want to tell them where they ought to get to. Hence they expect a mirror of a certain kind that will help them with that process. Sometimes also it's not comfortable for them when the group has Jewish participants who really are liberal. Maybe because they make it hard for you to build your liberal self-image at the expense of the Jewish participants.

In just that way I, as an Arab facilitator, am uncomfortable with Arab participants who are uncritical and grovel before the Jewish group, and I am sometimes tempted to show them the light. In both these cases, this is our personal need, and it's not certain that this helps the participants.

M: You're right, this is a well-known trap. There's a desire to show them the light. The other thing seems to me to be even more dangerous—that is, to remain above them. This comes from the difficulty in accepting the fact that this is my people and I am part of the ruling group, with all that that implies. We hear about this from the Jewish groups mainly in the uninational meeting, that they feel they are disappointing the Jewish facilitator, that they are not okay. Sometimes no possibility is created for them to examine their positions, and from where they are the participants feel they are being judged. We have to be careful to distinguish between our personal needs and those of the group.

There was something else you said, that in the end we have a problem with people in the group who are really liberal. I think that sometimes we give them a hard time. The way we work emphasizes the group interactions and blurs the role of people who have unusual positions in the group, and to be really liberal is definitely an unusual position. In addition, the Jewish facilitator is frequently uncomfortable with a participant who is too liberal. I have found myself several times tending not to believe an opinion like that, so I cast doubt on what they say. For example, a Jewish woman related that she was riding in a car with members of the Arab group. She was the only Jewish woman, and they were speaking Arabic. She reported that this didn't bother her at all—to hear Arabic for the entire trip and not understand one word. It was hard for me to believe her because it bothers me to be in that kind of situation.

You have to facilitate with the participants from their discomfort points, so it is important to make the effort and identify what each one or the group wants to learn and to clarify. Generally we're dealing with obscure points that the participants don't fully grasp themselves or are not in a hurry to expose in the meeting. The obscure point of the Jewish facilitator that you revealed just now is part of this reality. Sometimes what moves us is the desire to be seen as more liberal than the participants.

R: This brings me right back to the role of facilitation because according to this description a strong Arab group is needed in order to enable the Jews to deal with their lack of liberalism, which turns the Arab group into an instrument. It would seem that the Arab facilitators think they are helping the Arab groups, but together with the Jewish facilitators they are in fact helping the Jewish group, although it looks as if they are attacking that group.

M: We have already noticed that the number of our interventions with the Jewish group is greater; it turns out that we invest more in the Jewish group. This maintains the situation as it is on the outside and is therefore problematical. However, there is a contradiction with political aspects that we haven't fully clarified because for many years and to a great extent justifiably we thought that the main responsibility was with the Jews. In recent years, maybe mainly since the intifada, we see that there is another party to this process and that if someone is going to make the change, it is usually the oppressed group. It's not reasonable that the ruling group would try to change the status quo. This has begun to be reflected in the way we work, and we are much more confrontational with the Arab group than in the past.

R: It seems to me that our being so preoccupied with the Jewish group is not coincidental because the Jewish group is in the stronger position; it has the power, and that gets us going as facilitators in the encounter. If the Jewish group turns to the Jewish facilitator and ignores me, this gives me the feeling that I am being obliterated as an authority. And it doesn't matter if I am a super-professional facilitator who is totally in control and in charge of all the dialogue; the Jewish group still has power that can affect me, in spite of my being aware of that.

This is a power that the Jewish group has more of than does the Arab group. In this matter, for instance, there is an interesting dynamic between the group and the facilitators. The Jewish groups try to nullify the authority of the Arab facilitators in order to delegitimize the facilitators' intervening and confronting it. Sometimes a Jewish group tries to delegitimize both facilitators with a comment like, "You are one-sided," or "You're with the Arab group." This is a mechanism for control, and in my opinion we fall into that trap sometimes. Such statements have a lot of influence on and power over the Arab facilitator, in my experience—more in the past than they would today, but there is still an influence.

M: This also has a tremendous influence on the Jewish facilitator because there is a big effort to be accepted by the Jewish group. I am affected by it when they are critical and angry, and I want to please them—mainly because what makes them critical and angry is deep distress from loss of control. What happens when a group verbally attacks a facilitator? I remember that we had a case like this when the group attacked you, and I didn't come to your aid; when we took a break, one of the observers turned to me and asked why I hadn't helped you. There is a question as to what we feel at that moment and what should be done in such a case. At that moment I thought that for me to help you would be patronizing because I thought that you could cope with the attack; however, many times not defending the other facilitator is to cooperate with the attack. It's important to say that almost always if this happens, it's the Jewish group that attacks the Arab facilitator.

R: Truly in that particular situation I didn't feel that I needed help, but there is an issue here. Mostly, when the Jewish group attacks the Arab facilitator, the attack is part of the relationship between Jews and Arabs in the meeting, and we should deal with these elements of the relationship. Sometimes the Jewish facilitator tells the Arab facilitator, "They attacked you for good cause; you weren't being fair." Then there is an argument between the two facilitators, and the same argument that is taking place in the group occurs between the facilitators. To me, it seems that in any case this is going to be an issue. If the Jewish facilitator helps, it will be perceived as patronizing or as the facilitation team defending itself at any price without relation to the Jewish-Arab question. If the Jewish facilitator also attacks the Arab facilitator—that is, does not agree with the Arab facilitator and expresses this disagreement to the group—then the Jewish facilitator also is getting into the argument and at that moment becomes sort of a participant.

M: We see how complicated this is. We are simultaneously perceived as a facilitation team, one unit, and also separately, as individual facilitators. Maybe this also relates to how we introduce ourselves and how we behave in the group. We move back and forth between the two situations.

R: It seems to me that the groups perceive us as two partners in one facilitation unit. Sometimes they aren't even able to distinguish between us except, as you said, when they want to split us up for their own reasons. Here there's an important question of principle: Why in fact do we appear as similar and intervene so similarly? Why don't we give more expression to the dispute between us and to our divergent views of what goes on in the group, especially considering how fundamental placing the conflict at the center is to our work? Why don't we demand of the participants that they talk about what separates them and what distinguishes them? There is a hidden message here.

M: The hidden message is evidently an outcome of the complexity of the task of facilitation. In our approach, the conflict is at the center of the group's existence; it raises the level of anxiety, tension, and aggression. There is a need for a framework, provided by the facilitators, that can contain all these feelings; so it stands to reason that if the two facilitators begin to be adversarial with one another, this will increase the anxieties and threaten the framework.

However, it seems to us that to express our disagreements will immediately be perceived as confrontational; hence we are cautious and don't even contribute our different points of view to the group—viewpoints that could enrich the learning experience of the participants. In my opinion the basic world-view of the Jewish and Arab facilitators on the team is similar, and we do express it; but the prism through which I experience and analyze what happens in the group is different in many cases from that of the Arab facilitator, and this diversity is not given expression openly.

R: What you are describing about the dangers of bringing the dispute between us to the group is correct with respect to short-term groups and groups of young people and also with respect to the beginning of longer encounters. But I don't see anything preventing our bringing up the differences between us when the groups get to a more confident stage and begin opening up the conflicts between them. I think that this concern of ours is exaggerated and that it tends to protect us as facilitators because as long as the facilitation is vague, our authority is maintained and not challenged.

About the similar world-view that we have as facilitators, facilitators have to have a common language, but my feeling is that we get carried away, and the cross-fertilization that can emerge from this partnership turns into castration sometimes. In any case we have to continue to examine and delve into this issue in our work.

M: You spoke metaphorically of a common language, but the most outstanding thing dividing us has to do with language as an instrument of communication, and this we cannot conceal even if we wanted to. That I don't speak Arabic and that you do speak Arabic and Hebrew make real the different worlds and cultures in which we are operating and make real our necessarily different points of view when we are facilitating a meeting.

R: Certainly, language as the most outstanding marker of identity distinguishes us from each other even if sometimes we deny these differences. This subject is especially conspicuous in the meetings between young people, when language is such an issue in the dialogue between the two groups (because the Arab group has difficulty with Hebrew and the Jewish group does not speak Arabic). The Arab facilitators become more active because they have mastery of both languages and serve as a channel of communication between the two groups, as translators. But in these cases the Arab facilitators feel a devaluation of their role as facilitator; they see translation as technical and inferior to facilitation. In any case, my experience is that translating offers a certain element of power to the Arab facilitators. Considering that the Jewish facilitators don't know Arabic at all, they are out of the dialogue during those moments when the Arab group is speaking Arabic.

M: As opposed to the Arab group, which doesn't perceive a knowledge of Arabic as a resource, the facilitators believe — or at least profess to believe — that a knowledge of both languages is an asset. This is definitely an advantage, but despite that we hear often that the Arab facilitators feel neutralized because they translate. And we don't hear from facilitators what you added, that maybe the translating bestows a certain power. We are always dealing with the fact that it is hard to translate, and evidently the difficulty colors and overshadows the advantage you mentioned.

   In my view, the Arab facilitator is definitely more dominant, and this fact creates a big problem: on the one hand, I want to say something so as to be also present; and, on the other hand, I see that often the presence of the Arab is not by virtue of the professional role as facilitator but rather the role as translator. I don't want the Jewish facilitator to intervene in the group as a facilitator while the Arab facilitator intervenes as a translator, which is perceived as a merely technical role.

   This division within the team between facilitation and translation is hierarchical: the translation is perceived as inferior. But, most of all, when Arabic is spoken, it reinforces the gap between what I do and what I say. The fact that I can't translate, that in many cases I can't even understand exactly what is being said in Arabic, puts me in a difficult situation alongside the Arab facilitator. Hence I always prefer that the groups speak Hebrew so as not to expose my weakness, although from an ideological standpoint I want the dialogue to take place in Hebrew and in Arabic.

R: What you said explains the reason for translation being turned into something technical and thus an inappropriate necessity; it creates a relationship between us, as facilitators, in which the Arab facilitator is made marginal and the Jewish facilitator sits there and analyzes what is going on in the group. I think that this does something to us also as Arab facilitators. We, too, have internalized this interpretation and have allowed it to become our reality. I think that usually the Arab facilitators can both translate and also be involved in the process. The two are not mutually exclusive — on the contrary, when they translate they can go on and also give their interpretation. Maybe the agreed-on reality we have created, in which the translation is a technical activity and inferior, is a joint effort by the two sides, the Jewish facilitator and the Arab facilitator, to neutralize the option of speaking in Arabic or to reduce it to a minimum.

M: We have created a dichotomy between the intervention of facilitation and the intervention of translation. This dichotomy is artificial because if our role is primarily to enable the dialogue between the two groups, then translating is the most important thing in that situation. We have created this hierarchy.

R: The matter of language relates to the dynamic that exists between the facilitators and the group, mainly between the Arab facilitator and the group. If the Arab facilitators have patience and translate with forbearance, this radiates to the Arab group. This is a statement to the Arab group that the Arab facilitators respect the Arabic language and accept the group. On the other side, the Jewish groups address all their questions to and speak mainly to the Arab facilitators as the translators, and the facilitators become central personalities; the Jews need them and test them. The Jewish groups try to find out to what degree the Arab facilitators are trustworthy as translators.

In my first year as a facilitator, I sometimes tended to change small details of what had been said. Sometimes I tried to strengthen and sometimes to moderate what had been expressed. Once a Jewish participant in the group knew Arabic and caught me when I translated in a way that wasn't exact. To this day I recall that situation as a hard experience.

In any case the group is preoccupied with the facilitators, with what we think and with what we expect of the participants. That's true of both groups and more of the Jewish group. I experience this mainly from the Jewish young people, but also adults think that we have something in our heads and that we want to steer them in a specific direction. They don't buy so easily that we are trying to help them to cope with their own attitudes.

M: I think this happens because we don't confide in them very much. It could be that if we knew how to translate what we ourselves are doing, expressing

it as a well-ordered world-view, this might make it easier for them and reduce their suspicions. Only recently have we begun to make our view known
to the group. I think that more dialogue is beginning to happen between the
facilitators and the groups, but this still doesn't neutralize what you say, that
they want too much to know exactly what we expect of them and what the
right answers are. This is only human, to want from us the recognition that
they are okay.

R: I think you're right. We do have to declare our world-view. Lately, at least in
working with adults and in the long-term courses, we are doing this, but it is
only fair and proper to also tell our world-view to the young people. That
doesn't mean we are going to educate them in a certain direction, but we
have our basic world-view, and our interventions flow from that.

      Sometimes we are asked who gave us the right anyway to come and
intervene, and some go further and claim that we have no right to intervene
in any direction. I tend to agree with Paolo Freire, who says that we have not
only a right but also a moral obligation to intervene and reveal the reality
for the people who are involved in building and shaping this reality, so that
they will have the option to make decisions based on knowledge and awareness. Sometimes I won't like their decisions, but they are still legitimate. Our
intervention is intended to bring the participants to an awareness regarding
reality as it is, or as close as possible, so that on the basis of knowledge and
awareness they can decide on the direction they want to go.

M: From one meeting to the next, when we talk about this with, for instance, the
students in our course, I am amazed at how much the encounter we facilitated has opened up for them additional options about how to look at things.
I don't know what they'll choose afterward, but I see that they had a blind
spot that was revealed to them, and I think that this is our obligation as
socially and politically aware educators. I think that the participants don't
know about the aspect we are revealing to them. In my view this is a duty
and a major privilege, but it also demands a lot of courage. I see how much
I, having worked so many years already in facilitation, from year to year
dare more—for example, to say to Jews that they have to cope with their
racism. At one time I didn't dare use a word like *racism*. It demands a lot of
courage to intervene in a group in the way that we do.

R: I have noticed that when the group reacts strongly, we react by drawing back,
by retreating a bit. My feeling is that the idea that we have a right to intervene doesn't sit well with us, and maybe some of the facilitators have doubts.
This is especially likely to be the case with the Jewish facilitators when they
work with Jewish groups. There's a contention that this is hard work and
sometimes even impossible.

M: We sometimes facilitate in uninational groups that are not meant to meet with the group of the other nationality. Facilitating with Jews by themselves is hard because, if we confront them with their racism, their anger is directed at us. The situation is slightly different when you're talking about the nature of the connection of facilitators with the group of their own nationality in the uninational forum that takes place during the course of an Arab-Jewish encounter workshop. The facilitation is easier; there is a homey feeling, and the way we facilitate is softer. I find it comfortable to be alone without the other facilitator, just as it is comfortable for the participants to be without the other group. One needn't work so hard or be so considerate as when you cofacilitate.

R: That's true, for me also there is a feeling like that. In the uninational forum the work feels good and is comfortable—although it's hard too. The work is good when the facilitator knows what he or she is getting into. One of the dimensions that is added in the meeting of the Arabs is that they speak Arabic, and this gives a homey feeling both literally and figuratively. Sometimes when working alone without the other group, it's as if there are no stimuli, and there's nothing to talk about. Then the facilitator also has to be a stimulus to get the talking going, and that is not at all easy.

M: The same with us. I have the feeling that I, as the facilitator, am expected to supply the stimulus that the Arab group supplies in the joint meeting. This puts me in a situation that is not simple: as if I am the counterforce for the Jewish group. You remember that I said that the link between the Jewish facilitator and the Jewish group isn't easy? In the uninational forum, there is a double test. The participants need support because their distress is severe, but there's also a desire to challenge them, and one must be careful not to fall into the trap of "us versus them."

   Have you noticed how usually, after returning from the separate forum to the combined group, the Jewish facilitators are determined to find out during the break what happened in the uninational Arab forum, but the Arab facilitators are not so eager to say what happened? And the Jewish facilitators want to relate in detail what happened in their meeting.

   This is a pattern that repeats itself, so evidently it is not coincidental. I think something in the uninational meeting strengthens the Arab group and gives it a feeling of independence that the group doesn't want to lose in such a hurry. As for the Jewish facilitators who have to know exactly what happened with the Arabs or else they can't be in control of the situation— this also is typical of our way of being. It took me a long time not to ask what happened in your meeting, and then also not to want to know, to go along with a lack of knowledge of what went on there, not because it's not important to me but in order to allow myself not to know everything all the time about the other group.

R: What you are describing is very much typical of me. I don't know exactly why, but that's how it is. I am absolutely not interested in what happens in the uninational meeting of the Jews, and it's also hard for me to talk about what happened in the uninational meeting of the Arabs when I am asked. It's really hard for me, and there are tensions around this all the time.

By the way, the Arab group in its uninational meeting mostly does not talk about the Jewish group; it is busy with itself and its behavior and is less preoccupied with what is going on with the Jewish group. I, too, am uninterested in what happens in the Jewish group, and this hampers me when I am asked what happened with us in the uninational Arab meeting. I accept that this is a need to be in control all the time from the Jewish side, and evidently on my side there is a need to let go of this control. And when we are finally alone, then it's a private matter, and we don't want to share and give out information. Maybe this gives me a little power and separation and autonomy. Apparently this is the situation because the feeling rests on something completely personal—but nothing in our work can be separated from either the personal or the group.

The foregoing dialogue is not the first such exchange we have pursued together, but this is the first time we have shared our thoughts and feelings with others. There was power in the writing: In being committed to paper, problems and dilemmas that we and other facilitators have confronted were given a voice and a new measure of legitimacy. In the wake of the dialogue shared here, we now devote more attention to the connection between gender and nationality. We are also more aware of what the Arab groups experience, and we've progressed in our understanding of how to enable them to learn from the encounter. The question of authority, which we discussed at length in this dialogue, continues to preoccupy the staff because the power relationships between Arabs and Jews are fundamental to the conflict between us.

Some of the questions we have raised here remain open. Evidently, we should be creating opportunities for facilitators to express different, even conflicting, voices in the group so as to enable participants to learn from the different perspectives. This may be the only way to sustain the facilitation model we have created and ensure its relevance in times of violent conflict.

A chapter like this one is difficult to close. The dialogue we began here became the start of a continuing process—in fact, it's an open-ended learning curve because, to stay in touch with and try to comprehend reality in all its complexity, we have to remain flexible and attentive. We have to make the effort to go on developing along with the reality around us. It's not a simple task because we are part of that reality and yet must cultivate the ability to interpret it and even address it critically.

The intriguing dialogue we have shared here has been eye opening for us both, drawing our attention to points of which we were previously unaware. We hope that the reader has derived at least as much benefit from this process as we have.

9

"HOME GROUP"

The Uninational Framework

NAVA SONNENSCHEIN
and AHMAD HIJAZI

What we at the School for Peace have termed the uninational framework is an integral part of the meetings we run. In the uninational format, the binational group separates into two national (sub)groups, the Jewish group with the Jewish facilitator and the Arab group with the Arab facilitator. The use of this framework follows from our point of departure—the encounter between two national groups, each with its own identities, its own needs, and its own unique work to do in the encounter—as well as from our view of the meeting as a microcosm of reality. The larger reality subdivides into two separate if overlapping realms, and life is certainly not lived jointly all the time. Hence a consideration of what takes place in the respective uninational frameworks helps us to understand this dual reality in its totality.

The uninational gathering is more relaxed than the joint meeting: one sits together with members of one's own nationality, and one's own native language is spoken (an important factor, particularly for the Arab group). The relatively relaxed atmosphere gives us a chance to look at what is happening to the workshop participants and to analyze and try to understand these processes critically. This also happens in the binational meeting, but to a lesser degree. The binational sessions are typically stormy, a cauldron of so many powerful forces that the groups are deeply occupied with the dynamic evolving between them, and there is simply less opportunity than in the uninational meeting to analyze these processes in a more leisurely way. Furthermore, certain subjects and concerns come up only in the uninational environment because the two groups avoid dealing with them in one another's presence. This is especially true when the binational process becomes competitive or stressful because participants worry that internal divisions will weaken their own national group and strengthen the other. Participants may also be cautious or embarrassed about bringing up these subjects in the joint environment.

Historically, when the School for Peace first began working, the uninational framework did not exist. Only later did we come to the conclusion that it ought to be added, in light of research we conducted about the encounter process. The findings indicated that what takes place is experienced differently by the Jewish and Arab participants and that the encounter evokes for each national group unique dilemmas and questions that demand a separate framework for discussion. Initially, the facilitators often found it difficult to cope with this new framework. What happens in the encounter between the two sides, they felt, is the main thing. They related to the uninational forum as an unnecessary addition or, in the best case, as a kind of preparation for the joint meeting. Over time, after much hard work by staff and participants, the uninational framework achieved its own status. Today we think of it as an integral and autonomous part of the meeting by means of which we can illuminate additional aspects of the Jewish-Arab conflict.

The facilitation in the uninational forum is a little different than in the binational meeting. When the two sides gather separately, the stimulus provided by the other group is absent. This task then falls to the facilitator, in addition to which she or he must function without a partner. Indeed, a number of difficulties confront the facilitator in this forum. The main challenge is to forge a connection with the members of the group: not to be alienated from them, not to patronize them, and not to exploit the fact of being alone with them to "indoctrinate" them as preparation for "doing battle" with the other group. The main task is to help the participants understand themselves as belonging to either the majority or the minority group. To do this, they must feel free to be spontaneous in bringing up what they feel, think, and believe. Often things come up with which the facilitators have difficulty dealing or empathizing—usually for reasons of which they are unaware, mainly because these feelings represent aspects of themselves that they don't like. For the Jews, these involve oppressive, controlling, superior, or racist elements; for the Arabs, they involve submission and the internalization of their oppression. The danger is that facilitators in such situations will confront the participants or will try to prove to them how much better they cope with all this than the participants do—and thereby block their learning. Because the processes taking place in the uninational framework are important for the group and because the role of these groups in this kind of work is not self-evident and may even be thought controversial, we devote a separate chapter to discussing it.

The chapter is the work of coauthors, a Jew and an Arab (and indeed could hardly have been written in any other way); each facilitator has written the section about his or her group. In other words, the Arab facilitator wrote about working with the Arab group, and the Jewish facilitator wrote about working with the Jewish group. In drafting this analysis, we have relied on written records from five long-running encounter groups. In all these groups, the uninational sessions alternated with the encounter sessions in a ratio of about three encounter sessions to one uninational forum. The groups used as sources were (1) two year-long university courses, one at Tel-Aviv University in 1996–97 and the other at the Hebrew University in 1997–98, and (2) three group facilitators' courses from 1996, 1997, and 1998. Names of individuals appearing here are fictitious. The chapter ends with a comparative look at what goes on in the respective groups plus some general comments on the uninational framework and the phenomena that characterize it.

THE ARAB UNINATIONAL MEETING

When we come to analyze the uninational process, which is an integral part of the workshop, we cannot totally ignore what happens in the meeting between the two sides because these two processes are, after all, parallel and complementary; hence some reference is also made to the joint encounter in the pages that follow.

Here I describe the general characteristics of the Arab uninational forum and illustrate how these are expressed in the uninational meetings from the standpoint both of what participants say and of their behavior. I sketch the general outlines of the process that the Arab group undergoes, as a group, and provide examples from the written record.

In the first uninational meeting, the Arab group usually expresses astonishment at the fact of the separation, at the unexpected situation:

"What is the goal of separating the two groups? I don't understand who asked for this. Or does the program require it?" "I meet [other] Arabs and talk to them all the time; here it seems like a waste of time." This may be a response to the fact that the Arab group has expended a lot of energy to prepare itself for the encounter and the dialogue with the other side, and the separation comes as a surprise. But the response evidently also expresses something deeper, something arising from the Arab group's dependence, as a minority, on the majority. Hence the pressing need of the Arabs to talk with the Jews and persuade them of the rightness of the Arab side: "We can talk here among ourselves until the sun rises tomorrow, but that won't change anything; we came to meet the Jewish group and relate our arguments and see if they agree or not."

Beyond the matter of dependence, there is a tendency manifest here toward lowered self-worth: a feeling that only the Jewish group has the power to change the situation and that what remains for the Arab group to do is to talk with the Jews, to influence them, to persuade them, so that they will take some action. The Arab group may even be scared by the option of taking responsibility, cut off from the Jews. By the nature of things, the attitudes and behavior of the Jewish group occupy a large share of the Arab group's attention at this stage: "My impression is that the people we are meeting with are all leftists and in favor of giving rights to Arabs; this will not be a difficult meeting because this is the Israeli left, who think as we do." "It seems to me that this meeting ought to be between left-wing Jews and right-wing Jews; they could persuade them better than we can that we deserve rights because they are from the same people, and anyway they are the ones who decide what happens, not us."

At the second stage, which comes at the second or third meeting, the Arab group begins focusing increasingly on itself, the roles it fulfills in the encounter, and the processes it is undergoing. At this point in the workshop, the conflict between the Arabs and the Jews is beginning to emerge in the joint forum, where the two groups engage in a struggle over who will determine the agenda and who will "win" the arguments that develop between them. The Arab group tries to get itself organized for the struggle that is obviously imminent and to put its house in order in preparation for the coming "campaign." The facilitator serves as a source to which the participants turn for reality checks: "Let's hear what the facilitator's general evaluation is of what's going on, how we [the Arab group] are behaving in the meeting."

Members of the group also appraise one another, checking to see where everyone stands. They attempt to fortify one another and encourage those who have been keeping quiet to be more involved in the discussion so as to strengthen the group: "The Jews, they all talk, but with us it's only two people talking all the time. That's not enough. Everyone has to join in the discussion, even if we repeat things someone else has already said."

At this stage, we hear talk of dissatisfaction with the group's functioning and an aspiration to do better, and people's feelings of frustration are put on the table so they can be addressed, analyzed, and dealt with: "I feel that the group can be more lively and do better. I know that there is a goal, but the goal is unclear, and I feel that we are treading water here. . . . The issues that come up are interesting but we aren't being open enough."

Some of the mutual appraisal going on in the group revolves around the question of which strategy is better for the negotiations with the Jewish group or how the Arabs can organize themselves to deal most effectively with the Jews in a way that will advance their own group: "I agree that some of the issues have not yet been opened up because they are very sensitive, like the subject of '48. Now we have an opportunity to look at this within the Arab group, before we talk about it with the Jews."

Often in this meeting and in the ones to come, the discussion returns to the question of whether the Arab group should have a single, coherent position or whether its members should be free to express themselves individually. The discussion revolves around the question, What in fact strengthens the Arab group's position and status? Unity and unanimity in its positions, its approaches, and its demands? Or to be seen to be liberal and allow freedom of action for its members? Naturally there are disagreements within the group on this point. Different positions and opinions are brought forward concerning this particular subject as well as others that are emerging in the mixed forum. To concretize this debate about unity, which is one of the central topics of discussion in the Arab uninational group, let us take a look now at part of an actual discussion from one of the groups.

> WAFA'A: I want to tell the Arab group something. We don't have one unified opinion like they [the Jews] do. For example, when we introduced the matter of religion, this split us. *(Turns to Mu'ad.)*
>
> MU'AD: We don't all have to agree.
>
> WAFA'A: It's a problem that we are not united, when the Jews are.

IKHLAS: We have genuine disagreements among us, and there is no need to conceal that.

AMAL: Each of us talks in another direction and that weakens our position.

This exchange expresses the dilemma between personal expression and the collective unity that can strengthen the Arab group in its encounter with the Jews. The stronger tendency is usually for unity, even at the expense of denying the self: "Whatever happens, when the person speaking is an Arab, I identify with him no matter what he says. This is a very important subject. I've worked on myself a lot in this regard—this is what she thinks and that's her opinion; why should I bring up some other subject that will stifle hers? Sometimes I identify with every Arab participant—even before he opens his mouth." The need for group cohesion is so strong that sometimes an injustice is perpetrated vis-à-vis participants who are not inclined, simply out of good will, to relinquish the right to express themselves as individuals: "I don't feel that we are democratic in our thoughts. Yusuf almost wanted to hit me before because I felt something else, different from the group. We have to have a collective position, but on the other hand every one of us has his own opinion and feelings; we are not robots."

These arguments are a part of humanity's heritage and have been studied for many years by social psychology. There is constant oscillation between the individual's need for a self and the need to belong to a group and have a collective identity. The Arab group, as a minority, frequently expresses the need for unity and for a united position to be presented to the Jews. The Arabs prefer to conduct their internal arguments in the uninational forum. However, there is also a sense that to make such a demand is undemocratic, not liberal, with Western-style individualism serving as the compass point in this regard.

As the uninational meetings progress, the Arab group gathers itself together and, aside from the arguments mentioned, focuses on the problems that relate only to itself. Thoughts even come up about leaving the meeting. One man says: "What we need is to sit, just ourselves, and talk, and pull together strategies and tactics to initiate and do things among our own Arab population, so that they will be more aware of their rights and their own way of behaving, so that they will be prouder of their own identity, and so that automatically the Jewish group won't have any choice except to relate to the change that has begun within us, and change their approach to how they relate to us."

This marks a sharp departure from the initial idea that the uninational forum isn't necessary and that the Arab participants came to the encounter to talk to and persuade the Jews. The Arab group has arrived at the conclusion that what will change reality is what is done internally, proactively, by Arabs. At this point voices are sometimes heard within the Arab group expressing a reluctance to return to the meeting and to the endless struggle with the Jews, which now seems devoid of purpose. A man explains: "Personally, I feel that I have become more extreme and because of this I prefer the uninational [environment]." Another participant, a woman, expresses the revulsion she felt at the joint encounter and the discussions that took place there: "From the beginning they don't acknowledge [our] existence at all; this really infuriates me."

Thus the Arab group abandons the Jewish group during a discussion that takes place in the uninational meeting and begins to engage with internal problems and dilemmas. The main issue that generally emerges, during prolonged meetings, is that of the national identity of the members of the Arab group, an identity that is sharpened via the encounter but that the Arabs prefer to clarify when they are alone: "When, in the discussion we had with the Jewish group, Hussein said that he is not a Palestinian, I felt that the more important argument for me is with him and not with the Jewish group. I had some kind of need to argue with him, and I felt that that was not the place. I would like very much to clarify that now, between us."

The discussion of this topic is usually lively. Everyone pays close attention and participates periodically, and the group has trouble winding up and going back to the encounter. One of the main points that comes up in this discussion is the tension between national affiliation (Palestinian) and identity as a citizen (Israeli). Mostly, the Arab group's identity is clear and unequivocal when facing the Jewish group, and most if not all the Arabs identify themselves without reservation as Palestinians; whereas in the uninational forum the change to these less unequivocal positions provokes discussion and a profound process of clarification. One woman comments: "I can't be in Jordan or in Egypt, for example. I want to be in Israel; I like the lifestyle here. There are things I have to struggle over, but Israel gives me things I won't get somewhere else." A man says: "None of us wants to move elsewhere. The question is, Does Israel want to accept you? Israel is a Jewish state; how can you call yourself an Israeli? Besides, why should we compare ourselves with Palestinians from the Arab states? If the Palestinians in Egypt don't have rights, that doesn't mean that I shouldn't ask for my rights here. I'm here by right, not by charity. I want to be Palestinian and still have the rights I am entitled to."

Central threads in the discussion in this regard are the essence of

Palestinian identity and the comparison with Palestinians living beyond the Green Line [in the Palestinian Autonomous Areas]. This debate is sharp and became especially so after the Oslo agreements. A man says: "Palestinians' identity is clear, their boundaries are clear, their peoplehood is clear, and they behave accordingly. We are Palestinians, but we live in a different reality, a completely Israeli reality that has nothing Palestinian about it. Not only that, but the Palestinians from the territories see us as not Palestinian. They sometimes even see us as traitors or at least they describe us as *Arab el-shamenet* [the "cream-puff" Arabs, i.e., pampered]. They don't understand us because there's no connection between us." Another man reinforces this line of thought: "They [the Palestinians] have clear-cut demands and aspirations. But for us, as Arabs in Israel, our national aspirations are unclear. When I met Palestinians from Ramallah, I understood what Palestinian is. And then I understood that our Palestinian identity as I define it is different, and we are not like them." A woman in that group rejected these arguments: "We have feelings of inferiority vis-à-vis our Palestinian brothers in the political context because we are not struggling and suffering as they are. We live in a different reality, and so our struggle is also different. We have to oppose with all possible force being turned back into Israeli Arabs again, and this time by whom? By our Palestinian brothers." The clarification of this issue is one of the more fascinating and profound discussions engaged in by the Arab group on its own.

Another issue that usually arises in the Arabs' uninational discussion is the subject of one's inward affiliation: the subidentities subsumed under the umbrella of a national identity that itself is not totally clear. In this context, ethnic-religious affiliations come up for discussion, principally Muslim and Christian, and sometimes these are joined, though marginally, by the third element in the picture, the Druze. A Christian woman comments: "I would like to understand when members of the Knesset and other people, in our group too, talk about cultural autonomy for the Arabs: Do they mean Arab culture in general or Muslim Arab culture?!'"

The discussion that develops around this subject is interesting and most edifying for the Arab group, especially for the Muslim participants. An unfamiliar dynamic is operating here as the Christians bring up their feelings as a minority within a minority, and the Muslims become a majority and have to cope with a situation that they find not only novel but even hateful and repellent. The dynamic between these two groups somewhat resembles that between the Jews and the Arabs. We have found that the phenomena that occur between a majority and a minority are uni-

versal and tend to repeat themselves everywhere; they are not unique to
the Jewish-Arab conflict, as, for example, when the Muslims forcefully
oppose raising the religious issue, arguing that the subject is not relevant
to the group's discussion: "This is not the time to debate our internal
problems; we as a national minority have to stand together first of all
against our oppressor, against the serious problems. Other things, which
in my opinion are negligible, can be attended to after we finish our struggle with the Jews." This subject, such a core issue for the Christians participating, is, for this Muslim, "negligible." Generally a lot of courage and
effort are required of the Christian participants to get this issue onto the
group's agenda: "I think that we can't separate the two issues. If we want
freedom of expression and freedom of religion, education, etc., then we
have to first of all actualize this among ourselves; otherwise we won't be
able to ask it of others."

This and other issues I have described here, which are a source of
acute disagreement within the Arab group, are brought up for the most
thorough discussion and exploration in the uninational meetings. But the
Jewish group remains unaware of these discussions and tends to accuse
the Arab group of being overly united and of refusing to discuss their internal problems and differences.

Later on, after having withdrawn into itself and debated mostly
internal issues, the Arab group turns outward once again. It tries to examine the quality of its connection with the Jewish group and its options
for coping with the necessity of living with this conflict on a daily basis:
"Those we are meeting with here are a leftist group, and even with them
talking isn't simple. What would happen if we were to meet with an extremist right-wing group?" "What was it one of the sages said? You don't
pick your enemies." At this stage, the group is ready to take a look at itself and its part in the difficulties that arose during the earlier stages of the
dialogue: "We said very hard things to them. In their place, I don't know
what I would have done if someone had told me I was a racist."

Toward the end of the uninational meetings, the Arab group sums
up the forum with a retrospective look at what happened to them, both
on their own and in the encounter as a whole: "In the uninational meeting I felt more comfortable. I could express myself and my opinions freely,
something I couldn't do in the meeting with the Jews. Maybe also because
of the language." "I also felt really good in the uninational meeting. At
first I didn't understand why we Arabs were sitting by ourselves, or what
there was for us to talk about. I was surprised by how many issues there
are for us to discuss."

THE JEWISH UNINATIONAL MEETING

The processes and issues described in this next section emerge with most of the Jewish groups in the uninational framework in our workshops. Generally, in the first meeting, people figure out where they belong in the group (leftists-rightists, pessimists-optimists, nationalists-universalists; leaders emerge). At the initial separation into subgroups, the reason for the uninational framework is not immediately evident to the Jews. Some of them wonder aloud why this framework is necessary: "I have trouble with the notion of a 'home team.' I am closer to the women's group and don't identify here as part of the group. It bothers me being pushed into a Jewish group, opposite to them [the Arabs]."

Because the Jewish participants at this stage see themselves as individuals and not as belonging to a national group, they view this framework as superfluous and even as compelling them to cohere as a group against their will. The Arabs are seen as a separate, different national group because they are a minority, but the members of the majority group don't conceive of themselves as an ethnic or national group because they are the norm that is taken for granted—the model for others. In addition, possibly unconsciously, they are trying to postpone coping on an intergroup level with the conflictive issues.

Another phenomenon that emerges early in the Jewish uninational framework is that the participants are overwhelmed by the force of their first encounter with the Arab group. This entire experience is new to them because most have no prior experience with such a meeting. Hence the uninational gathering is quickly laden with the feelings and content that arose for the participants following the joint encounter. They have a tendency to project: to talk about the Arabs, to place responsibility for the difficulty on the other side, and not to look inward too much. Various subjects come up, among them the question of whether these are "easier" Arabs or "harder" Arabs. There is a desire to shape the other side. A woman says: "I have a hard time with Mahmoud; Marwan is easier. It's unpleasant to bring up the associations of lack of security, but Mahmoud is carrying so much stuff inside it could really explode. With Marwan, exactly because he is aware and he brings [these things] up, I feel more secure with him despite his saying things that are hard to hear." Sometimes there is an attempt to classify the members of the Arab group as either militants or moderates. This split offers a way to delegitimize the power emerging in the Arab group by ascribing negative attributes to it, even to the point of negating the humanity of its representatives: "For me, Mona is no more than an article in the newspaper. She has no uncertainties, like a manifesto. Adnan on the other hand vacillates between his Israeli and his Palestinian identity, just as we Jews do. With him it is possible to talk, to argue."

After both groups begin dealing with the conflict, and the Jewish participants come to understand that there are two groups in the encounter, each with a distinct national identity, they lose the feeling that the uninational framework is not particularly necessary and begin to experience a powerful need to talk among themselves. This need for uninational discussion grows when the members of the Jewish group begin to be distressed by the Arab group's increasing strength and by the image that now confronts them of Israeli society as immoral in relation to the Arab minority. The Jewish group generally finds it difficult to reveal its distress in front of the Arab group lest its weakness be perceived. The uninational framework allows the participants to vent their distress and analyze their feelings. At this point, they feel a need for support from other members of the group. They want to draw together and be reinforced for persevering in the dialogue with the Arab group. The framework, again, is now perceived not as superfluous, but rather the opposite. The participants feel tremendous relief at being able to express what is in their hearts: "There's a lot to talk about today. There's a feeling of the need to be in the uninational forum, to clarify things among ourselves. After yesterday's meeting I felt a need to defend Israeli youth who go into the army."

The need for the uninational framework is clearly intensifying in the wake of the growing distress felt by the Jewish participants. Sometimes they prefer to continue to clarify issues among themselves and have trouble returning to the joint meeting. The sessions at this stage are less stormy than they were earlier in the process, as the group now turns to the task of confronting itself: "Until the meeting before last, I wasn't comfortable arguing with them. Now I'm uncomfortable with myself because we've started talking about my part, more personally. It's hard in a different way. More connected with me; this time it's me and not them."

The uninational meetings midway through the workshop are the meetings in which the group does intensive "work" to understand the processes it is undergoing, with the level of insight and awareness varying with the participants. Gradually they are less preoccupied with the Arab group, and they can turn their attention to dealing with their own group and the problems that emerge in the wake of the encounter.

At this stage, the Jewish group is coping with a growing realization that in the room are two national groups between whom there is a conflict. This recognition opens up a host of questions about their Jewish-Israeli identity and their identity as the majority in the state. They explore how they want to view their own identity and how they are viewed by the others. They discover nationalistic parts of themselves of which they were previously unaware. They discover that even if they thought of themselves as liberals and non-nationalistic, the encounter with the Arab identity brings out those parts of themselves that they had hitherto preferred to suppress. One woman says: "I am too quick to insist that the nationalist identity is not a part of me. I don't want to go away from this country. Abroad, I find myself explaining right-wing positions. The ugly side is part of me, not someone else." This discovery is hard and evokes anxiety. The Jews fear that the nationalism they have discovered within themselves will be perceived as right-wing or racist by the other side and their own as well.

Aside from the developing inner conflict, another difficulty arises: the gap that opens up, in light of the awareness the participants acquire through the encounter, between them and those close to them, whether friends or family. The uninational forum, for participants in such cases, becomes a source of support and a warm place to which they can bring these conflicts and explore them: "In the last meeting I was uncomfortable. I come from a right-wing home, and I felt an unpleasant sensation in the earlier meetings. There I am considered leftist, and here I felt almost rightist. I am a nationalist Zionist." "After the first meeting, it really scared me. I am on the left, but more to the center. It infuriates me that I have to be afraid to say where I come from, who my parents are. Especially when I clash with my home and family, I have to be very strong. My father is a sociologist and my uncle is a military man; both of them are very right-wing, and I have to stand up to them. My father claims that it's impossible to rely on them [Arabs], that they aren't trustworthy, that they don't speak the truth. Aside from the fact I don't care about the Greater Land of Israel, my arguments are emotional and humanistic. The only thing I could tell him was that he didn't know Arabs personally."

The difficulties that come up in the Jewish group at this stage are on two levels: One level concerns problems generated by the dissonance evoked by the emergent gap between image and reality: participants' Jewish-Israeli image of the group and the reality of Israeli society, especially the discrimination and oppression it harbors, as reflected in the mirror that the Arab group provides. On another level, the Jewish group is reeling from hard blows: the encounter with a strong Arab group that refuses to be intimidated and the fearful sense of losing control.

These issues greatly trouble the Jewish group and dominate the uninational meetings. Sometimes distinguishing between the two levels is hard because both relate to the sense of identity. Because the element of power is an important one in the Jews' sense of identity, a feeling of losing power or an intensification of power on the other side is experienced as a loss of identity. There is also a connection between the two levels, as described by one of the Jewish women: "As we feel less and less that we're right, we lose power in the room." At this point a host of feelings emerge: anxiety, anger at loss of control and loss of power, and a sense of emptiness and depression following this loss. Because the meeting between the two (national) identities evokes a comparison of one group with the other, the Jewish uninational forum is now intensively preoccupied with the identity of the participants as Jews and as Israelis who belong to the majority group in the state. Building their national identity is a complicated and painful journey with many stages: "Suddenly when I am confronting them [the Arabs], I feel that my opinions aren't well formed compared with theirs. If before I came I thought that my ideas were clear, suddenly it all falls apart. It's hard for me to put something coherent together. The confrontation with another group brings us to a real search for identity and demands of me that I define my identity."

Before the meeting with the Arab group, the Jews can live long years in a state of denial and avoidance simply because they have not been forced to confront certain ethical dilemmas. The first meeting with the Arabs (for most of the Jewish participants, this is their first significant group encounter) moves the participants from denial to confrontation with these ethical dilemmas. The revelation creates dissonance, which is accompanied by feelings of guilt, emptiness, depression, powerlessness, and anxiety. The Jewish participants are trapped with an image of Israeli society that doesn't match the image they had of themselves and of their group as ethical and humane. They cannot help seeing that the ethical principles of equality that they believed were characteristic of Israeli society are not extended to Arab society. The injustice, oppression, and racism in the behavior of the Jewish majority toward the Arab minority, behavior that the Arab group reveals to the Jews, creates an ugly picture of Israeli society that the Jews dislike having to see. This dissonance is painful because it harms the individual and group self-image and creates an empty feeling. Among other things, the feeling that everything is falling apart comes from the sense that for the Jews to acknowledge this reality of oppression would nullify their right to exist here. "There is a gap here between how I would like to describe myself and what I am. I have sentimental feelings toward my grandparents' generation, who were pioneers; on the other hand the price [was paid by] another group. I wouldn't like to know that I had caused that. This really touches on identity, as a people and as a state."

Some of the myths on which participants were raised begin to show cracks, and moral dilemmas begin to peek through. "This is awfully hard. Yesterday I saw the news, the tape of the Border Patrol soldiers who beat up Palestinians. That tape sat around for five weeks, . . . and then today just before the meeting it was broadcast. . . . This is always current; it's exhausting. My problem is standing in front of the mirror. You don't really want to see that that is what is really happening in reality." "For me, to leave here [Israel] is not an option. Home, army, education . . . because the soldiers, they are us. The problem is not how to divide up the country, but how I can live here. Because to live here, as a conqueror and with what is happening here, it destroys all the sacred cows."

Shattering the myths and the accompanying confusion create a feeling that the group identity is jeopardized. This brings on a reaction: the Jewish group becomes unified and returns to a Jewish-Israeli national identity, as described by one of the women: "Usually with friends I am considered to have opinions that are not extreme. Outside [this meeting] I am on the side that defends the Arabs, and my grandmother even called me "you Arab-lover"; and here I am trying to clarify things that in everyday life are buried in my unconscious. I play two roles within myself— when I am confronting her, what I believe is clear and strong, and here in this room I suddenly bring up things that she says, not that I say. Suddenly my grandmother's arguments come up on the other side."

At this stage there is a demand periodically from all the participants in the Jewish group to fall into line and conform. Those setting the tone are those who express the nationalist voice. Usually they attack the others, who, they say, are *"mityafyefim"* [attempting to look good] and whom they accuse of avoiding the conflict and impeding real clarification of the relations between Jews and Arabs. Sometimes, though, those who had declared themselves to be leftists draw the line at this stage and "come home" or are silent or lower their tone against the voice of nationalist ultimatum. Let us sample a dialogue along these lines:

> LIAT: I was angry, in the room, at Yaron and Dahlia, not at their opinions but at their way of evading the conflicts. I was angry at them, and I asked myself, Where is their connection with the state, with this place?
>
> DAHLIA: There are two groups here now. Yaron and I are with them [the Arabs], and this isn't easy for me although it may sound that way. I envy you, that you feel such a connection to here.

Sometimes in such cases the pressure on those who "step out of line"—those who express a liberal voice, authentic though it may be—is strong, to the point that an atmosphere is created in which these voices are delegitimized. The Jewish group becomes cohesive and united and doesn't allow its members to deviate. Those who insist on doing so pay a heavy price within the group. A woman says: "I know that I am the one who has caused you [the Jewish group] problems. I felt uncomfortable with this, that I bothered you. Even so it is hard with the conflict. From now on I'd rather be silent." These processes and clarifications take place only in the uninational forum and not in front of the Arab group. Generally the Arab participants are not aware at all of the phenomenon just described, unless the "leftist" Jewish participants confide in them outside the framework of the meeting.

At this stage, the Jewish group divides into other subsets that are explored in the uninational framework. Disagreements come up now between "religious" (observant) and secular participants, natives and new immigrants, and especially Ashkenazim ("European Jews") and Mizrahim ("Oriental Jews"). "The social issue is close to my heart, and it bothers me that the Israeli left is outstanding in its humanism and pluralism only toward the Arab minority but not internally. This bothers me, and I resent it; I think the left are hypocrites." Generally those who put this subject on the group's agenda are Mizrahi participants who try to explode the myth that the typical Ashkenazi is a leftist and the typical Mizrahi is a rightist. They try to clarify their complex identity within the conflict: "When I am in a Jewish environment, people don't know that I am not an Arab; I am a black [i.e., dark-skinned] Jew. . . . On the Mizrahi side there are groups who are more traditional, and more people vote right-wing, but on the other hand they talk with Arabs as equals [literally, "at eye level"]."

Complex indeed is this issue of people who are oppressed within the oppressor group; they tend to be relatively more extremist in their pronouncements and generally are identified with the nationalist camp. Perhaps this comes from a need to prove that the "Israeliness" more identified with Ashkenazim applies to them as well. By contrast, on the level of behavior the Ashkenazim tend to act superior toward Arabs, whereas Mizrahim strike up a direct connection and talk with Arabs as equals. This subject is a sensitive one within the Jewish group, perhaps because the Ashkenazim take pains to suppress it in the discussion.

Toward the end of the entire process, when the Jewish groups feels less pressured, the need for unity decreases; this change facilitates in-depth inquiry, which allows for a variety of opinions in the group, and promotes a profound examination yielding many insights. Participants try to cope with the dilemmas that arose earlier and with the ruins of the myths shattered by the encounter with the Arabs. At this stage there is an acceptance of Jewish identity with all its ramifications, including its less attractive aspects, and there is a tendency to take responsibility for these: "This is the second meeting in which I feel a lot of anger toward people, toward militant expressions on the Jewish side to protect our being on top." "We took to ourselves the privileges of a majority and acted accordingly. We permitted ourselves to agonize and to let them share in these processes we went through. A minority cannot allow itself to do this; it has to present a united front. To me this emphasizes our power, our control over everything." Taking responsibility in the Jewish group for racism or power or discrimination rehabilitates to a great extent the group's damaged national identity and builds a more positive and healthier one. This examination is conducted first in the uninational meetings. Only afterward is the discussion imported to the meeting with the Arabs, where it changes the interaction between the two groups and opens the option for another kind of dialogue.

Approaching the last of the uninational meetings, participants are dealing with the processes they have undergone. The Jewish group is busy dealing with feeling that, in order to arrive at a change in their awareness, they have invested great effort that involved much pain. For this effort they want recognition from the Arab group. They see their new awareness as an achievement, and they express frustration that their achievement has not been acknowledged by the Arabs. "There are two separate processes here that do not converge, one positive and the other negative. Here in the uninational framework I see that I have come a long way and have developed, and on the other hand it's as if they are telling me, So what?"

This frustration is evidently difficult to prevent in a Jewish-Arab encounter. Generally the Arab group avoids expressing this recognition because it is reentering the daily reality—which is unchanged—and also because it doesn't want the Jews to leave in too self-satisfied a mood and then not do anything to change the way things are out there. The Jews long for this acknowledgment of the process they have gone through because that would release them from the role of oppressor and give them back their humanity. Even if they don't get it explicitly, there is still some feeling of release from the burden of that role, but the overt recognition is important in validating the change they have undergone.

The Jewish participants at this stage evaluate what has happened to them in the uninational meetings. "At the beginning a kind of critique took place in this room about what was being said there [in the joint meeting]. Afterward we analyzed things. I remember that the analysis dealt many times with who was stronger and what that does to us." "I understand that the insights we have achieved here will not always be actualized in the binational forum. Lots of times when we tried to bring insights from here, it didn't work out. As time went on, we brought key statements. The uninational forum was like a secure anchor in which we were able to understand many things. Many things became clearer."

DISCUSSION

At the beginning of the uninational forum the two groups, each for its own reasons, opposed the framework itself and did not see the logic of having it or its potential usefulness. As things progressed, this framework became significant for the participants—to the point where, at certain stages, they even preferred it to the encounter with the other group. This happened when the tensions in the meeting escalated and the conflict emerged in full force. Under those circumstances, the uninational meeting became a kind of homecoming, an anchor to which the participants could cling, during the hours that were toughest for them. Thus the uninational environment promoted real, hard, and painful coping in the encounter because it encompassed the distress, the troublesome feelings, of the participants while providing a basis from which they could "go out to do battle" and to which they could return at the end of the day.

Alongside this function, the uninational forum was also a framework in its own right. In it, a unique kind of exploration went on, parallel to that taking place in the encounter, in which there were characteristic processes and phenomena that we will pinpoint here. Some of these processes are also evident in the binational encounter but appear more conspicuously and sharply in the uninational meetings, while others are possible only in the uninational framework. From a comparative look at the process that each of the two national groups undergoes, one may distinguish a kind of inverse double track on which they are marching. The Arab group supposedly came into the meeting as a unified entity and with a coherent identity, and then in the course of the meeting this identity came unglued and was debated seriously and investigated courageously. Not only that, but here also subjects were opened up concerning which there was disagreement within the Arab group. The feeling was that at home among ourselves anything may be clarified, but to the outside we have to appear united and all together. As the saying goes, dirty laundry shouldn't be washed in public.

By contrast, the Jewish group came into the meeting with less of a group feeling, indeed with a tendency to stress each participant's individuality and the conflict vis-à-vis the Arab group. Over time, the Jewish group gathered itself to itself and got in touch with its national identity. And at a certain point heavy pressure was even brought to bear within the group to get everyone in line and "back home" so as to appear in front of the Arab group speaking in one united, unanimous voice.

If we examine these processes via the model suggested by Janet Helms (see Chapter Five), a useful model that speaks about the development of ethnic identity among whites and blacks, it appears that each group researched and built its identity via interaction with another identity. Or as Helms would put it, in our context, the Jews and the Arabs were developing their identity from a "primitive" stage to "higher" stages, but each on its own ladder because they are two different groups, majority and minority, strong and weak.

The Jewish group, as the majority, has the privilege of not having to cope with its national identity and the meaning of that for others. In the encounter, the presence of the Arab group wedged its way into the consciousness of the Jewish participants and disturbed their peace of mind; it forced them to connect with their identity in all its ramifications. They had to come to grips with the moral dilemmas that lie between being basically liberal and humane and the more difficult challenge of truly coming to accept the Arabs as equal in every way. The distress arising from this dissonance brought part of the Jewish group to reown its nationalism and look for ways to justify an unjust and immoral situation. The others took responsibility for the situation and tried to examine their unexamined assumptions about their own superiority and the inferiority of the Arabs in a serious and in-depth way. These members became more dominant in the last phase of the group process and spoke in the name of the group as a whole.

Nearly all the Arab group, as a minority, came to the meeting with an awareness of its national identity and an awareness of the conflict that divides the two groups. The meeting brought the Arab group at first to gather even more to itself. This is the stage of extremism and anger discussed by Helms, in which a minority group idealizes its identity and rejects anything to do with the majority—as we saw when the Arab participants in their anger wanted to boycott the meeting with the Jews and preferred the uninational forum. After exhausting this stage, the Arab participants looked deeply and thoroughly at their national identity, going beyond declarations and clichés, and also looked into the options for dialogue and cooperation with the Jews in order to change the situation.

Thus, each group became a mirror and a catalyst for the other, so that the other could change and develop a healthy, positive identity, as Helms puts it, through a fruitful and egalitarian dialogue. The uninational forum contributed greatly during a painful journey navigated by the two groups and moreover gave us the option to examine carefully and at close quarters the processes of change that occurred along the way.

The matter of identity is the heart of the encounter, which is in fact an encounter between two identities. But the uninational forum makes possible a profound exploration of, and a more leisurely manner of analyzing, the question of identity. The uninational forum also enables an exploration of subidentities on both sides, something that simply does not happen in the meetings between the two groups: for example, with the ethnic-religious (Muslim, Christian, Druze) issue in the Arab group and with the ethnic (Ashkenazi-Mizrahi) issue in the Jewish group. Without the uninational framework, the meetings would be partial, and our insights concerning the encounter between Jews and Arabs would be less complete and more flawed. One might come away with the mistaken impression, for example, that the encounter is one between a unified and cohesive Arab group and an open Jewish group that emphasizes individuality. The uninational framework rounds out what is lacking structurally to allow us to learn about other, complex processes—crucial processes involved in the encounter between a minority and a majority in conflict.

10
IDENTITY PROCESSES IN INTERGROUP ENCOUNTERS

GABRIEL HORENCZYK

Despite its vagueness, the notion of identity is gradually emerging as a central component of the discourse on intergroup relations and intergroup conflict. Burton (1986) and Azar (1986), for example, suggested that identity-related conflicts dominate the contemporary world scene and that any attempt to resolve these conflicts must acknowledge and address the basic human needs associated with group identities. The approach to intergroup intervention proposed and discussed in this book gives a prominent role to social identities (particularly, but not solely, to national identities) and to the processes of identity construction and negotiation.

Some of the contributors to this book have found the "intergroup-interpersonal continuum" (Tajfel 1981) useful both in conceptualizing the intergroup strategy adopted and refined by the School for Peace and in analyzing and interpreting the group and intergroup processes taking place at the School for Peace encounters. In Chapter Two Ramzi Suleiman insightfully suggests that the two interacting groups are frequently located at different points on the continuum: typically, the Arab group positions itself close to the intergroup end, whereas Jewish participants strive for interpersonal contact. Suleiman further proposes conceptualizing the two options—the intergroup and interpersonal—as two orthogonal dimensions.

In this concluding chapter, I locate social identity within a broader sociopsychological framework. A broader context can take us beyond the theoretical role of identity as a central factor in the analysis of strategies for intergroup contact and permit us to view identity-development processes themselves—participants' examination and reconstruction of their own identity—as an important and implicit goal of intergroup encounters. Use of this framework assumes that the intergroup encounter can serve, and in fact it often does serve, as an optimal arena for the exploration, construction, and reconstruction of group and cultural identities.

I argue that some strategies for intergroup encounters are likely to put more emphasis on identity-development processes than are others. The "categorized" group-contact approach, during which group categories and identities are kept clearly defined and salient, seems most effective in promoting change in—and development of—ethnic and national identities on the part of the participants. The approach to intergroup encounters developed and implemented at the School for Peace can be clearly classified as "categorized" contact.

Hewstone (1996) distinguished three types of outcomes that intergroup interventions might seek to achieve: (1) A "change in attitudes toward the social category" may ensue when mutual perceptions are improved within the contact situation and group members come to feel differently about the out-group social category. In other words, more positive attitudes toward out-group individuals participating in the intergroup contact may be generalized to the out-group as a whole. This is the outcome that is most frequently associated with the idea of the intergroup encounter, and it is based on the assumption that negative attitudes are generally a result of lack of contact and of mutual ignorance. (2) Growing familiarity with out-group members gained in the intergroup situation may lead to more differentiated interaction within that setting. Such interaction is likely to result in "increased complexity of intergroup perceptions." If this complexity is achieved, following intergroup interaction the out-group will be perceived as more heterogeneous, comprising people with diverse traits, beliefs, and attitudes. (3) In "decategorization," a third potential successful outcome of intergroup encounters, there is a change in a social category's perceived usefulness for interpersonal contact. Individuals may realize that other, more personal, attributes should be preferred for identifying and classifying people within the wider intergroup context rather than the social categories that tend to lead to hostile relationships.

For decades, structured and unstructured intergroup encounters have aimed primarily toward outcomes of the first and third kind—the fostering and enhancement of positive intergroup attitudes and a reduction in the use of group (racial, national, ethnic) labels. These are the types of goals participants themselves generally have when entering the intergroup situation. This book provides some evidence that change in group perceptions or concepts is indeed achieved during the encounters at the School for Peace. According to Michal Zak, Rabah Halabi, and Wafa'a Zriek-Srour in Chapter Six, for example, Jewish participants report a change in their image of the Arab as a result of their intergroup experience.

Aside from such changes involving the perceptions of and the relationship with members of the other group, intergroup contact can also set in motion valuable processes that touch on the individual view of the self and on participants' own group identities and identifications. This is a central goal of School for Peace activities. The intergroup encounter can be a powerful context in which people can explore, define, and redefine their own group identities and affiliations. The dialogue with the other, sometimes calm and sometimes challenging, impels the participant to examine his or her own cultural and national identity.

The belief that the intergroup encounter can and should help foster development of a positive and healthy cultural identity rests on certain assumptions and arguments. First, identity processes are often seen as necessary steps toward the attainment of higher intergroup goals. In the Introduction, Halabi argues that only an encounter between clear, confident identities can lead to an authentic encounter of equals and thereafter, perhaps, to the creation of a more humane and just society. This assumption is particularly relevant to national and ethnic conflicts, which involve a struggle for the legitimization and recognition of group and cultural identities.

Second, psychologists have also argued for the positive effects of a healthy ethnic identity on personal well-being. Much research evidence suggests that both strong attachment to group identities and higher levels of ethnic-identity development are related to psychological and sociocultural adjustment, especially among minority individuals (Phinney 1995). Thus if the intergroup encounter has the potential to promote the development of healthy group identities, indirectly it could exert a positive influence on the minority individual's self-esteem and well-being. In addition, as noted throughout this book, the structured intergroup encounter may be even more important for members of majority or dominant groups, who typically have little contact with minority individuals in their daily lives. According to various racial-identity models, such as the one formulated by Helms (1990b), intergroup contact is essential, although not sufficient in and of itself, for the development of group identity among both minority and majority group members.

Third, promoting an enlightened and growing awareness of participants' group and cultural identities is deemed, by many observers, an inherently valuable goal all by itself, obviating the need for any further sociological or psychological rationale on that score. Many scholars have proposed that education should include among its aims the fostering of identity development, primarily—from an Eriksonian perspective—through the processes of exploration and commitment (Archer 1989; Marcia 1989).

Structured intergroup encounters can serve as powerful educational interventions that can contribute significantly to identity development in general and to group (cultural, ethnic, national, racial) identity in particular. Hewstone's (1996) insightful analysis also classifies strategies of intergroup interventions according to the way in which they deal with the group identities involved; he arrives at four types of intergroup contact: (1) In "decategorized" contact the intergroup interventions should be "differentiated" (allowing for distinctions to be made among out-group members) and "personalized" (allowing for perceptions of the uniqueness of out-group members). (2) The intergroup ("categorized") strategy argues that positive contact between groups must be defined as an intergroup, and not an interpersonal, encounter. (3) The "crossed-categorization" model suggests introducing into an encounter (such as Arab-Jewish) additional group identities (such as gender) in order to reduce the importance of any one category. (4) The intervention model of "common in-group identity" argues that intergroup attitudes and behavior can be improved by "recategorization," by transforming individuals' perceptions of group boundaries from "us" (for example, Jewish) and "them" (Arabs) to a more inclusive "we" (Israelis, youngsters).

How does each of these intergroup encounter strategies deal with group identities? Briefly, both decategorized contact and interventions based on common in-group identity tend to ignore, or attempt to overcome, the group identities brought by the participants to the encounter situation. Decategorization aims at dissolving these group identities in favor of personalized contact, whereas the model of common in-group identity suggests superseding other existing but divisive categories with one superordinate (but still group) identity. Cross-categorization does not ignore potentially colliding group categories but suggests reducing the level of conflict by adding a crossed-group category. Only under categorized intergroup contact do the initial group categorizations and identities brought by participants remain central to the encounter, even as they evolve over the course of the interaction.

The approach developed by the School for Peace is mainly an intergroup one, although the chapters of this book clearly show the complexity of the intergroup processes: aside from categorized intergroup processes, elements of decategorization, cross-categorization, and recategorization emerge at various stages and demand careful attention. The categorized intergroup approach has the highest chance of bringing about generalized change in intergroup perceptions, precisely because participants are perceived as representatives of their respective groups.

As to the identity-related goals so central to the approach developed at the School for Peace, these are more likely to be achieved when group identities are accorded legitimate visibility during the meeting instead of being regarded as interfering factors to be ignored. In encounters based on the intergroup approach, such as those held at the School for Peace, group identities and boundaries are indeed central subjects of discussion and objects of negotiation.

EPILOGUE

TOWARD A HUMANE AND
EQUAL RELATIONSHIP

RABAH HALABI

An epilogue usually ties up all the loose ends in an orderly package. A concluding section also usually signifies, in one way or another, that the matter is now finished. In this instance, however, such an ending would be antithetical to the content and nature of the book itself. This is a dynamic anthology that attempts to track and report on what is happening in the changing reality in which we are living. Our reality is so crazy that by the time we have begun to discern some logic in all the confusion, events overtake us and leave us standing there, open-mouthed.

Yet, some closing comment is called for. I use this opportunity to say a few words about current reality as it revolves around the second intifada, which erupted after most of this book was written. I address the enduring argument over the questions of how useful Arab-Jewish encounter is and what relevance our model has for groups in conflict in general. I interpret what is happening to us right now, utilizing the insights we have gained from the continuing encounter in which we, as organizers and directors of these meetings, are perpetually engaged.

The dialogue between Arabs and Jews in Israel has been extensively studied, and much as been written about it. Some of the research has cast doubt on the effectiveness of such encounters. Arab researchers in particular have been critical. Ramzi Suleiman (in Chapter Two), Rouhana and

Korper (1997), and Abu-Nimer (1999) are harshly critical of the encounters that have been conducted in Israel over more than two decades. They argue that such meetings, which generally take place on the interpersonal plane and ignore or suppress political reality, serve mainly the Jews and support a continuation of the status quo.

The question of the effectiveness of Jewish-Arab encounter is crucial and central. It touches a raw nerve because it goes to the crux of the matter: Is an educational process as such capable of altering the profile of a society? We at the School for Peace tend to a somewhat skeptical outlook on this point, believing that our reality is shaped, above all, by processes of a political and economic nature. Yet the encounter can, ideally, contribute to awareness. Participants can come away with a better understanding of the reality in which they are living and, in that sense, be better equipped to grapple with it.

We think that if there is value in having Jewish-Arab encounter, the model developed at the School for Peace is optimal because it offers a breakthrough in two key areas. First, it narrows the goals of the encounter, locating them within the realm of examining identity and broadening awareness, and doesn't pretend to change attitudes. Second, the encounter as conducted at the School for Peace takes into account overall reality and its social, economic, and political structures; it does not relegate the encounter solely to the personal dimension, severed from any broader structural context. On the contrary; in this model, the encounter promotes scrutiny both of the political issues and of participants' identity and views as central to the conflict.

As we have repeatedly emphasized, the main contribution of Jewish-Arab encounter is broader awareness. In its wake, participants can better chart their course. Some put the encounter behind them and move on, making no meaningful changes in their lives; others try to act on the experience, each in his or her own fashion. We have trained hundreds of facilitators over the years, and most people working in this field in Israel today are School for Peace graduates. In addition, many of our graduates are now activists with various social-change organizations, where they attempt to integrate our philosophy into their work. We have seen the impact of our approach in women's organizations, legal-advocacy and defense organizations, Jewish and Arab high schools, local government social services departments, voluntary organizations, and protest movements.

The model we have developed at the School for Peace can be adapted for use in any situation of intergroup conflict. Over the years, we have worked in Israel with various groups in conflict—men and women,

Mizrahi and Ashkenazi Jews, Muslims and Christians, and others—as well as Jews and Arabs. We have had instructive experiences working with groups in conflict outside Israel, among them people of color and whites in the United States, Catholics and Protestants in Northern Ireland, and representatives of the various national groups in the former Yugoslavia. We have run a course for Cypriot bicommunal practitioners—Greeks and Turks—from both parts of the island.

Those of us who organize encounters have found that we, too, undergo changes in our own awareness. The modest contribution we can make to society is to attempt to share the insights we have from our work, and thereby promote a better understanding of the reality around us. This contribution is especially important in the troubled times we are living through now, when the conflict is in such an acute phase—both within Israel and, especially, between Israel and the Palestinian Authority.

Relations between Jews and Palestinians in Israel following the events of October 2000 have been deflected sharply in a new direction, to the point of estrangement or even a complete break. The level of hostility between the two peoples has risen to new heights; there is widespread frustration and despair, and a terrible fear of what the future may bring. Ostensibly, according to what we hear many people saying, there has been a deterioration in the relations between the two peoples: a regression, relative to the "ideal" situation that obtained beforehand. We at the School for Peace have our own perspective, informed by our extensive experience with encounters and the insights we've evolved from our work, as presented in this book. Our view is that, with all the pain entailed, what happened in October 2000 constituted a necessary step on the path to equal and more humane relations between the two peoples.

In this book (notably Chapter Four, on university-level courses on the Jewish-Arab conflict), we have described a dynamic web of relations between Jews and Arabs in the encounter. For the sake of description, the typical pattern can be simplified into five distinct stages. In the initial stage, one of exploratory overtures, the atmosphere is cordial and relaxed. During the second stage, the Arab group begins to feel stronger and to act accordingly; this change causes the Jewish group to feel threatened and anxious. In the third stage, the Jewish group attempts to return to the status quo ante (before the Arab group became stronger); its doing so engenders an acute conflict, and the atmosphere turns bitter, sometimes intolerably so. In the fourth stage, when the Arab group refuses to retreat, the atmosphere becomes one of treading water, of impasse. The fifth stage brings a breakthrough, and relations between the two groups become more reciprocal and egalitarian. This breakthrough occurs because the Jewish group comes to terms with the new power relationship and accepts the Arab group as it is, rather than as the Jews would prefer it to be—with all the ramifications that entails.

If, as we firmly believe, the encounters we facilitate are a microcosm of the reality outside, the pattern they so reliably display should enable us to deduce what is currently going on between the two peoples in the larger reality around us. Let us quickly revisit, in the light of the model we have described, the history of the relations between the two peoples since 1948.

Between 1948, when the State of Israel was founded, and the late 1960s or, more precisely, until the 1967 war, relations between Jews and Arabs inside Israel were in the nature of exploratory overtures (stage one). The Arabs were trying to learn how to live as a small minority under Jewish rule, and the Jewish establishment was trying to figure out how to proceed and what to do with the Palestinians living right there among them—underfoot, so to speak. During that era, the Palestinians sought to efface themselves as best they could, and they relinquished, insofar as possible, their national identity in order to go on living and surviving—to the point that the Jews were often unaware of their existence. This situation engendered a false atmosphere of coexistence, the illusion of an ideal shared life.

After 1967, the Palestinians in Israel encountered their brothers and sisters from over the border (in the West Bank and Gaza). This renewed contact—along with various concurrent social and political changes too complex to be addressed here—was tremendously invigorating for Palestinians in Israel, who felt themselves becoming stronger, individually and collectively. Their national identity and pride were rehabilitated. This process evolved gradually over a period of years, and then reached an abrupt peak in October 2000. The events of that fall were the inevitable explosion toward which the entire dynamic had been unfolding, as the growing Palestinian strength and repeated demands for absolute equality with Jews in all spheres was experienced by the Jews as a threat to themselves (stage two).

Over the years, Jews had responded harshly and disproportionately to Arab attempts to protest against the existing reality. That dynamic, too, reached a peak in October 2000, when the police shot and killed thirteen Palestinian Israelis who were demonstrating against the discrimination leveled at their community in Israel and against the policies promulgated against their brothers and sisters in the Palestinian Authority. The ease with which live fire was aimed at Arab demonstrators evidently arose from the old sense of threat, overlaid with panic and the longstanding imperative to stop the Palestinian group from growing stronger. The police were acting to put the Arabs in their place, back where they belonged, so they would resume behaving as they were supposed to: as "nice" Arabs, just as in the early years of the state (stage three).

Today we seem to be mired down somewhere in the fourth stage: The Jews are trying to rewind the movie, to repress the changes that have taken place in Israel and the region. They are refusing to accept any change in the balance of power between them and the Palestinians. They are profoundly reluctant to acknowledge the new, proud Palestinian, who will accept nothing less than complete equality with Jews.

Looking to our encounter model as a guide to what is happening, we can see that we are somewhere in the middle of the period of the most profound conflict, with hard and bitter times still to come. Yet the situation as it stands now, tough as it may be, marks tremendous progress in comparison with the counterfeit cordiality of the first stage. If we can weather the storms ahead without entirely losing our way, a more humane and equal relationship with one another awaits us, around the next bend in the road.

References

Abu-Nimer, M. 1999. *Dialogue, Conflict Resolution, and Change: Arab-Jewish Encounters in Israel.* Albany: State University of New York Press.

Adar, L., and H. Adler. 1965. *Teaching Values in a School for Children Immigrants.* Jerusalem: School of Education, Hebrew University.

Adorno, J. W., E. Frenkel-Brunswick, D. J. Lewinson, and R. N. Sanford. 1950. *The Authoritarian Personality.* New York: Harper.

Al-haj, M. 1996. *Education among the Arabs in Israel: Control and Social Change* (in Hebrew). Jerusalem: Magnes Press.

Allport, G. W. 1954. *The Nature of Prejudice.* Reading, Mass.: Addison-Wesley.

Altemeyer, B. 1988. *Enemies of Freedom: Understanding Right-Wing Authoritarianism.* San Francisco: Jossey-Bass.

Amara, A., and S. Kabaha. 1996. *Divided Identity: A Study of Political Division and Social Reflections in a Split Village* (in Hebrew). Givat Haviva, Israel: Hamagon Leheger Hashalom.

Amir, Y. 1969. "Contact Hypothesis in Ethnic Relations." *Psychological Bulletin* 71: 319–342.

Amir, Y. 1976. "The Role of Intergroup Contact in Change of Prejudice and Ethnic Relations." In *Toward the Elimination of Racism,* edited by P. A. Katz. New York: Pergamon Press.

Amir, Y., and R. Ben-Ari. 1987. "Encounters between Jewish and Arab Youth in Israel" (in Hebrew). *Megamot* 30: 305–315.

Archer, S. L. 1989. "The Status of Identity: Reflections on the Need for Intervention." *Journal of Adolescence* 12: 345–359.

Argule, M. 1982. "Intercultural Communications." In *Cultures in Contact,* edited by S. Bochner. New York: Pergamon Press.

Asher, S. R., and V. L. Allen. 1969. "Racial Preference and Social Comparison Processes." *Journal of Social Issues* 25: 157–166.

Azar, E. E. 1986. "Protracted International Conflicts: Ten Propositions." In *International Conflict Resolution: Theory and Practice,* edited by E. E. Azar and J. W. Burton. Boulder, Colo.: Lynne Riner.

Barth, F. 1969. *Ethnic Groups and Boundaries.* Boston: Little, Brown.

Ben-Ari, R., and Y. Amir. 1988. "Intergroup Confrontations in Israel: Assessment and Paths of Change" (in Hebrew). *Psychology* 1: 49–57.

Berry, J. 1997. "Immigration, Acculturation, and Adaptation." *Applied Psychology: An International Review* 46:5–68.

Billing, M. 1995. *Banal Nationalism.* London: Sage.

Bion, W. R. 1961. *Experience in Groups and Other Papers.* New York: Basic Books.

Birman, D. 1994. "Acculturation and Human Diversity in a Multicultural Society." In *Human Diversity: Perspectives on People in Context*, edited by E. J. Trickett, R. J. Watts, and D. Birman. San Francisco: Jossey-Bass.

Bishara, A., ed. 1999. *Between "I" and "We": The Construction of Identities and Israeli Identity* (in Hebrew). Tel Aviv: Van Leer Jerusalem Institute, Hakibbutz Hameuchad Press.

Bizman, A. 1978. "Similarity in Status, Status Level and Reduction of Stereotypes Following an Encounter between National Groups" (in Hebrew). Ph.D. diss., Department of Psychology, Bar-Ilan University.

Bourdieu, P. 1977. "The Economics of Linguistic Exchanges." *Social Science Information* 16:645–668.

Bourhis, R. Y., and A. Gagnon. 2001. "Social Orientations in the Minimal Group Paradigm." In *Intergroup Processes*, edited by R. Brown and S. Gaertner. London: Blackwell.

Branscombe, N. R., N. Ellemers, R. Spears, and B. Doosje. 1999. "The Context and Content of Social Identity Threat." In *Social Identity: Context, Commitment, Content*, edited by N. Ellemers. Oxford, U.K.: Blackwell Science.

Brewer, M. B., and D. T. Campbell. 1976. *Ethnocentrism and Intergroup Attitudes: East African Evidence.* New York: Sage.

Brislin, R. W. 1981. *Cross Cultural Encounters.* New York: Pergamon Press.

Brown, R. 1995. *Prejudice: Its Social Psychology.* London: Blackwell.

Brown, R. 2000. *Group Processes.* 2d ed. London: Blackwell.

Brown, R., and M. Hewstone. 1986. *Contact and Conflict in Intergroup Encounters.* Basil, U.K.: Wheatsheaf Books.

Bukhurst, D. 1990. "Social Memory in Soviet Thought." In *Collective Remembering*, edited by D. Middleton and D. Edwards. Thousand Oaks, Calif.: Sage.

Burton, J. W. 1986. "The Procedures of Conflict Resolution." In *International Conflict Resolution: Theory and Practice*, edited by E. E. Azar and J. W. Burton. Boulder, Colo.: Lynne Riner.

Burton, J. W. 1991. "Conflict Resolution as a Political System." In *The Psychodynamics of International Relationships*, edited by D. Volkan, J. Montville, and D. Julias. Lexington, Mass.: Lexington Books.

Byrne, D. 1971. *The Attraction Paradigm.* New York: Academic Press.

Campbell, D. T. 1965. "Ethnocentric and Other Altruistic Motives." In *Nebraska Symposium on Motivation*, edited by D. Levine. Lincoln: University of Nebraska Press.

Carnevale, P. J., and D. G. Pruitt. 1992. "Negotiation and Mediation." *Annual Review of Psychology* 43:531–582.

Clark, K. B., and M. P. Clark. [1947] 1955. "Racial Identification and Preference in Negro Children." In *Basic Studies in Social Psychology*, edited by H. Proshansky and B. Seidenberg. New York: Holt, Rinehart and Winston.

Cook, S. W. 1978. "Interpersonal and Attitudinal Outcomes in Cooperating Interracial Groups." *Journal of Research and Development in Education* 12:97–113.

Cross, W. 1978. "Models of Psychological Nigrescence: A Literature Review." *Journal of Black Psychology* 5 (1): 13–31.

Darley, J. M., and P. H. Gross. 1983. "A Hypothesis Confirming Bias in Labeling Effects." *Journal of Personality and Social Psychology* 44:20–33.

Erikson, E. 1964. *Insight and Responsibility*. New York: Norton.

Erikson, E. 1968. *Identity, Youth and Crisis*. London: Norton.

Freire, P. 1972. *Pedagogy of the Oppressed*. Ringwood, Australia: Penguin Books.

Gaertner, S. L., J. F. Dovidio, J. A. Nier, C. M. Ward, and B. S. Banker. 1999. "Across Cultural Divides: The Value of a Superordinate Identity." In *Cultural Divides: Understanding and Overcoming Group Conflict*, edited by D. Prentice and D. Miller. New York: Russell Sage Foundation.

Giles, H., R. Y. Bourhis, and D. M. Taylor. 1977. "Towards a Theory of Language in Ethnic Group Relations." In *Language, Ethnicity and Intergroup Relations*, edited by H. Giles. London: London Academic Press.

Grossman, D. 1992. *Present Absentees*. Tel Aviv: Siman Kriaa.

Hamers, J., and M. Blanc. 1989. *Multilingualism and Intergroup Relations in Bilinguality and Bilingualism*. Cambridge: Cambridge University Press.

Hamilton, D. L., and G. D. Bishop. 1976. "Attitudinal and Behavioral Effects of Initial Integration of White Suburban Neighborhoods." *Journal of Social Issues* 32:47–67.

Helms, J. E. 1989. "Considering Some Methodological Issues in Racial Identity Counseling Research." *Counseling Psychologist* 17 (2): 227–252.

Helms, J. E., ed. 1990a. *Black and White Racial Identity: Theory, Research, and Practice*. Westport, Conn.: Greenwood Press.

Helms, J. E. 1990b. "Towards a Model of White Racial Identity Development." In *Black and White Racial Identity: Theory, Research, and Practice*, edited by J. E. Helms. Westport, Conn.: Greenwood Press.

Hewstone, M. 1996. "Contact and Categorization: Social Psychological Interventions to Change Intergroup Relations." In *Foundations of Stereotypes and Stereotyping*, edited by C. N. Macrae, C. Stangor, and M. Hewstone. New York: Guilford Press.

Hobsbawm, E. 1995. "The National Movement of the 20th Century" (in Arabic). In *Nationalism: The Malady of the Era of Deliverance*, edited by A. Fallah. Beirut: Dar al-Saki.

Hoffman, Y., and K. Najar. 1986. "Willingness for Normal Social Relations amongst Jewish and Arab High School Students" (in Hebrew). *Iyunim Behinuch* 43/44:103–118.

hooks, b. 1994. *Teaching to Transgress*. New York: Routledge.

Hutnik, M. 1991. *Ethnic Minority Identity: A Social Psychological Perspective*. Oxford: Clarendon Press.

Isaacs, H. 1989. *Idols of the Tribe: Group Identity and Political Change*. Cambridge, Mass.: Harvard University Press.

Katz, Y., and M. Kahanov. 1990. "A Review of Dilemmas in Facilitating Encounter Groups between Jews and Arabs in Israel" (in Hebrew). *Megamot* 33 (1): 29–47.

Kimmerling, B., and J. Migdal. 1999. *Palestinians: The Making of a People* (in Hebrew). Jerusalem: Keter.

Levine, R. A., and D. T. Campbell. 1972. *Ethnocentrism: Theories of Conflict, Ethnic Attitudes, and Group Behavior*. New York: Wiley.

Levy, S., and A. L. Guttman. 1976. *Values and Attitudes of Adolescents Studying in Israel* (in Hebrew). Jerusalem: Institute for Applied Social Research.

Lewin, K. 1948. *Resolving Social Conflicts*. New York: Harper & Row.

Lewin, K. 1951. *Field Theory in Social Science: Selected Theoretical Papers*. New York: Atarper.

Libkind, K. 1992. "Ethnic Identity—Challenging the Boundaries of Social Psychology." In *Social Psychology of Identity and the Self-Concept*, edited by G. M. Breakwell. London: Surrey University Press.

Lukes, S. 1974. *Power: A Radical View*. London: Macmillan.

Lustick, I. 1985. *Arabs in the Jewish State: Israel's Control of a National Minority.* Austin: University of Texas Press.

Marcia, J. E. 1989. "Identity and Intervention." *Journal of Adolescence* 12:401–410.

Mar'i, S. 1978. *Arab Education in Israel.* Syracuse, N.Y.: Syracuse University Press.

Mar'i, S. 1985. "Arab Education in Israel: Pupils as Educators." *Politics* (Jerusalem) (November-December):34–36.

Michelovitch, Y. 1986. *Palestinian Identity as an Issue in Jewish-Arab Encounters* (in Hebrew). Jerusalem: Van Leer Jerusalem Institute.

Morris, B. 1987. *The Birth of the Palestinian Refugee Problem, 1947–1949.* Cambridge: Cambridge University Press.

Nagel, J. 1994. "Constructing Ethnicity: Creating and Recreating Ethnic Identity and Culture." *Social Problems* 41 (1): 152–171.

Ng, S. H., and J. Bradac. 1993. *Power in Language and Language Behaviours.* Vol. 3. London: Sage.

Padilla, F. 1986. "Latino Ethnicity in the City of Chicago." In *Competitive Ethnic Relations,* edited by S. Olzak and J. Nagel. New York: Academic Press.

Peres, J., A. Ehrlich, and N. Yuval-Davis. 1968. "National Education for Arab Youth in Israel." *Race* 12 (1): 151.

Peres, Y., and N. Yuval-Davis. 1969. "Some Observations of the National Identity of the Israeli Arabs." *Human Relations* 22:219–223.

Pettigrew, T. F. 1998. "Intergroup Contact Theory." *Annual Review of Psychology* 49:65–85.

Phinney, J. S. 1989. "Stages of Ethnic Identity in Minority Group Adolescents." *Journal of Early Adolescence* 9:34–49.

Phinney, J. S. 1990. "Ethnic Identity in Adolescents and Adults: Review of Research." *Psychological Bulletin* 108 (3): 499–514.

Phinney, J. S. 1995. "Ethnic Identity and Self-Esteem: A Review and Integration." In *Hispanic Psychology: Critical Issues in Theory and Research,* edited by A. M. Padilla. Thousand Oaks, Calif.: Sage.

Phinney, J. S., and D. Rosental. 1992. "Ethnic Identity in Adolescence: Process, Context, and Outcome." In *Adolescent Identity Formation,* edited by G. Adams, T. Gulotta, and R. Montemayor. Newbury Park, Calif.: Sage.

Rabinowitz, D., and K. Abu Baker. 2002. *The Stand Tall Generation: The Palestinian Citizens of Israel Today* (in Hebrew). Jerusalem: Keter.

Rouhana, N. 1984. "The Arabs in Israel: Psychological, Social and Political Dimensions of Collective Identity." Ph.D. diss., Wayne State University.

Rouhana, N. 1993. "Accentuated Identity of the Protracted Conflicts: The Collective Identity of the Palestinian Citizens in Israel." *Asian and African Studies* 27:97–127.

Rouhana, N., and S. Korper. 1997. "Power Asymmetry and Goals of Unofficial Third Party Intervention in Protracted Intergroup Conflict." *Journal of Peace Psychology* 3 (1): 1–17.

Sampson, E. 1993. *Celebrating the Other: A Dialogic Account of Human Nature.* Boulder, Colo.: Westview Press.

Seago, D. W. 1947. "Stereotypes: Before Pearl Harbor and After." *Journal of Social Psychology* 29:55–63.

Sherif, M., O. J. Harvey, B. J. White, W. R. Hood, and C. W. Sherif. 1961. *Intergroup Conflict and Cooperation: The Robber's Cave Experiment.* Norman, Okla.: University of Oklahoma Press.

Shohamy, I. 1995. "Issues in Language Policy in Israel, Language and Ideology" (in Hebrew). In *Education Towards the 21st Century*, edited by D. Chen. Tel Aviv: Tel-Aviv University Press.

Smith A. 1998. *Nationalism and Modernism*. London and New York: Routledge.

Smooha, S. 1980. *The Orientation and Politicization of the Arabs in Israel*. Haifa: Jewish-Arab Center, University of Haifa.

Smooha, S. 1983. "Minority Responses in a Plural Society: A Topology of the Arabs in Israel." *Journal of Sociology and Social Research* 67 (7): 436–456.

Smooha, S. 1988. *Arabs and Jews in Israel*. Vol. 1. Boulder, Colo.: Westview Press.

Smooha, S. 1990. "Minority Status in an Ethnic Democracy: The Status of the Arabs in Israel." *Ethnic and Racial Studies* 13 (3): 389–413.

Sonnenschein, N., R. Halabi, and A. Friedman. 1998. "Legitimization of National Identity and the Change in Power Relationships in Workshops Dealing with the Israeli-Palestinian Conflict." In *The Handbook of Interethnic Coexistence*, edited by E. Weiner. New York: Abraham Fund.

Stephan, W., and C. Stephan. 1984. "The Role of Ignorance in Intergroup Relations." In *Groups in Contact: The Psychology of Desegregation*, edited by N. Miller and M. Brower. New York: Academic Press.

Suleiman, R. 1999. "Minority Self-Categorization: The Case of the Palestinians in Israel" (in Hebrew). *Iunim Bachinuch* 4 (1): 172–186.

Suleiman, R., and B. Beit-Hallahmi. 1997. "National and Civil Identities for Palestinians in Israel." *Journal of Social Psychology* 132 (2): 219–228.

Tajfel, H., ed. 1978a. *Differentiation between Social Groups: Studies in the Social Psychology of Intergroup Relations*. London: Academic Press.

Tajfel, H. 1978b. *The Social Psychology of Minorities*. London: Minority Rights Group.

Tajfel, H. 1979. "Human Intergroup Conflict: Useful and Less Useful Forms of Analysis." In *Human Ethology: Claims and Limits of a New Discipline*, edited by M. Von Cranach, K. Foppa, W. Lepenies, and D. Ploog. Cambridge: Cambridge University Press.

Tajfel, H. 1981. *Human Groups and Social Categories*. Cambridge: Cambridge University Press.

Tajfel, H., and J. Turner. 1986. "An Integrative Theory of Intergroup Conflict." In *Psychology of Intergroup Relations*, edited by W. G. Austen and S. Worchel. Monterey, Calif.: Brooks/Cole.

Tarrow, N. 1992. "Language, Interculturalism and Human Rights." *Prospects: Quarterly Review of Education* 84:489–509.

Tessler, M. 1977. "Israel's Arabs and the Palestinian Problem." *Middle East Journal* 31:313–329.

Triandis, H. C. 1983. "Essentials of Studying Cultures." In *Handbook of Inter-Cultural Training*, vol. 1, edited by D. Landis and R. Brislin. New York: Elmsford.

Turner, J. C., and R. Brown. 1978. "Social Status, Cognitive Alternative and Group Relations." In *Differentiation between Social Groups*, edited by H. Tajfel. London and New York: Academic Press.

Turner, J. C., and K. J. Reynolds. 2001. "The Social Identity Perspective in Intergroup Relations: Theories, Themes and Controversies." In *Intergroup Processes*, edited by R. Brown and S. Gaertner. London: Blackwell.

Waters, M. 1990. *Ethnic Options: Choosing Identities in America*. Berkeley: University of California Press.

Weber, R., and J. Crocker. 1983. "Cognitive Processes in the Revision of Stereotypic Beliefs." *Journal of Personality and Social Psychology* 24:14–21.

Wilder, D. A. 1984. "Intergroup Contact: The Typical Member and the Exception to the Rule." *Journal of Experimental Social Psychology* 20:177–194.

Yalom, I. 1975. *The Theory and Practice of Group Psychology.* New York: Basic Books.

Notes on the Contributors

Ariella Friedman was born in Haifa in 1940. She earned her B.A. in social work from Hebrew University in 1963 and her Ph.D. in psychology from UCLA in 1970. She is an associate professor of psychology in the department of psychology and School of Social Work at Tel-Aviv University. She is the author of *Coming from Love: Intimacy and Power in the Female Identity* (1996) and coauthor of *Women in a Bind: On the Status of Women in Israel* (1982) and *Sex, Gender, Politics* (2000).

Rabah Halabi was the director of the School for Peace from 1998 to 2002. Today he is the head of the Research Center at the School for Peace. He is currently working on his Ph.D. in the Department of Education at Hebrew University and also lectures there. He has published more than ten articles about the dialogue between Israelis and Palestinians.

Ahmad Hijazi was born in 1967 and has been involved in Arab-Jewish encounters since 1987. He has been a resident of Neve Shalom/Wahat al Salam and a member of the School for Peace management team since 1992. Ahmad codirects adult and facilitation-training programs locally and abroad and speaks at international conferences. From 1995 to 1997 he also served as general secretary of Neve Shalom/Wahat al Salam.

Gabriel Horenczyk is a senior lecturer at the School of Education at Hebrew University. His teaching and research areas include the psychological study of cultural and ethnic identity; education and immigration; and cultural identity processes during intergroup contact. He has coedited two books: *Language, Identity, and Immigration* (2000) and *National Variations in Jewish Identity* (1999).

Arie Nadler has been a professor of psychology at Tel-Aviv University since 1988. His research interests include the study of cooperation and conflict behavior, bargaining situations, and computer simulation of social phenomena. He served as the dean of social sciences at Tel-Aviv University and is currently the incumbent of the Argentina Chair for Research on the Social Psychology of Conflict and Cooperation there.

Deb Reich is an author, editor, translator, and freethinker. She was born in Manhattan, raised in Westchester County (New York), and educated at Barnard College. A mother of two, she lives and works in Karkur, a small town in Israel.

Nava Sonnenschein is one of the founders of the School for Peace and is currently its director. She has trained hundreds of people to facilitate groups in conflict in Israel, Palestine, and in other areas. She is working on her Ph.D. at Hebrew University.

Ramzi Suleiman is currently chair of the Department of Psychology at the University of Haifa. He is cofounder and coeditor of the *Journal of Artificial Societies and Social Simulation*. He has edited two books and published more than forty articles and book chapters. His research interests include the study of social dilemmas, social identity, and intergroup behavior.

Michal Zak is a manager at the School for Peace and editor of its annual report. She has a master's degree from Hebrew University in the role of language in the Arab-Jewish conflict and is a member of Neve Shalom/Wahat al Salam. Michal is Jewish and a mother of three.

Wafa'a Zriek-Srour is a senior staff member of the School for Peace, where she is a manager and the director of the women's department and the youth-programs department. She is a trainer of new facilitators for groups in conflict and is teaching a joint course for the School for Peace and Hebrew University.

Index

Adar, L., 37
Adler, H., 37
Adorno, J. W., 15
affiliations, social, 18
Allport, G., 22
Al Naqba, 2
Amara, A., 120
Amir, Y., 31, 32, 33, 35, 37, 38
assimilation, 6, 122
autonomy, cultural, 166
awareness, 47–57; consciousness and, 49;
    development of, 49–50; group, 48;
    identity, 61; individual, 48; raising, 33;
    of reality, 57, 76
Azar, E. E., 179

Babin, P., 106
Babtiste, A., 106
Belisle, C., 106
Ben-Ari, R., 33, 35, 37, 38
Ben-Gurion University, 60
Billing, M., 121
Bion, W. R., 51, 79
Bishara, A., 4, 5
Bourdieu, P., 120
Bourhis, R. Y., 19, 121
Bradac, J., 121
Braidotti, R., 139
Brewer, M. B., 18
Brown, R., 15, 22, 23, 24, 41, 43, 51,
    78
Burton, J. W., 51, 179

Campbell, D. T., 18
cofacilitation, 141–158; objectivity
    and, 143; process of transference and,
    142; technical equality and, 142;
    understanding both sides and, 142;
    uninational forum and, 142. *See also*
    facilitation
communication: intergroup levels, 35–38;
    interpersonal, 34, 35–38, 45, 49; lan-
    guage issues and, 119, 120; techniques,
    49
competition: geographical proximity
    and, 18; hatred and, 16, 17; over re-
    sources, 17, 18, 20; social, 41; tolerance
    and, 17
Compulsory Education Law (1949),
    123–124
conflict, intergroup: academic study of,
    60; blame on "sick mind," 15; centrality
    of psychological aspects of, 13, 14; cog-
    nitive processes and, 13; competition
    and, 16; contact hypothesis and, 22–
    27, 47, 48; dialogue in, 28, 29; ethnic,
    2; externalization of blame, 16; group
    commonalities and, 29; group identi-
    fication and, 26, 27; intergroup, 13–
    30; intergroup favoritism and, 19–20,
    28; maintenance of, 28; management
    of, 32; multicausal nature of, 13; na-
    tional, 2; nature of, 59; objective-
    rational model, 18; origins of, 15–22,
    27–28; outgroup favoritism, 20–21,

199